Between the Street and the State

POLITICS AND CULTURE IN MODERN AMERICA

Series Editors: Keisha N. Blain, Margot Canaday, Matthew Lassiter, Stephen Pitti, Thomas J. Sugrue

Volumes in the series narrate and analyze political and social change in the broadest dimensions from 1865 to the present, including ideas about the ways people have sought and wielded power in the public sphere and the language and institutions of politics at all levels—local, national, and transnational. The series is motivated by a desire to reverse the fragmentation of modern U.S. history and to encourage synthetic perspectives on social movements and the state, on gender, race, and labor, and on intellectual history and popular culture.

BETWEEN THE STREET AND THE STATE

Black Women's Anti-Rape Activism amid the War on Crime

Caitlin Reed Wiesner

PENN

UNIVERSITY OF PENNSYLVANIA PRESS

PHILADELPHIA

Published by
University of Pennsylvania Press
Philadelphia, Pennsylvania 19104–4112
www.pennpress.org

Printed in the United States of America on acid-free paper
10 9 8 7 6 5 4 3 2 1

A Cataloging-in-Publication record is
available from the Library of Congress

Hardcover ISBN 978-1-5128-2826-9
eBook ISBN 978-1-5128-2827-6

For Steven

CONTENTS

ABBREVIATIONS

AFDC	Aid to Families with Dependent Children
CAPTA	Child Abuse Prevention and Treatment Act
CASAPP	Child Assault, Safety, and Awareness Prevention Program
CCVA	Citizens' Committee for Victim Assistance
CCWWC	Coalition of Concerned Women in the War on Crime
CSASN	Chicago Sexual Assault Services Network
CRC	Combahee River Collective
DCRCC	Washington, D.C. Rape Crisis Center
FAAR	Feminist Alliance Against Rape
FNCTWWV	First National Conference on Third World Women and Violence
GJC	Governor's Justice Commission of Pennsylvania
ICASA	Illinois Coalition Against Sexual Assault
LBW	League of Black Women
LEAA	Law Enforcement Assistance Administration
MARCC	Metropolitan Atlanta Rape Crisis Council
NABF	National Alliance of Black Feminists
NBFO	National Black Feminist Organization
NBWHP	National Black Women's Health Project
NCASA	National Coalition Against Sexual Assault
NCCAN	National Center on Child Abuse and Neglect
NCPCR	National Center for the Prevention and Control of Rape
NIMH	National Institute of Mental Health
NOW	National Organization for Women
NYWAR	New York Women Against Rape
PEPP	Public Education and Policy Program
PGH	Philadelphia General Hospital
PRWORA	Personal Responsibility Work Opportunity Reconciliation Act

RAINN	Rape, Abuse, & Incest National Network
RVA	Rape Victim Advocates
SRCC	Baton Rouge Stop Rape Crisis Center
TANF	Temporary Aid for Needy Families
TWC	Third World Caucus of Philadelphia WOAR
TWWA	Third World Women's Alliance
VAWA	Violence Against Women Act
VOCA	Victims of Crime Act
WOAR	Women Organized Against Rape

Introduction

One October afternoon in 1977, radical Black activist and feminist thinker Angela Y. Davis arrived at Sonoma State College (now Sonoma State University) to address the student body about "rape from a Black woman's perspective."[1] It was not the first time Davis broached the topic. Two years earlier, the national feminist organ *Ms.* magazine published her commentary on the widely publicized trial of Joan Little. Little, a young Black woman, had murdered Clarence Alligood, her white middle-aged jailer, when he attempted to sexually assault her in her cell.[2] Davis issued a stern warning to the feminist faction of the interracial freedom movement that rallied around Little. The feminist movement against sexual violence, which had been steadily building across the United States since the late 1960s, championed Joan Little as a symbol of women's vulnerability to rape and rapists' near-immunity to consequences. Davis reminded them Little was a Black woman and her sexual assault and subsequent defense trial reflected racism at least as much as it did sexism. She concluded that a successful freedom movement for Little required "racism and male supremacy" to be "projected in their dialectical unity" because "in the case of the raped black woman, they are mutually reinforcive."[3]

By the time Davis arrived at Sonoma State, Joan Little had won her freedom and avoided the electric chair. But Davis only sharpened her critique of the feminist movement against sexual violence. "In order to anticipate the involvement of larger numbers of Black women, and women of color," she argued, "the character of the anti-rape movement must change."[4] She explained that the underrepresentation of African American women in the feminist movement against sexual violence—a persistent anxiety of the movement's white leadership—was not due to Black women's disinterest in the issue of rape. As a Black feminist scholar, Davis was well-versed in the routine rape of Black women by white men during and after slavery, lynch mobs' weaponization of rape accusations against Black men, and the generations of Black women who had valiantly attacked these conjoined violences since the nineteenth century.[5] Rather, she argued, Black women were repelled by the practices adopted by the feminist anti-rape movement, specifically "the frequent reliance on law-and-order methods to curb the rise of rape—the reliance on police, harsher prison terms."[6]

The uneasy partnership between the feminist movement against sexual violence and law enforcement entities was well underway by October 1977. Three years prior, the Law Enforcement Assistance Administration (LEAA), a central agency orchestrating the federal "war on crime," identified feminist rape crisis centers as candidates for funding through block grants.[7] The feminist anti-rape organizers who applied for and accepted these monies departed from the founders of their movement. Early anti-rape feminists had categorized law enforcement among the patriarchal oppressors of women and deliberately created feminist rape crisis centers to serve as "an alternative to the police" for assaulted women.[8] This partnership rested upon an assumption that a more vigorous police response to reports of sexual assault and harsher punishments for convicted rapists could provide a path to women's safety from male violence. Davis pointed out that this assumption failed to recognize how frequently law enforcement entities were a source of violence and harm in Black women's lives. Police remained wedded to historically entrenched myths about Black women's lasciviousness and declined to regard them as victims whose bodily violations demanded redress. "There have been numerous instances . . . where Black women are raped and they report it to the police, only to be raped, assaulted, a second time by a police officer," Davis added. An invigorated criminal justice response to rape also seemed destined to exacerbate the hypercriminalization of Black men. Davis asked her audience, "How do you deal with the fact that when you go into a prison and you look at the rapists, the ones who have committed rape who are there, you find a large number of Black men?" Finally, Davis noted that calls to protect vulnerable women and capture their assailants provided convenient moral subterfuge for the ongoing expansion and militarization of urban police forces. She pointed to the nearby city of Berkeley, where a community-led movement to abolish the city's SWAT team was opposed by a female city commissioner who endorsed the tactical unit as a necessary measure for confronting the city's rape epidemic. Davis concluded that for Black women, "it's hard to in any way have confidence in the ability of the police to deal with that when we know that they will use this as a further pretext to escalate the repression they mete out in any event."

The change Davis sought was not just a stronger racial consciousness and intersectional analysis within the feminist movement against sexual violence. She envisioned a movement where Black women's presence and leadership would problematize the casual acceptance of law enforcement as an effective solution to gender violence and usher in a wider range of activist possibilities. The First National Conference on Third World Women and Violence (FNCTWWV), convened in Washington, D.C. in August 1980, brought together more than one hundred Black, Latina, Asian American, and Native American women working in feminist rape crisis centers across the country.[9] They formed the vanguard of the change prescribed by Davis. The conference attendees agreed that the anti-rape movement's penchant for close cooperation with law enforcement posed a major hurdle for women of color. Loretta Ross, an organizer with the Black-led D.C. Rape Crisis Center (DCRCC), stated in her summary of the conference proceedings that "Third World people share a collective experience with law enforcement officials, usually one of intense mistrust on the part of the community and racism / insensitivity on the part of the police. This collective experience tends to make the police one of the last options Third World women choose."[10] Ross and her fellow conferencegoers identified the arms of the American carceral state—the police, the courts, and the prisons—as consistent purveyors of violence for both Black men and Black women and urged the feminist movement against sexual violence to implement "alternatives to the criminal justice system" in its praxis.[11]

Like Angela Davis, the attendees of the First National Conference on Third World Women and Violence pinpointed rape as an enduring feature of Black women's historical experience and a mainstay of Black women's activism. The conferencegoers elaborated on the distinctive character of this activism, which consisted of "giving [Black women] some control over their lives and assistance in times of crisis."[12] Within the mainstream feminist movement against sexual violence, the operative definitions of control and assistance centered carceral actors. Rape crisis centers believed rape could be controlled by punitive state machinery, and they could best assist victims by connecting them to that machinery. By contrast, the Black anti-rape organizers who attended the First National Conference on Third World Women and Violence understood controlling rape and assisting victims as functions of care work. This deep-rooted ethic and practice of care began with nineteenth century Black women's paid and unpaid efforts to sustain the bodies, minds, and souls of their communities, mitigating the damages incurred under the shifting visages of white supremacy.[13] In the 1970s, care work typified Black women's activism within the feminist movement against sexual violence. For Black women, care could and did serve as a functional alternative to criminalization.

The intertwining of the feminist movement against sexual violence with carceral entities born of the "war on crime" created inhospitable terrain for the changes sought by Angela Davis and the First National Conference on Third World Women and Violence. Although the LEAA folded in 1981, a steady rotation of federal laws and agencies advancing a crime control agenda, including the National Center for the Prevention and Control of Rape (NCPCR), the Victims of Crime Act of 1984 (VOCA), and the Violence Against Women Act of 1994 (VAWA), extended financial support to the feminist movement against sexual violence throughout the 1980s and 1990s. This book is, in one sense, an account of that intertwining and activists' efforts to challenge it. It gives this account from the perspective of African American anti-rape organizers in Philadelphia, Washington, D.C., the San Francisco Bay Area, Chicago, and Atlanta who upheld a broader vision of anti-rape activism despite the unfavorable terms set by an increasingly carceral state. They were compelled by the resurgent Black feminist consciousness of the early 1970s to confront Black men who assaulted Black women, but were also cognizant of law enforcement's escalating hostility toward all Black bodies. To resolve this contradiction, they drew upon a storied tradition of Black women's caring labor to develop a diverse arsenal of practices that centered the needs of Black women and girls while eschewing the remedies mandated by "law-and-order" entities. This arsenal included the subversive use of state funds within spaces controlled by the feminist movement against sexual violence to oppose carceral imperatives; the diversion of anti-rape advocacy from feminist rape crisis centers to other institutions where advocacy was premised on a default Black victim; and outspoken resistance to carceral solutions to rape. They would not completely turn back the carceral co-optation of the feminist movement against sexual violence or divorce anti-rape advocacy from an intractably racist criminal justice system. But for the Black women and girls they served, Black anti-rape organizers acted as crucial space-keepers between the interpersonal gender violence encountered on the street and the institutionalized violence imposed by carceral actors. They preserved this space through simple yet profound acts of care, standing athwart an increasingly conservative state that relinquished all obligations to care for Black women in its narrow quest to control violent crime.[14]

In Defense of Themselves in the Post–Civil Rights Era

In the three decades since historian Darlene Clark Hine first described a "culture of dissemblance" obscuring Black women's sexual lives in the archive, scholars have documented a centuries-long tradition of African American women testifying about their bodily violation.[15] *Between the Street and the State* extends this literature by mapping the shifts in Black women's anti-rape discourse during the "post–civil rights era."[16] For all of the nineteenth century and much of the twentieth, the Black-initiated anti-rape tradition was strictly limited to interracial rapes committed by white men against Black women. To be sure, Black men did (and do) victimize women within their own communities and Black women did (and do) resist their victimization.[17] But, as a rule, Black women focused exclusively on interracial white-on-Black rape to avoid breathing life into the dreaded myth of the Black rapist that animated white violence. This also allowed anti-rape activity to fit snugly in a civil rights agenda primarily geared toward combatting white supremacy.

While African American women had long organized "in defense of themselves," their terms, conditions, and goals changed significantly from the 1970s onward.[18] In the years following the passage of the Voting Rights Act, an uncompromising focus on interracial assaults was no longer a political necessity. Disillusionment with the male chauvinism and misogyny that permeated civil rights and Black Power coalitions gave rise to Black feminist organizations including the National Black Feminist Organization in New York (1973–1975), the National Alliance of Black Feminists in Chicago (1976–1980), and the Combahee River Collective in Boston (1975–1980).[19] These groups predicated their politics on the inseparability of racism and sexism and a refusal to continue shelving gendered concerns to present a unified racial front. All three featured anti-rape activity in their agendas. Unlike their foremothers in the Black women's club movement and civil rights movement, none abstained from implicating Black men as assailants of Black women. Bucking a longstanding strategic reticence, Black feminists of the 1970s spoke openly about intraracial rape committed by Black men against Black women.

The shift toward explicitly naming Black men as perpetrators of violence against Black women, induced by the political currents of organized

Black feminism, drew more Black women to the fledgling feminist movement against sexual violence in the early 1970s. It also raised thorny questions about relying upon the criminal justice system as an appropriate line of defense against sexual assault. Black women's lived experience—as veterans of Black radical organizing, as social service professionals attempting to staunch the bleeding of urban divestment, and as Black residents of American cities besieged by law enforcement since the 1960s—taught them that policing, prosecution, and punishment contributed to, rather than controlled, the violence that buffeted their lives. As Black feminist scholar Beth Richie explains, Black anti-rape organizers' distaste for law enforcement was twofold. As individuals, Black women hesitated to report their assaults to the police out of fear that police officers, who imbibed destructive stereotypes of Black women's promiscuity and untrustworthiness, would simply dismiss their complaints out of hand. Frequently, law enforcement would overlook the assault committed against a Black woman and arrest *her* instead for outstanding crimes such as drug offenses, theft, or prostitution.[20] Worse, some police officers followed up their dismissal with physical and sexual assaults.[21] At the level of the community, Black women feared that inviting a hostile police force to intervene in situations of gender violence would reinforce the assumption that Black communities were anarchic and crime-ridden. This would all but ensure the infliction of greater state violence through aggressive policing and disproportionate incarceration.[22]

Black feminist sexual politics represented a new venture in Black women's organizational history, but did not require the total abandonment of older strategies. Black anti-rape organizers who operated within or alongside the feminist movement against sexual violence understood their duties as a form of care work: the provision of services to uphold human survival and promote individual and communal wellbeing. The care work performed by Black anti-rape organizers was rooted in a tradition of community uplift that stretched back to the nineteenth century, when state services were always inadequate for (and oftentimes actively hostile toward) mitigating Black suffering. This tradition of paid and unpaid caring labor was first identified by historians like Jacqueline Jones and Stephanie Shaw.[23] It has since been elaborated on by scholars such as Annelise Orleck, Alondra Nelson, and Cheryl Hicks, who point to it as a basis for political action that changes the structure of power, and not merely a balm for racialized harm.[24] In the post–civil rights era of the 1970s, the tradition of care work was inflected by the Black feminist argument that women's safety within the community was not an insignificant distraction or a means to a different activist end. Rather, it was an integral concern deserving open discussion and a permanent place in any Black movement's political analysis.[25] The combination of new Black feminist sexual politics and traditional Black women's care work proved essential for navigating the merger of the feminist "war on rape" and the federal "war on crime."

The War on Rape Meets the War on Crime

Though attempts to curb men's sexual privilege can be found in antebellum abolitionist literature, the formal feminist movement against sexual violence emerged during the women's liberation movement in the late 1960s.[26] What separated the formal movement from its forerunners was consciousness-raising, the practice of groups of women gathering in unstructured settings to discuss the problems that dogged their lives. Through consciousness-raising, women realized that sexual assault was neither a personal misfortune nor a private shame, but a pervasive symptom of living within a patriarchal society that drove men to objectify and possess women.[27] This realization sparked concerted protest against women's vulnerability to sexual assault. Some of these early protests took the form of confrontational vigilante justice, with women forming "Anti-Rape Squads" in Michigan, California, and New York that took to the streets to humiliate and intimidate alleged rapists who had evaded the law.[28] More representative of the movement to come was the Rape Speak-Out organized by the New York Radical Feminists on January 24, 1971. Hundreds of women gathered at St. Clement's Episcopal Church and dozens of them testified about their experiences of sexual assault, declaring rape to be "a political crime" targeting their gender and not a sexual act.[29]

In 1972, the first feminist rape crisis centers opened within months of one another in Berkeley, California, and Washington, D.C. That August, Elizabethann O'Sullivan of the D.C. Rape Crisis Center compiled a free manual, "How to Start a Rape Crisis Center," and distributed hundreds of copies of the booklet to seed the formation of similar centers across the country.[30] By the end of the decade, nearly five hundred rape crisis centers dotted the United States.[31] As the "backbone of the anti-rape movement," these centers were committed to the admittedly utopian goal of eradicating sexual violence from American society.[32] In the long term, they would achieve this by educating professionals who managed the fallout of sexual assault as well as the general public. In the short term, they worked to insulate survivors of sexual violence from the callousness of the medical and criminal justice systems by providing services, including hotlines, emergency room counseling, court accompaniment, and group counseling.

The earliest feminist rape crisis centers consisted of rented apartments, shared telephone lines, and a devoted cadre of women volunteers. As the demand for services ballooned, rape crisis center operators hunted for funding to hire full- and part-time staff and secure permanent space. They tapped an unexpected and unprecedented source of funds in federal acts and agencies established by the long "war on crime" announced by President Lyndon B. Johnson in the wake of the Black-led urban rebellions that detonated in the 1960s.[33] Alongside its primary objective of beefing up urban police departments, the LEAA began offering substantial operational grants to feminist rape crisis centers in 1974.[34] Later, President Ronald Reagan would disband the LEAA in his quest to eliminate what he saw as bloated and inefficient federal bureaucracies. He kept up the federal commitment to funding the feminist movement against sexual violence for crime control purposes through the Victims of Crime Act (VOCA) of 1984, which extended grants to "victim assistance" groups that shepherded the assaulted through criminal justice proceedings. Couched within the landmark Violent Crime Control and Law Enforcement Act of 1994 (the so-called "Clinton Crime Bill") was the Violence Against Women Act (VAWA). VAWA provided $1.6 billion in support for feminist anti-rape activities through the newly minted Office on Violence Against Women within the Department of Justice.[35] Between these major legislative initiatives, policymakers created the National Center for the Prevention and Control of Rape (NCPCR) in 1975 and refocused the National Center on Child Abuse and Neglect (NCCAN) on child sexual abuse in the early 1980s.[36]

At first glance, the synergy between the feminist movement against sexual violence and the federal "war on crime" appears obvious. Anti-rape feminists pointed to abysmally low reporting and conviction rates for sexual assault as positive proof of women's subordination.[37] Courts frequently declined to convict accused rapists because prosecutors, judges, and jurors bought into the sexist and racist myth that rape was an exceptionally rare crime committed solely by non-white or otherwise depraved men against respectable women. Judges instructed juries that women's testimony was fundamentally untrustworthy and required intense scrutiny. In the eyes of the law, the slightest suggestion of a less-than-chaste lifestyle could immediately disqualify a woman's rape complaints. For Black women, assumptions of lasciviousness prevailed irrespective of personal conduct.[38] As early as 1973, groups like the National Organization for Women's Rape Task Force and the Michigan Women's Task Force on Rape dedicated their energies to reforming rape laws and court procedures to counteract the traditional disbelief of rape victims and make convictions easier to sustain.[39] At the agitation of feminist groups, many states adopted piecemeal legal reforms, such as disaggregating sexual offenses according to severity, easing the evidentiary burdens of "utmost resistance" and third-party corroboration, and "shielding" victims by rendering their sexual histories inadmissible as evidence.[40]

Feminist demands for rape laws that empowered victims gained traction in the 1970s at least in part because of the "cracking down" mentality stoked by the ongoing "war on crime."[41] Feminists of all stripes demanded rape be regarded as a serious crime. A sizeable portion of the feminist movement against sexual violence earnestly hoped more rapists would be duly convicted and lengthily incarcerated. This demand neatly dovetailed with the prevailing political ethos that promised to "get tough" on crime and repudiate leniency toward offenders.[42] State entities created to fight the "war on crime" looked to feminist activists and service providers as allies who also wished to see more violent criminals behind bars. But they did not share feminists' trademark analysis of patriarchy as the wellspring of sexual violence.[43] They promoted carceral tactics—more consistent police reporting, swifter prosecution, and harsher punishment—as the only viable means of controlling rape. They expected the anti-rape feminists they subsidized to enthusiastically embrace their tactics to the exclusion of all other forms of advocacy, such as community education, self-defense training, and therapeutic counseling. Through coercive strings-attached grantmaking practices, carceral entities cynically exploited a sincere feminist desire to change the cultural consensus about rape and estranged feminist rape crisis centers from their original commitment to function as "an alternative to the police." In their attempt to transform the sexual politics of law enforcement, the feminist movement against sexual violence inadvertently transformed itself into a node of late twentieth century carceral state building.

In the last two decades, political scientists, historians, and legal scholars have traced the rise of the modern American carceral state to the policy interventions that mutated the "War on Poverty" into the "war on crime."[44] Most studies have focused on the aggressive enforcement of narcotics control, and with good reason: the racialized harm wreaked by the drug wars can hardly be overstated.[45] But as historian Anne Gray Fischer reminds us, "women matter in the history of police power."[46] Cracking down on gender-based violence was a significant aim of the long "war on crime" that stealthily contributed to mass incarceration. The rate of incarceration for sexual assault at state and federal prisons in the United States rose threefold between 1980 and 1996, a faster pace than the general incarceration rate.[47] In 2015, the Bureau of Justice Statistics confirmed that while drug offenders comprise 15.7 percent of the U.S. prison population, sex offenders follow closely behind at 12.4 percent.[48] In addition to the sheer number of sex offenders behind bars, carceral technologies developed by the state to control rape, such as lifelong sex offender registries, extend the "collateral consequences" past the period of incarceration.[49] Although federal funds invested in drug enforcement and prosecution far surpassed those allotted to feminist rape crisis centers, funding victim service provision delivered outsized rhetorical benefits for the state. Banking upon the cultural consensus that rape (putting aside divergent opinions about what qualified as "real rape" and who a "real" rape victim was) was an egregiously harmful crime whose perpetrators needed to be restrained, politicians could frame the unprecedented expansion of the carceral state as unambiguously just.[50]

Carceral studies scholars have attended to the ways the feminist movement against sexual violence became both a casualty of and an accessory to the ascendance of mass incarceration.[51] Throughout the twentieth century, political scientist Marie Gottschalk observes, "women's groups and feminists . . . played central roles in defining violence as a threat to the social order and uncritically pushing for more enhanced policing power to address law-and-order concerns."[52] Some scholars have claimed that feminists were not intrinsically committed to carceral tactics to end violence against women, but securing operating funds from the state required them to moderate their politics. State agencies and offices were willing to materially support anti-rape organizers "so long as they fitted into a mode of operation that was acceptable to the state."[53] Thus, Kristin Bumiller argues, "the desire for stable funding sources pushed [rape crisis centers] onto the terrain of the state," making the feminist movement against sexual violence "a partner in the unforeseen growth of a criminalized society."[54]

Between the Street and the State shows that Black anti-rape organizers were keenly aware of the conservatizing influence of state funding on the feminist movement against sexual violence and contested it through a diverse arsenal of practices. The care work undergirding this diverse arsenal overlapped with aspects of the early feminist movement against sexual violence, such as the consciousness-raising sessions that encouraged victims to regard their assaults as undeserved and community education initiatives that aimed to overturn patriarchally sanctioned "rape culture." But as white anti-rape feminists' commitment to care work faltered under the growing pressures of carceral state co-optation, Black organizers' commitment to care only deepened. In this way, this book joins Treva Lindsey, Sarah Haley, and Erica Edwards in reexamining Black women's caring labor in the context of accelerating state violence toward Black bodies since the 1970s. As crime control officials and their white feminist allies sought to control rape through the actively violent logics of law enforcement, Black anti-rape organizers challenged the carceral approach while also contesting the state's passively violent neglect of vulnerable Black victims. They insisted upon care as the opposite of crime control and engaged in a "contra-state form of repair" that promised survival and healing in the short-term and transformation of the communal and societal structures that endangered Black women and girls in the long run.[55]

Framing Black anti-rape organizers' activism as an evolution of care work complicates the trajectory of U.S. feminism, particularly the "narrative of decline" that has characterized recent studies of the feminist movement against sexual violence. According to this declension narrative, while the earliest rape crisis centers were guided by a comprehensive understanding of patriarchy, this radical vision evaporated once these groups transitioned toward a systems advocacy approach adopted to attract and retain state funding sources. In 2018, scholars Maria Bevacqua and Carrie N. Baker declared the narrative of decline "oversimplified and incomplete."[56] The influence of state-sponsored crime control entities undeniably contracted the terrain of the feminist movement against sexual violence to activities that served the state's interest in crime control. But that contraction was always disputed, though not by the movement's white feminist leaders and not in explicitly anti-carceral language. Despite mounting pressures, Black anti-rape organizers maintained intersectional perspectives and Black-centered practices that challenged the hegemony of crime control approaches. Their care for Black women and girls upheld the Black feminist ethical framework described by Treva Lindsey in which "to be handled warmly is oppositional to the handling that occurs under conditions of antiBlackness, misogynoir, multiple jeopardy."[57]

Subversion, Diversion, and Resistance

In recent years, scholars have adeptly illustrated the longstanding sexual vulnerability of Black women and girls, the growing currency of policing and punishment in the late twentieth century United States, and the exponential harm inflicted upon Black women and girls as a result.[58] *Between the Street and the State* follows their lead by explaining how Black anti-rape organizers prevented and redressed the sexual violation of Black women and girls outside the punitive framework imposed by the carceral state upon the feminist movement against sexual violence. Building upon organized Black feminists' unapologetic appraisal of the reality of intraracial rape faced by Black women in the 1970s, Black anti-rape organizers articulated a flexible and nuanced dissent from the narrow carceral solutions to rape endorsed by state agencies and supported by much of the white leadership of the feminist anti-rape movement. Instead, they created a diverse arsenal of practices that cared for Black women and girls and downplayed criminal justice responses to rape. This arsenal consisted of the alternating tactics of subversion, diversion, and resistance enacted by Black organizers within (and eventually outside of) feminist rape crisis centers during the 1970s, 1980s, and 1990s. Their tactical choices shifted with the variable configurations of state funding for the feminist movement against sexual violence during these decades.

State support for the feminist movement against sexual violence was predicated upon a myopic interest in controlling crime that animated much of American politics during the last third of the twentieth century. Every funding overture, whether direct or indirect, shared the same goal of expanding police power over rape. However, the means for achieving this expansion would shift substantially with the collapse of large federal grantmaking in the late 1970s and the rise of neoliberal governance during the 1980s and 1990s.[59] Subversion was an effective tactic for the grantmaking modality of the late 1970s. During this period, the feminist movement against sexual violence took advantage of large (to the tune of hundreds of thousands of dollars), renewable grants offered by the Law Enforcement Assistance Administration (LEAA) and National Center for the Prevention and Control of Rape (NCPCR). This grantmaking style, cribbed from the community action programs of the "War on Poverty," invested in the institutionalization of feminist rape crisis centers and feminist knowledge production about rape to ensure the survival of a grassroots movement that would improve police performance in the apprehension and incarceration of rapists.[60] Black organizers within the movement skillfully repurposed some of those resources for projects that were not intended by politicians and policymakers. The LEAA subsidized up to 90 percent of Philadelphia WOAR's operating budget between 1976 and 1980, with the clear intent of bolstering the City of Brotherly Love's police performance in containing sex crime.[61] Yet Black staff members whose salaries were paid with LEAA monies opposed reporting-centric anti-rape advocacy, as shown in their internal memos and outreach materials. They subsequently restructured Philadelphia WOAR with Black volunteers at the helm and Black victims at the center. Although the NCPCR refused to fund direct service provision alongside research initiatives, that did not stop Black anti-rape organizers from employing subversion. They commandeered the NCPCR's 1977 "Special Populations" conference to stage a confrontation with the white researchers the agency was funding about the ineffectiveness of police reporting as a rape prevention strategy for Black women and the importance of financially supporting caring labor.[62] Subversion was also present in the narratives offered by non-activist Black women who participated in an NCPCR-funded study of the incidence of rape in the San Francisco Bay Area. Their narratives, which did not appear in the study's final published form, undermined the NCPCR's claims about proactive policing while demanding proactive care work.

The lean years of the 1980s required Black anti-rape organizers to substitute diversion for subversion. With the onset of fiscal conservatism in the 1980s, large grantmaking fell into political disfavor, as evidenced by the disbanding of the LEAA and NCPCR. Those feminist rape crisis centers that survived the pronounced die-off of the early 1980s found grants offered by the National Center on Child Abuse and Neglect (NCCAN), the Victims of Crime Act (VOCA), and the Violence Against Women Act (VAWA) to be much more modest.[63] Federal politicians and policymakers remained interested in extending police power over rape, but elected the less costly strategy of bringing individual victims of sexual violence in regular direct contact with the criminal justice system through mandatory reporting laws, victim's compensation, or simply proliferating the carceral infrastructure of police and prisons. With the state abandoning a wholesale strategy in favor of a retail approach, feminist rape crisis centers remained useful assets only insofar as they referred individuals to law enforcement. The NCCAN offered only meager backing for anti-rape feminists to operate child sexual abuse prevention programs through the 1980s. State officials instead relied upon mandatory reporting laws to extract victimized children from sexually abusive households after the fact of their violation. VOCA deployed the bulk of its financial resources as compensation for individual victims of sexual abuse who successfully pressed their claims in a court of law. Leftover scraps went to groups who assisted victims by retaining them through grueling investigations and court procedures. With state anti-rape funding reduced to a trickle and tainted by law enforcement, Black organizers carried their anti-rape advocacy outside the formal boundaries of the feminist movement against sexual violence. They embedded themselves in local institutions where the reporting-centric model held less sway and Black-centered care could proceed unfettered. A wide array of urban institutions availed themselves to the diversion of Black anti-rape organizers, from Black-majority public school districts to embattled community welfare agencies. In the District of Columbia, the Black-majority public school system welcomed Nkenge Tourè of the D.C. Rape Crisis Center and her pathbreaking child sexual abuse prevention courses.[64] Against the backdrop of a moral panic that spurred punitive state intervention to "save" children, Tourè built a radical curriculum that sidelined police and other state actors that were eager to remove Black children and punish Black parents. The Black-led Chicago Sexual Assault Services Network (CSASN) turned to the embattled community welfare agencies on the city's underserved South and West Sides as a launchpad for no-cost counseling services for sexual assault.[65] The Victims of Crime Act of 1984 (VOCA) required prompt police reporting from those hoping to receive compensation for assaults and excluded applicants whose "contributory misconduct" may have instigated the crime.[66] This prerequisite, in conjunction with the slashing of social safety nets during the Reagan Administration, branded poor Black women as undeserving victims. By attending to the physical, mental, and emotional health of the poor Black woman, CSASN affirmed her worthiness to use the resources of the state while evading the crime control impetus that saw victims only as potential reporters.

By the advent of the Violence Against Women Act of 1994, the material and rhetorical zenith of carceral investment in feminist anti-rape activity, Black anti-rape organizers initiated the third practice within their arsenal: direct resistance to laws that ran contrary to caring for Black victims. The eye-popping $1.6 billion promised by VAWA to the feminist movement against sexual violence reversed the previous decade's austerity. But the decision to establish the Office on Violence Against Women within the Department of Justice, like the decision to attach VAWA to the "Clinton Crime Bill," guaranteed that this funding would emphasize controlling the crime of rape and relegate caring for victims to an afterthought. [67] Before VAWA, the Atlanta-based National Black Women's Health Project wielded the tool of diversion to safeguard the care of Black women and girls threatened by gender violence.[68] Community-engaged care formed the basis of their signature self-help method that regularly occurred in the Center for Black Women's Wellness and Atlanta's public housing projects. They shifted tactics to resistance in opposing the otherwise popular VAWA, arguing that the carceral legislation formalized the state's negation of the care that they deemed essential to individual healing and community transformation. NBWHP's resistance anticipated the explicitly anti-carceral interventions of groups like Critical Resistance and INCITE! Women, Gender Non-Conforming, and Trans people of Color Against Violence (formerly INCITE! Women of Color Against Violence) in the new millennium.

Between 1974 and 1994, Black anti-rape organizers turned from subversion to diversion to resistance as a means of adequately caring for assaulted Black women and girls. In doing so, they occasionally found themselves at odds with the white-dominated feminist movement against sexual violence and its state-informed mission to control sexual assault. *Between the Street and the State* refrains from extensive commentary on the oftentimes fractious relationship between Black women and white women within the feminist movement against sexual violence. Other scholars have capably analyzed this facet of the second "wave" of the U.S. women's liberation movement.[69] Black women's position within the feminist movement against sexual violence has always been "at once full of possibility yet fraught with frustration."[70] White feminists often failed to recognize their racial privilege within the movement, enshrining their experience of sexual violence as universal and marginalizing the perspectives of women of color. This tendency, which Beth Richie has termed the "everywoman analysis," played a part in the intertwining of the war on rape and the "war on crime."[71] The white feminist leadership of rape crisis centers did not share key aspects of Black women's historical experience, such as the chilling effect of the myth of the Black rapist, the heightened disbelief of Black victims by police, or the destruction wrought on Black communities by "law and order" measures. Thus, they were more likely to look toward law enforcement as a suitable partner for controlling rape. Certainly some radical pockets of the white anti-rape movement were sensitive to Black women's distinctive experience of rape, worked to check their racial biases, and vocally objected to allying with the carceral state.[72] But most were opposed to actions that might jeopardize state funding streams, and others genuinely sought more aggressive policing as a path to women's safety.

Between the Street and the State concurs that Black women's anti-rape politics were fundamentally different from those of white women. But it focuses on how racist thinking continued to shape the response to rape waged by state crime control agencies and accepted by the mainstream feminist movement against sexual violence. Historians have exhaustively documented the racist assumption that Black men posed a constant sexual threat to white women, the denial of Black women as violable victims, and the mobilization of violence to "punish" presumed Black rapists both within and outside of the law.[73] Even as the lynch mob dissipated and feminists professed an understanding of the myth of the Black rapist, the solutions to rape endorsed by state actors (and the white leadership of the feminist movement to whom they dispensed funding) were inextricable from the pathologizing of Black communities and the dyad of state violence and abandonment.[74] State agencies' commitment to increased police reporting as a means of preventing and controlling rape effectively excluded Black women and girls through its refusal to consider how law enforcement routinely enacted violence against them. White feminists' general acceptance of this method resulted in anti-rape advocacy that was, as Kimberlè Crenshaw and Beth Richie have argued, inherently racialized.[75] Of course, feminist anti-rape organizations wielded far less power to shape these systems than their state benefactors. They too were victims of the drift from the welfare state to the carceral state as the United States' primary social apparatus in the late twentieth century.[76] But their adoption of carceral technologies to control rape implicated them in anti-Black processes as a group, even as they opposed racism as individuals.

Sources, Strands, and Styles

To expose this strand of Black-led anti-rape activism amid the "war on crime," *Between the Street and the State* draws upon a wide array of sources. These include the archival collections of feminist anti-rape organizations and activists, publications created by government agencies that supported anti-rape activity, state-sponsored research on rape, journalistic coverage of the anti-rape movement, and oral history interviews with Black women active in the anti-rape movement. The textual records of state actors, such as the congressional testimony of federal policymakers who supported the "war on crime," illuminate the state's motivations, goals, and biases in addressing rape as a violent crime issue. Periodicals, including the *Chicago Defender*, *Washington Post*, and *Ebony* are useful for gauging popular opinion toward the feminist movement against sexual violence and the "war on crime." Materials generated by feminist anti-rape organizations, such as grant applications, training materials, and movement publications like the *Feminist Alliance Against Rape Newsletter / Aegis* and *off our backs*, reveal how the anti-rape movement responded to the state's crime control overtures and provide glimpses of Black women's activities within the movement. Oral history interviews are vital for capturing aspects of their experiences that escape the archival record. Black women's voices offer a bottom-up perspective of the entanglement of the "war on crime" and the feminist anti-rape movement, a story previously told from the vantage points of policymakers and white middle-class feminists.

Black anti-rape organizers did not constitute a discrete movement that could be totally separated from the broader feminist movement against sexual violence. With the lone exception of the National Black Women's Health Project in Atlanta, all the anti-violence organizations examined in *Between the Street and the State* counted white feminists among their leadership and membership. More accurately, Black anti-rape organizers comprised a geographically diffuse and chronologically nonlinear insurgency within the anti-rape movement that sought care for Black victims while keeping them at arm's length from carceral machinery. This insurgency was anchored by several national points of connection, including the Women of Color Caucus of the National Coalition Against Sexual Assault, regional conferences sponsored by the National Center for the Prevention and Control of Rape (NCPCR), the First National Conference on Third World Women and Violence, the annual meetings of the National Black Women's Health Project, and issues of the *Feminist Alliance Against Rape Newsletter* (later *Aegis*).

Writing the history of a still-evolving social movement requires use of terminology that remains in-flux and contested by various parties. A brief clarifying note follows. "Second wave feminism" and "women's liberation movement" refer interchangeably to the period of women's activism roughly stretching from the 1970s to the 1990s that gave rise to the feminist movement against sexual violence. This chronological shorthand should not suggest an allegiance to the outmoded "wave metaphor" of American women's movements, which frequently obscures the activism of Black women who participated in multidecade movements like the feminist movement against sexual violence.[77] Though some contemporary activists prefer the term "survivors" to refer to individuals who have endured rape and abuse, this book primarily employs the term "victims" for the sake of historical accuracy. "Survivor" did not come into regular usage within anti-violence organizations as an empowering alternative to "victim" until the early 2000s. Some Black anti-rape organizers interviewed for this book expressed annoyance with the shift in language, feeling it erased the systemic turmoil experienced by victims.[78] In keeping with the most recent stylistic and editorial conventions, "Black" is capitalized throughout this book except in primary source quotations.

The term "Third World" was introduced to anti-rape discourses by Black organizers to qualify the needs and activism of non-white women, as in the Third World Women's Caucus of Philadelphia WOAR and the First National Conference on Third World Women and Violence. Black feminist Fran Beal, founder of the Third World Women's Alliance, implemented the term in its feminist context to indicate a political affinity between Black women suffering under the internal colonialism of white supremacy in the United States and African, Latina, Asian, and Indigenous women living under colonial and imperial conditions throughout the world.[79] In practice, Black anti-rape organizers used "Third World" mostly as a synonym for "Black" or "Black feminist," signaling the anti-racist commitments at the core of their anti-violence advocacy.

This book employs the word "carceral" in a similarly flexible manner. It does not simply connote prisons or the experience of imprisonment but describes a governmental ethos in which punishment is the primary remedy for all that ails society. This broad application captures the varied methods, technologies, and actors engaged by the state to execute this punishment outside of prison walls. As Beth Richie has noted, America is a "prison nation" for poor people of color, whether they reside inside or outside the physical structure of the prison.[80] However, *Between the Street and the State* stops short of designating anti-rape activists who in any way collaborated with carceral actors as "carceral feminists." In the same way that Black anti-rape organizers were not omniscient anti-carceral warriors, neither were their white colleagues enthusiastic cheerleaders for mass incarceration. They shared Black women's yearning for systemic solutions to rape that interrogated systems of power, such as undermining patriarchal rape culture through preventative education, and viewed police engagement as a means to that end. By contrast, their state funders who were unapologetically carceral saw aggressive policing as an end in and of itself.

CHAPTER 1

Black Feminists Confront Intraracial Rape

In November 1974, the *Chicago Defender* advertised an upcoming meeting of the local chapter of the National Black Feminist Organization (NBFO) at the Blue Gargoyle community center on the city's South Side. Founded by Margaret Sloan in New York City one year prior, the NBFO seeded the development of local chapters across the nation, some of which blossomed into autonomous Black feminist organizations.[1] Beverly and Barbara Smith transformed the Boston chapter into the Combahee River Collective in 1975, and Brenda Eichelberger spun off the Chicago chapter into the National Alliance of Black Feminists (NABF) in 1976.[2] Ahead of this rebranding, Eichelberger proclaimed that the Chicago Chapter was "alive and well," boasting a membership of more than three hundred Black women, and was "especially concerned with the problem of rape and is working with other anti-rape groups."[3] Inches above this announcement in the newspaper, the Coalition of Concerned Women in the War on Crime (CCWWC) profusely thanked those who participated in its organizational meeting the previous Saturday. Led by *Defender* editor Ethel Payne and Arnita Young Boswell of the League of Black Women, the CCWWC was also appalled by Black women's vulnerability to rape. They expressed their "concern with the crime of rape" by operating a hotline on the South Side, through which "the victims are encouraged to cooperate with the police."[4]

The anti-rape activity of the Black feminists and the Concerned Women in the early 1970s continued the historical tradition of African American women speaking publicly about their sexual violation. But the Black women who joined the NBFO, NABF, and CCWWC differed from their foremothers on one crucial front: they were willing to address the rape of Black women by Black men. Throughout the nineteenth and twentieth centuries, white Americans had stoked the "myth of the Black rapist," insisting that Black men were inherently hypersexual beings whose urge to rape white women could only be curbed through rigid segregation and retributive extralegal violence.[5] Black men became the default rapist in American cultural imagination, and Black women, who supposedly lacked the sexual morality to qualify as victims of rape, disappeared from the discourse altogether. African American women would fight to be recognized as violable victims whose bodies were not freely available to white men, but remained mostly silent about the Black men who abused them. Through their strategic silence, they avoided reinforcing the "myth of the Black rapist."[6] Moreover, protesting the sexual predations of white men proved politically useful for delegitimizing white supremacist social structures from slavery to Jim Crow.

By the 1970s, Black women from across the political spectrum were bucking this tradition. Brenda Eichelberger asserted at a consciousness-raising session sponsored by the Chicago NBFO that "when one considers that in most major metropolitan areas 70% of the rape victims are Black women who have been raped by Black men, it becomes paramount that Black men address themselves to the issue."[7] The CCWWC also called upon Black Chicago to focus on the sexual violence that occurred within its borders. "The real tragedy is that we in the ghetto seem to take out on each other our anger and resentment over the black condition," Ethel Payne surmised. "In this era of violent crime, we must become part of the solution, or we will become part of the problem."[8] Both Eichelberger and Payne claimed the same duty to care for assaulted Black women and girls in their communities that Black women had honored for generations.[9] They diverged when it came to taking political action toward rectifying and preventing those assaults. Eichelberger pointed directly to Black men's culpability, while Payne's use of the first-person plural gestured toward a broader community responsibility.

Though committed to the same project of combatting intraracial rape, Black feminists and the non-feminist Concerned Women advanced competing understandings of the issue. Eichelberger and her Black feminist colleagues approached the rape of Black women by Black men as a symptom of the sexism within the Black community that had gone unchecked for too long and compounded the destructive impact of racism. Meanwhile, Payne and other Concerned Women never grappled with the effects of patriarchy. Instead, they categorized intraracial rape as a form of "Black-on-Black crime," a term invented in the 1970s to connote a sudden surge of criminality among Black urbanites that was ultimately more destructive than the effects of white supremacy. Whereas Black feminists directly challenged the interlocking systemic oppressions of racism and sexism, the Concerned Women called for personal responsibility and expanded policing as the salvation of the Black community. In this way, their anti-rape activities aligned with the goals of the federal "war on crime," the constellation of pro-criminalization public policies from which they derived their name. Conversely, Black feminists understood the potential of their anti-rape advocacy to further the criminalization of their communities. They calibrated their ethic and praxis of care for Black women and girls accordingly.[10]

The Concerned Women and the Black feminists represented a fork in the road of Black women's tradition of caring for assaulted Black women and girls. The road of the Concerned Women, with their disinterest in the dynamics of patriarchy, moralizing tone, and appeals to the protection of extant systems, would resonate with pockets of non-activist Black women beleaguered by seemingly uncontrollable rates of community violence through the 1970s and 1980s. But the road cut by Black feminists, however short-lived their formal organizations, would place African American women from across the political spectrum in feminist rape crisis centers and anti-rape organizations founded by white feminists.[11] There, they continued to dismantle the enforced silence that shrouded rape within the Black community while opposing the steady encroachment of carceral solutions to rape.

Black Feminists Confront the Black Rapist

Formal Black feminist organizations proliferated in the 1970s, including the Third World Women's Alliance (1968–1979), the National Black Feminist Organization (1973–1975), the Combahee River Collective (1975–1980), and the National Alliance of Black Feminists (1976–1980). Their founders—Fran Beal, Margaret Sloan, Brenda Eichelberger, and Barbara and Beverly Smith, to name a few—had spent the previous decade in Black liberation organizations like the Student Non-Violent Coordinating Committee (SNCC), the Congress of Racial Equality (CORE), and the Black Panther Party (BPP) but found that the male leadership of these groups frequently indulged in sexism. Offenses ranged from relegating female members to menial tasks to demanding unrestricted sexual access to women comrades. The severity of the masculinism varied widely across and within Black liberation groups, even between chapters of the same organization.[12] Some Black liberation leaders conflated first-class citizenship with ownership of Black women's bodies, creating the conditions for sexual violence within these spaces.[13] Many of the Black women who were drawn to these organizations by their revolutionary potential challenged their sexually charged subordination, altering political and intellectual foundations as they did so.[14] Others elected to split off into separate Black feminist organizations where they could tackle the problems facing Black women, including intraracial sexual violence.

bell hooks detected a disturbing strand of misogyny coursing through radical Black politics in the 1960s in which "black men . . . idolized men who exploited and brutalized women" and "use violence against women to restore their lost sense of power and masculinity."[15] The most forceful assertion of Black men's "castration" under white supremacy came from early Black Panther Party leader Eldridge Cleaver. His widely read prison memoir *Soul on Ice* (1968) repeatedly identified the author as a "Black Eunuch" whose impaired state was partly relieved by raping Black and white women prior to his incarceration.[16] Historian Robyn Spencer concurs that "Cleaver's uncritical embrace by such a wide swath of movement activists speaks to the consensus around patriarchy and the promotion of manhood that was so central to movement culture at that time."[17] This vein of objectifying and possessive masculinism was neither uniform nor unshakable throughout the movement.[18] Historian Ashley Farmer points out that Eldridge Cleaver, alongside Amiri Baraka and Maulana Karenga, retracted their patriarchal cultural nationalism by the early 1970s in response to the ascendance of Black Power women like Ericka Huggins.[19] But for many Black women, this introspection arrived too late. Several Black women who were active within civil rights and Black Power groups during the 1960s retrospectively disclosed the rape, assault, and harassment they encountered within these organizations. In June 1964, Gwendolyn Zoharah Simmons (born Gwendolyn Dolores Robinson) was assaulted by a respected Black male activist while attending the Mississippi Summer Project Orientation at Western College for Women in Oxford, Ohio. A second male SNCC leader dismissed her report of the assault, suggesting that "you should have given him some anyway."[20] Panther women like Elaine Brown, Kathleen Cleaver (the former partner of Eldridge), JoNina Abon, Tondalela Woolfolk, and Regina Jennings later reported sexual abuse from their male comrades in Oakland, New York City, and Chicago.[21]

Gender-based violence also afflicted smaller Black Power groups, as well as unaffiliated Black men who claimed to work toward Black liberation. Years before joining Philadelphia Women Organized Against Rape, Wadiyah Nelson learned firsthand about the machinations of male violence through her husband, a Pan-Africanist teacher who physically and sexually abused her. Nelson quickly discovered that her husband's commitment to racial justice did not imply a commitment to gender equality. She recalled: "He had been married to a white woman, and admitted to physically abusing her. And he said to me 'I would never do that to a Black woman.' . . . That was a trap. Because I was thinking, 'He wouldn't do it to me, because he's a Black man and I'm a Black woman.' I had not yet grown into a feminist."[22] Nelson eventually divorced her abusive husband. But her experiences with a reading group in a Black bookstore on 52nd Street in West Philadelphia reinforced her belief that Black Power discourses accommodated sexual violence. She bristled over the group's decision to study *Soul on Ice* and fumed as male members minimized Cleaver's assaults on Black and white women. Nelson tired of what she saw as a "dick thing" masquerading as revolutionary politics.[23] In her view, the tacit permission to assault Black women was the most severe facet of the sexism that hamstrung the Black Power movement.

Black feminist social scientists have elaborated upon the anecdotal evidence of sexual abuse offered by women who participated in male-led civil rights and Black Power organizations. Patricia Hill Collins suggests that a "prevailing Black gender ideology," warped by Western cultural mores, requires Black men to violently seize control of the Black women in their lives in order to prove their masculinity and ward off their own victimization.[24] This ideology also requires Black women to prove their femininity by "assuming the position" and quietly complying with abuse, never allowing their complaints of gender oppression to upstage the community's focus on racial oppression.[25] Beth Richie adds that under the combined stressors of criminalization and economic divestment in the late twentieth century, "the community embraces a set of dynamics that conspire to foster an environment where individual men can use physical and sexual violence against Black women with few real or long-term consequences."[26] Both Collins and Richie add empirical merit to the pronunciation made by bell hooks decades prior that "Black male / female relationships (like all male / female relationships in American society) are tyrannized by the imperialism of patriarchy which makes oppression of women a cultural necessity."[27] The models and theories developed by Collins, Richie, and hooks make clear that Black liberation circles were not particularly abusive toward Black women compared to the wider Black community or American society at large. Nor was the violent subjugation of Black women a central goal or even enduring feature of movements for Black freedom in the 1960s and 1970s. But their lingering commitment to patriarchy and slow-building admission of their own masculinism left little space for the comprehensive reckoning with intraracial sex violence that Black activist women sought.[28] Separate Black feminist organizations seemed the only viable venue for these conversations.

Sexual violence occupied a prominent place in the theorizing and organizational agendas of Black feminist organizations from their earliest days.[29] In the spring of 1973, Margaret Sloan juggled a nationwide speaking tour with rising feminist luminary Gloria Steinem and steady editorial work with *Ms.* magazine, which had become the official organ of the burgeoning women's liberation movement. That same year, she connected with a handful of politically engaged Black women in New York City, including Eleanor Holmes Norton, Florynce Kennedy, and Michele Wallace.[30] The group did not officially announce the formation of the National Black Feminist Organization until August 1973, when Sloan and Norton spontaneously called for a regional conference of Black feminists to take place in New York that December. Sloan was quickly inundated by phone calls from hundreds of Black women requesting information about joining local chapters or forming their own. Hundreds more attended the Eastern Regional Conference at Manhattan's Cathedral of St. John the Divine from November 30 through December 2.[31] Sloan was unprepared to meet this demand, and the NBFO would falter two years later due to lack of organizational structure. Sloan packed the short life of the NBFO with consciousness-raising and organizing that spoke to the rape and abuse Black women encountered within their communities. The attendees of the Eastern Regional Conference of November and December 1973 listed rape as a special concern for African American women, convincing Sloan to prioritize the issue on the NBFO's agenda.[32]

In August 1974, Sloan sat down for a televised interview with Sandra Elkin, the white host of the "Woman" segment on WNED Buffalo.[33] She retraced for Elkin the origin story of the NBFO and her own Black feminist politics. Sloan was an alumna of both CORE and the SCLC, two prominent male-led civil rights organizations. Though she did not disclose any sexual abuse within CORE or SCLC, she maintained that "the civil rights organizations [and] Black liberation organizations were born out of a patriarchal society." As a result, they were "carrying on the same kinds of oppressions that we as Black people, men and women, were fighting so desperately to be free of." As Sloan saw it, no issue better encapsulated the deadly combination of racism and sexism in Black women's lives than sexual violence. "As Black women," Sloan explained to Elkin, "we see this is a clear issue that Black women must address ourselves to . . . We see rape as the female lynching." Statistics confirmed that in New York City nearly 70 percent of reported rape victims were Black and / or Hispanic women, with the most common victim being a Black girl between the ages of eleven and nineteen. These numbers mirrored what Brenda Eichelberger reported for Chicago. Sloan also announced before Elkin that the NBFO had formed an internal "Rape Committee" that actively participated in New York City's Women's Anti-Rape Coalition alongside other white-led feminist groups, including the Manhattan Women's Political Caucus, the New York Radical Feminists (NYRF), the National Organization for Women (NOW), and the New York Women Against Rape (NYWAR).

Essie Mae Williams coordinated much of the NBFO's anti-rape activities in New York City. Her efforts began with holding a workshop on rape at the NBFO's Eastern Regional Conference in late 1973.[34] According to Williams, "the fact that women were in the workshop meant that rape was an issue for Black women."[35] After hearing the Black women in attendance share wrenching accounts of rape and the constant fear of assault that suffused their daily lives, Williams offered a course of action. She insisted that "members of black feminist groups who have the time or the commitment to the whole issue of rape should get involved with the New York Women Against Rape and the Manhattan Political Caucus to get the experience of rape counseling and public education as a preparation for setting up these same services in the Black community." While they could take advantage of the groundwork already laid by the feminist movement against sexual violence, Williams found it insufficient to simply direct Black women to existing rape crisis centers. Establishing freestanding rape counseling and preventative education in Black communities was essential because Black women were primarily assaulted within their own communities. "In dealing with the statistics, you find that most rapes are not interracial—that most Black women are raped by Black men," Williams declared. "A very high percentage of rape victims are Black and the persons committing the crime are Black also, so what is the Black community going to do about this?" The community-based anti-rape advocacy Williams envisioned aligned with the historic tradition of Black women's caring labor filling in the cracks left by a negligent state. It also promised to enact political change *within* the community itself. Williams remained optimistic about the prospect of community education to reduce the incidence of rape among African Americans and convince Black men to embrace Black feminism. She concluded that "if we keep on pushing, a lot of brothers will become aware of how feminism is a part of the struggle for the liberation of all people and how these issues such as rape work into that pattern."

Initially, the white feminist founders of NYWAR feared that "rape cannot be a priority of black feminists because it sets up too great a division between black men and women, and that black women's racial loyalty will prevent them from bringing complaints against black men."[36] This presumption reflected the older phase of Black women's anti-rape tradition, one that complied with male-led civil rights struggles and refrained from validating the dreaded myth of the Black rapist. The NBFO quickly defied NYWAR's assumptions. By January 1974, it was clear that Black women were surpassing white women as the most frequent callers on the hotline. Throughout the summer of 1974, representatives of NYWAR regularly attended NBFO meetings and events. Impressed by their awareness campaign on "rape in the black community," NYWAR welcomed NBFO members as volunteer counselors.[37] Just three weeks after Margaret Sloan's interview with Sandra Elkin, the NBFO and NYWAR cohosted a Speak-Out on Rape and Sexual Abuse at Junior High School 104 in Stuyvesant Town, Manhattan, complete with consciousness-raising sessions, an open mic, workshops, and self-defense demonstrations.[38]

In the wake of the wildly successful Speak-Out, NBFO members Elizabeth Bell and Hortense Barber took up the charge of "going out to areas where Black women are and speaking and educating and showing just what to do in case you've been raped."[39] Bell was instrumental in organizing the August 1974 Speak-Out to meaningfully include Black women's experience. A public health nurse by training, Bell was highly skilled in convincing Black women of their intrinsic worth in the face of a racist and sexist society that devalued them. This was not only a central goal of organized Black feminism, but also a foundational element of Black women's praxis and ethic of care. "Many black women don't feel that the rape issue deserves high priority, since there are so many other issues affecting them," Bell noted. "They need to be educated to understand the importance of the issue."[40] Bell also lent her voice as an official spokeswoman for the NYC Women's Anti-Rape Coalition, in which she vigorously campaigned for the city to recognize August as Rape Prevention Month. Hortense Barber, who held a day job as a computer systems analyst, aimed even higher than Bell and sought to "declare August as rape prevention month nation-wide to "make the nation safe for women!!!"[41] For Barber, making the nation safe for women meant expanding the work she was already performing in New York City under the auspices of the NBFO's Rape Committee and the NYC Women's Anti-Rape Coalition, namely "education regarding the facts of rape and rape prevention" and "funding of women-sponsored rape prevention projects" like rape crisis centers. Like Bell, Barber was committed to dismantling a rigidly patriarchal culture that silenced women—especially Black women—on the male violence that plagued their lives. In August 1975, she joined the roster of speakers for the New York City Rape Conference organized annually by the Women's Anti-Rape Coalition, where she lectured on the subject of "Rape Prevention and Self-Assertion."[42]

The Chicago chapter of the National Black Feminist Organization directed even more theorizing and organizing toward stopping the rape of Black women by Black men. Raised in Washington, D.C. and educated as a teacher and counselor, Brenda Eichelberger convened a meeting for Black women interested in Black feminism at the YWCA in Chicago's Loop District in the early summer of 1974.[43] She was thrilled by the news that a National Black Feminist Organization had been born in August 1973, but was unwilling to squander the energy and enthusiasm of Black feminists in Chicago by waiting for the blessing of Sloan and her associates in New York City.[44] Even without their guidance, Eichelberger arrived at the conclusion that sexual violence required urgent attention from Black feminists. Anti-rape politics suffused the early materials produced by the "provisional" Chicago Chapter of the National Black Feminist Organization. The inaugural meeting designated an "Anti-Rape Committee" alongside committees on employment, education, health, and media. During the July 24, 1974, meeting, member Michele Gautreaux reported on the rape crisis intervention classes she had been attending with the Northside Rape Crisis Intervention Line and urged all members to join her.[45] By the end of the summer, Eichelberger proudly announced that "our most active project to date has been working in the area of rape" in collaboration with the Northside Rape Crisis Intervention Line.[46] Like other Black feminists, she fully recognized that the primary sexual threat facing Black women came from within their communities, not from outside: "Many are not aware of the fact that in Chicago the rank order of victim and rapist are as follows: First, black women raped by Black men. Second, White women raped by white men. Third, Black women raped by White men. Fourth, White women raped by Black men. It is interesting to note that based on media coverage, the last order appears to be the first."[47] Eichelberger also drew attention to the enormous difficulties faced by assaulted Black women who turned to the criminal justice system of Chicago. "Many are not aware of the callous attitude of law enforcement officials, hospitals, and the courts have towards rape victims," Eichelberger explained. "Moreover, when the victim happens to be black, it is often assumed she is a prostitute" whose sexual immorality discredited her as a victim.[48] From late 1974 through early 1975, the Anti-Rape Committee of the Chicago Black Feminists forged partnerships with the Northside Rape Crisis Line, Chicago Legal Action for Women, Rape Victim Advocates, and a handful of sympathetic police commanders. Together, they developed counseling services and escort services for the hospital, police station, and the courts, and hosted regular public information sessions.[49] In a January 1975 piece in the *Chicago Daily News* on the flowering of Black feminism in the city, Michele Gautreaux confirmed that "the problem of rape in the black community" remained a "major concern of the Chicago chapter [of the NBFO]."[50]

By the summer of 1975, the Chicago NBFO had become the National Alliance of Black Feminists (NABF), secured permanent meeting space at the Blue Gargoyle, and appointed Brenda Eichelberger as chair.[51] Shortly thereafter, the NABF formulated the "Black Woman's Bill of Rights," which outlined the objectives of the NABF by listing ten broad fields in which organized Black women could turn back the racism and sexism that deprived them of full citizenship. All these fields foregrounded an ethic of care for Black women's bodies and minds, and several specified anti-violence initiatives. "The RIGHT to access to knowledge of and control of her own body" included supportive services for victims of rape and abuse.[52] "The RIGHT to equal protection under the law for her life, limb, and property" granted Black women "increased preventive [*sic*] measures to secure her protection from sexual abuse" as well as "appropriate assistance to victims and witnesses of crimes."

Crucially, the NABF did not define Black women's safety from sexual violence as the responsibility of an invigorated police force. In fact, they identified "freedom from police harassment" as constitutive of a right to "Individual Freedom," positioning law enforcement as an antagonistic element in the lives of Black women. In the construction of this wide-ranging "Black Women's Bill of Rights," the NABF saw safety from sexual violence as imbricated in Black women's political, social, medical, and psychological wellbeing. This care-based approach reflected what legal scholar James Forman Jr. has termed the "all-of-the-above strategy" that frequently characterized Black politics during the early 1970s, in which Black leaders tentatively accepted crimefighting policies so long as they were coupled with attacks on structural inequality.[53] Brenda Eichelberger elaborated on this "all-of-the-above strategy" for addressing sexual assault in an interview for the feminist periodical *Quest*. She recalled the "countless numbers of times" Black women approached her in public and agreed that they needed "increased protection from . . . sexual abusers" alongside pay equity, robust social welfare, and labor protections.[54]

By the summer of 1976, messages about intracommunal rape had percolated beyond Black feminist groups and gained traction with a wider audience of politically unaffiliated Black women. That June, Bernette Golden's groundbreaking article "The Ugly Crime of Rape" appeared in *Essence*, the flagship African American women's magazine.[55] Golden assembled an alarming array of statistics, anecdotes, and literary excerpts spotlighting Black women's vulnerability to sexual assault within their own communities and the sociocultural factors that maintained their vulnerability. Beginning with Eldridge Cleaver's infamous confession in *Soul on Ice* that he began "practicing on Black girls in the ghetto" before seeking white women to assault and continuing with a harrowing account of Janet Brown's rape at knifepoint under Manhattan's 155th Street Bridge, Golden castigated Black men who weaponized their sexuality to control Black women.[56] Like her Black feminist contemporaries, she emphasized the overwhelmingly intraracial nature of rape against Black women. "When a Black woman is raped, it is usually by a Black man," Golden averred. She attributed the prevalence of rape in the Black community to the combined effect of racism and sexism upon the socialization of Black boys and girls.[57] In keeping with the Black feminist arguments of Margaret Sloan and Brenda Eichelberger, Golden concluded that this cycle of victimization must be interrupted through consciousness-raising among Black women and feminist education among Black men. "Discussing rape with other Black women will help us become aware of and find ways to change our traditional psychological and physical vulnerability. Discussing this crime with Black men will also help them re-examine their attitudes about women and sex."[58]

Not everyone agreed with the interventions of Black feminists or appreciated the sudden about-face on intraracial rape in the Black press. In the spring of 1979, sociologist Robert Staples took to the pages of the *Black Scholar* to refute what he termed "the myth of the Black macho."[59] His title referenced NBFO founding member Michele Wallace's pivotal Black feminist text, *Black Macho and the Myth of Superwoman* (1979). Staples argued, contrary to Williams, that Black men were not oppressors of Black women. "Angry" Black feminists were naively copycatting white feminists who were flexing their racial privilege by attacking Black men. For Staples, the feminist response to rape was a case in point. "The black male had been spared as a target of feminists," Staples wrote. "White feminists generally left him alone in their assault on men . . . In the last few years, however, a few of them have taken off the gloves."[60] Staples pointed to prominent anti-rape texts crafted by white feminists, namely Diana E. H. Russell's *The Politics of Rape* (1974) and Susan Brownmiller's *Against Our Will* (1975), as proof that "Black males can now be attacked, not as the banker denying white women credit, but as the sadistic rapist lurking in the alley to terrorize and sodomize a white woman to whom he has no other access." According to Staples, Black feminists who spoke out against rape were derivatively participating in open season on the Black man and furthering his emasculation.

The Black feminist poet Audre Lorde forcefully answered Staples's diatribe in the very next issue of *The Black Scholar*. Lorde assured Staples that "Black feminism is not white feminism in blackface," but an organic articulation of Black women's dual suffering under racism and sexism.[61] Echoing bell hooks's assessment of capitalist patriarchy, Lorde stated, "No reasonable Black man can possibly condone the rape and slaughter of Black women by Black men as a fitting response to capitalist oppression."[62] In her response to Staples, Lorde reprised the message of Black feminists that rape was a devastating issue within the Black community and addressing it openly did not constitute a breach in racial solidarity. She concluded that "as Black women and men, we cannot hope to begin dialogue by denying the oppressive nature of male privilege. And if Black males choose to assume that privilege for whatever reason—raping, brutalizing, and killing Black women—then ignoring these acts of Black male oppression within our communities can only serve our destroyers."[63]

Staples also received a sharp rebuke from Black feminists operating in the grassroots. In October 1979, Barbara Smith of the Combahee River Collective composed "An Open Letter on Black Feminism" that ran in *Plexus*, a Bay Area women's newspaper.[64] She directed the predominantly white feminist readership to select issues of *Essence*, *Ebony*, *Jet*, and *the Black Scholar* "not only to familiarize themselves with what is going on in the Black community around issues of sexual politics, but also to see what we Black feminists are up against." Staples' "virulently anti–Black feminist article" in *the Black Scholar* was a case in point, illustrating how "sexual politics is finally up for discussion by Black people and that there is a massive amount of resistance to the idea of Black women being autonomous by many Black people." Black feminists' identification of Black men as potential rapists, though an outrage to Staples, clearly fell under the purview of sexual politics. Smith had another complaint with *Ebony*, the glossy monthly magazine on Black news, culture, and entertainment. A special August 1979 issue focusing on "Black-on-Black Crime" largely omitted "the epidemic of violence against women or sexual oppression and patriarchal notions of manhood as causes for Black women's abuse and deaths." In fact, other Black women were discussing sexual violence as an aspect of intracommunal violence in the Black media. However, they were omitting the requisite condemnation of patriarchy.

Rape as "Black-on-Black Crime"

In early November 1974, a woman going by the initials "W. E." submitted a disturbing letter to Ask Alice, the advice column of the *Chicago Defender*. According to W. E., her granddaughter had been sexually assaulted by her daughter's live-in boyfriend, who had a criminal record for assault and rape. W. E. reported that her daughter was "afraid to take any action" against her boyfriend. She begged Alice Claire for guidance on "what can be done to get this man out of the house and in jail where he belongs."[65] Alice Claire replied to W. E. and alerted her that she would be forwarding her letter to an organization of Black women who were committed to addressing rape within Chicago's Black neighborhoods. Claire did not have Brenda Eichelberger's National Black Feminist Organization chapter in mind. In fact, she adopted a distinctly anti-feminist tone, declaring W. E.'s daughter "the real culprit in this whole shameful situation" because "she is putting this man before the safety of her children." Bypassing the Black feminists, Claire directed W. E. to the Coalition of Concerned Women in the War on Crime (CCWWC). Members of the CCWWC jointly operated a rape crisis line on the South Side of the city with the League of Black Women. They also promoted dialogues between the community and the police on a long list of crimes that included sexual violence. Claire shared W. E.'s yearning for punishment, agreeing that "this man is a danger and should be confined." She assured her readers that the CCWWC was "concerned about repeat offenders who are turned loose to prey upon society" and endorsed incarceration as an effective form of rape prevention.

The harrowing story "W. E." told was not an isolated incident. Earlier that year, the *Chicago Tribune* ran several stories that anticipated Black feminist talking points: rape was "growing at an alarming rate" in Chicago, Black women comprised the majority of its victims, and they were almost uniformly victimized by Black men.[66] The surge of rapes and the overrepresentation of the Black population within it caught the attention of other Black women in

Chicago who did not label themselves as feminists. Chicago's League of Black Women (LBW), founded by Dr. Arnita Young Boswell as a vehicle for professional Black women's community leadership, was already holding rallies and dialogues "to educate the community at large about intraracial sexual violence, and to encourage black leadership in attempting to eradicate it."[67] The League of Black Women was represented among the forty women delegates from community organizations who gathered at the offices of the *Chicago Defender* in late February 1974 to "launch an all-out fight on crime in black neighborhoods," including sexual assault.[68] An ad hoc committee emerged from the meeting chaired by Ethel Payne, associate editor of the *Daily Defender*. Heralded as "the First Lady of the Black Press," Payne led a pathbreaking career in journalism as the first African American woman admitted to the White House press corps and regular commentator on milestones of the civil rights movement.[69] A lifelong resident of the South Side of Chicago who had held her position at the *Defender* since 1951, she saw combatting crime in her native city as the next logical step in the Black freedom struggle. She joined Black leaders across the nation who acknowledged a genuine uptick in violent crime within their constituencies and called for action to combat it.[70] By March 1974, the ad hoc committee crystallized into the Coalition of Concerned Women in the War on Crime, with Ethel Payne at its head.

The CCWWC addressed itself to "the spiraling crime wave in the city" by calling for "more cooperation on the part of the Chicago Police Department and greater citizen responsibility."[71] In practice, this meant establishing task forces to educate the public on forms of crime in a manner that sought "to improve community-police relations."[72] Police-community relations programs appeared in dozens of cities that had been engulfed by the urban rebellions of the late 1960s, created by Black denizens hoping to promote mutual understanding with local law enforcement.[73] The CCWWC innovated by dedicating a specialized rape committee that strove to foster better relations between the Chicago Police Department and Black rape victims. The committee met frequently and productively with Chicago Police Commissioner James Rochford, to whom they recommended the appointment of Black policewomen and "quick responses to calls for help" from Black women victims.[74] The CCWWC also "urge[d] all women to take advantage of the services of the Southside Rape Crisis Line." They hoped that callers would be convinced to "report and prosecute rapists in order to make the streets safer."[75]

The CCWWC never used the word "feminist" to describe their public statements and community organizing around rape. As self-proclaimed foot soldiers of the "war on crime," the CCWWC framed the rape of Black women by Black men as one facet of the explosion of violent crimes committed by Black people against their neighbors in blighted urban spaces. In keeping with the prescriptions of the "war on crime," they looked to stronger police presence as a solution to sexual violence in 1970s Black Chicago. Despite the invention of myriad police-community relations programs, calling for stronger police presence in Black neighborhoods remained controversial.[76] The police murders of Black Panther leaders Fred Hampton and Mark Clark in 1969 remained etched in the memory of many Black Chicagoans, reinforcing the consensus that law enforcement only added to the violence that plagued their communities.[77] In the founding meeting of the Coalition of Concerned Women in the War on Crime, Payne acknowledged the appalling record of the Chicago police, but doubled down on the need to forge a new alliance. "While recognizing the existence of police brutality and corruption and the need for police reform, the basis for the struggle against crime must be made in police-citizen cooperation," she argued.[78] One favorable write-up in the *Defender* in November 1974 agreed that the Coalition "achieved a remarkable record of cooperation with the Chicago Police Department in effecting dialogue between the police and the people at the neighborhood level . . . without compromising on the issue of police brutality."[79]

For Payne and her associates in the Coalition of Concerned Women in the War on Crime, intracommunal violence was not a longstanding problem finally brought to light. It was a sudden, new problem indicative of the changing values of Black America. Payne believed that during the 1960s, African Americans in Chicago were preoccupied with police brutality, an obvious and deadly manifestation of racism, and were therefore disinclined to seriously engage with the issue of crime at the community level.[80] But she insisted that times had changed. In the 1970s, "black-on-black crime showed that there is *personal responsibility* in the fight on crime."[81] Payne's allusions to personal responsibility should not suggest that she or the CCWWC were politically conservative. By "personal responsibility," Payne meant the necessity for individuals within the Black community to hold themselves to a higher moral standard. This recalled an older race improvement strategy honed by Black club women like Mary Church Terrell, Anna Julia Cooper, and Nannie Helen Burroughs since the nineteenth century. In addition to demanding criminal justice reform, they called for moral uprightness within the Black community as a tactical means of preventing Black women from being abused and proving to white authorities that Black people were worthy of protection.[82] Black club women's deployment of moral improvement in the Black community made sense in a Jim Crow political climate, where gaining recognition of Black people as citizens entitled to equal protections under the law was the undisputed goal. Payne's application of the rhetoric of moral improvement and police cooperation struck a different chord in the post–civil rights era as the target of Black women's anti-rape activism expanded to include Black men.

Payne's references to "black-on-black crime" reflected the new social narrative that percolated within the mainstream press in the decade that followed the civil rights movement. Criminologist Bernard D. Headley first described "Black-on-Black crime" in 1983 as a media narrative in which "the physical survival and well-being of the black community in America is threatened more by blacks killing or stealing from other blacks (threats from within) than from external or systemic forces (threats from without)."[83] According to Headley, racist media figures popularized the phrase to deflect attention from the racial capitalism that alienated poor Black people from their communities and compelled them to commit crimes as a means of survival. As a politically loaded media contrivance, "Black-on-Black crime" recast crime perpetrated by African Americans as an individual moral failing divorced from systems of oppression and placed the onus upon Black communities to sternly correct or disown their errant members. This line of reasoning proved persuasive in the 1970s, after the Civil Rights Act of 1964 abolished legal discrimination but poverty and violence kept a grip on Black urban centers. With white racists supposedly muzzled, Black communities could only blame themselves for their enduring problems. According to the narrative, intracommunal violence happened because the Black community tolerated it, and would continue to happen unless they set stringent internal standards for behavior and cooperated with police to enforce them. In this respect, the narrative of "Black-on-Black crime" ideologically bolstered the "war on crime," which also prescribed heavy-handed police intervention as the ultimate cure for crime and poverty among Black Americans.

Headley noted that "the myth that crimes committed by blacks against other blacks pose the single most dangerous threat to the black community is one that the black community itself (including the black press) has helped promulgate."[84] The *Chicago Defender*, where CCWWC's Ethel Payne served as editor, both trafficked in the narrative and interpreted intraracial sexual violence in Black Chicago through that lens. Pearl Reed's December 1974 op-ed "Calling the Kettle the Right Color" presented rape as a foil to arguments about the systemic roots of crime in the Black community. After agreeing with the premise that "violent crime is mostly black on black," Reed wrote that "Some black leaders say blacks commit crimes because they are hungry and unemployed. What has rape got to do with being hungry? After they rape, they are still hungry—lies and excuses."[85] By 1977, *Chicago Defender* police reporter Lawrence Muhammad proclaimed himself an "honest law and order convert," meaning one who was not cowed by the specter of burning cities, but by a sincere belief that increased policing would produce a healthier society.[86] He completed his conversion after reviewing the rape statistics furnished by Chicago Police Superintendent Michael Spioto. For one week, eighteen of twenty-four rapes were reported by Black victims, all of whom accused a Black assailant. That week was not an outlier. The four Chicago districts where reported rapes reached triple digits in 1977 all lay in the predominantly Black South and West Sides of the city: Wentworth (131), Englewood (111), Grand Crossing (101), and Westside-Harrison (100). The statistics convinced Muhammad that the Black community was locked in a self-destructive cycle that "cannot be remedied by traditional formulas of politics and civil rights." In Muhammad's view, rape and other violent crimes had no basis in poverty or discrimination. Intracommunal violence was not a problem of oppression but "a problem of the mind, the result of warped social attitudes." This "problem of the mind" was exacerbated by lax enforcement of the law, especially among Black police officers who inappropriately sympathized with accused Black rapists and released them without further questioning. Two years later, Muhammad released a nearly identical column in which high rates of intraracial rape once again served as the justification for more invasive police presence in Black Chicago.[87]

The Concerned Women's alarm over intracommunal violence and subsequent calls for more rigorous law enforcement were not unique within Black politics. Black activists and commentators' acceptance of the "black-on-black crime" media narrative across the 1970s demonstrated mounting frustration and desperation amid state retreat from anti-poverty initiatives and the intractability of systemic racism.[88] Historian Leah Wright Rigueur argues that Black voters in the 1970s were understandably alarmed by the crime that rendered their neighborhoods dangerous.[89] However, they consistently rejected narrow appeals to "law and order," insisting instead that "law and order" must be coupled with a broader recognition of unjust social conditions. What distinguished Ethel Payne and the Concerned Women in their anti-rape activities was that greater police involvement itself would catalyze a community movement to correct unjust social conditions.[90] Payne saw incarceration as a key mechanism of accountability in her grassroots "war on crime," warning that "unless the judge acts with deliberation, [criminals] could be out on the streets on bond to rape again." Payne's hopes for a successful grassroots movement against intracommunal violence sat uneasily beside a persistent moral condemnation of the Black populace for its self-destructive habits. She remarked that "Blacks are going to have to learn that rape is neither a laughing matter nor a stigmata [*sic*] that the victim must endure."[91] Though Payne saw Black Chicagoans as capable of controlling rape, such a change would require the firm guiding hand of a punitive criminal justice system to fully materialize. On that point, Payne and the policymakers behind the "war on crime" agreed.

Labeling the entirety of the Coalition of Concerned Women in the War on Crime as politically conservative due to their approach to controlling rape would be an oversimplification. Other committees within the group evinced deep concern with the structural causes of Black urban poverty and supported community action programs reminiscent of the "War on Poverty."[92] That said, the anti-rape activity of the Concerned Women certainly bore signs of a Black conservatism rooted in defensive reactions toward the white gaze, such as reinforcing patriarchal relations of protection and policing the morality of poor Black Chicagoans. In this respect, the Concerned Women straddled the shifting priorities of the "War on Poverty" and the "war on crime."[93]

At the time of their first anniversary celebration in February 1975, the CCWWC still regarded intracommunal violence as a key battleground in the grassroots "war on crime." They celebrated the expanded programming at the Southside Rape Crisis Line, which included preventative self-defense training for Black women in addition to counseling Black victims to report their rapes.[94] Ethel Payne recognized Mary Garden Williams, the director of the line and member of the League of Black Women, with an award for her "outstanding contributions in the city-wide effort to combat crime."[95] That spring, Payne attended Arnita Young Boswell's retirement send-off from LBW as a representative of the CCWWC. She praised Boswell and her colleagues for "helping to change attitudes of the public, hospitals, courts, and police about the treatment of rape victims," all of which "help the War on Crime program."[96]

Over the next few years, Payne continued demanding a more robust criminal justice response to intracommunal violence that would stir Black Chicago from its apathy. Speaking on behalf of the Concerned Women, Payne informed the Illinois State Legislature that "black women often do become resigned to rape as what they feel is an unavoidable fact of life" and "police in the inner city areas considered rape to be an accepted behavior pattern" among Blacks that did not demand punitive intervention.[97] In late 1978, Aurie Pennick would replace the outgoing Payne as the director of the Coalition of Concerned Women in the War on Crime. She concurred with her predecessor that "rape is but one of the many crimes that residents accept matter-of-factly."[98] Vera Hubbard, a member of the Concerned Women and resident of Henry Horner Homes, seconded Pennick. "It's like people are saying 'what the heck, it's black on black, no big deal.'" In their condemnations, Payne, Pennick, and Hubbard brushed against the systemic racism and sexism that exposed Black women to cyclical violence, just as the National Black Feminist Organization and National Alliance of Black Feminists did. But their genuine frustration over the pervasiveness of violence against Black women did not drive them to Black feminism. Instead, they locked their focus on the lack of moral fiber binding Black communities together and police as an instrument for forcibly rebinding them.

The CCWWC's anti-rape activities in Chicago ran parallel to those of the NABF. Both groups were fiercely committed to caring for assaulted Black women and girls. But their political frameworks for interpreting intracommunal violence differed substantially, shaping the type of care they provided. The *Chicago Defender* pinpointed the differences between these two organizations for readers who might conflate them.[99] The NABF was "about helping black women get themselves together psychologically and then working to help women—especially black women—attain full equality in this society."[100] NABF member LaVerne Bennett saw the NABF as "fill[ing] a void, a need for a common forum for black women from all stations in life to address the problems of discrimination and double jeopardy [of] being black and female." They confronted the rape of Black women by Black men through consciousness training and victim counseling, two care-based activities that did not necessarily require police involvement. By contrast, the Coalition of Concerned Women in the War on Crime sought first and foremost "to increase communication between black citizens and the police" and reduce the overall incidence of intracommunal crime. They identified intraracial rape as a gender-specific form of "Black-on-Black crime" and aimed to control it through the remedies prescribed by that narrative: greater police presence, swifter prosecution, and harsh punishment. The Concerned Women's allegiance to the "war on crime" and acceptance of the "Black-on-Black crime" media narrative precluded a deeper structural analysis of intracommunal violence. Though sincere in their attempts to shield Black women from violence, their limited framework directed them to control rape by shoring up existing punitive institutions. This stood in contrast to the NABF, who began with an understanding of how systemic racism, sexism, and capitalism colluded to produce a culture that devalued Black women. Their framework highlighted how state efforts to control crime multiplied the violences endured by Black women and directed the NABF to invest their energies in caring for them.

To Report or Not to Report: Black Feminists Seek Alternatives

While the Concerned Women welcomed law enforcement entities into their communities to control rape, Black feminists regarded state power suspiciously. Just as they recognized that holding their silence on the Black men who abused them perpetuated sexism, they also realized turning to the criminal justice system as the savior of Black women perpetuated racism without fully eradicating rape. Rather than working toward a new covenant with the criminal justice system, they developed what Barbara Smith of the Combahee River Collective has called "a nuanced Black women's perspective on how you address violence against women."[101] Scholar Beth Richie has similarly described Black feminists as forging a "third path" between silently enduring intraracial rape and enthusiastically embracing law enforcement that "addressed the issues of community violence and harm caused by state policy" with the same urgency.[102] This "nuanced Black women's perspective" or "third path" did not entail a total rejection of the tools offered by the criminal justice system to Black women who sought recourse for rape. At issue was the insistence that policing, prisons, and prosecution of rapists were the *best and only* tools for ending intracommunal violence. Black feminists countered that these tools were both blunt and unwieldy. They wished to expand the catalog to include defter tools that could strike at the anti-Blackness, misogynoir, and multiple jeopardy that, as theorist Treva B. Lindsey explains, render Black women's lives unlivable.[103] Historian Christina Greene remarks that, given this dire positionality, "not surprisingly, Black feminists were among the first to protest and theorize the contradictions of antirape activists' harnessing their efforts to the carceral state and the dangers of ignoring the long history of racialized sexual violence."[104]

Essie Green Williams of the National Black Feminist Organization invalidated the "Black-on-Black crime" narrative by situating intracommunal sexual violence within the context of systemic oppression, arguing that "what happens when people are oppressed is that they take it out on each other instead of against the oppressor."[105] In the same interview, she acknowledged that Black feminists shifting focus to intraracial rape would be "very difficult [and] very painful to address." Open discussion of sexual assaults committed by Black men could potentially concede to hostile law enforcement authorities that Black communities were hopelessly plagued by violence and required aggressive policing. This issue also surfaced at the inception of the feminist movement against sexual violence. Three months after organizing the first rape speak-out in January 1971, the New York Radical Feminists convened what was very likely "the world's first conference on rape" at Washington Irving High School in Union Square.[106] Several non-white women who attended testified that they chose not to report their rapes out of fear of betraying the men of their communities to hostile white law enforcement. One self-described Black Nationalist woman explained that: "I didn't report [my rape] to the police. Nationalism was all mixed up in this. It was partly being a Nationalist and the police were white, I felt I would be guilty in turning in another Third World person who raped me . . . that I shouldn't do that, that it was somehow wrong for me to do that, it was wrong for me to retaliate against another Third World person. It was partly that and partly because I was just terrified and partly because . . . I was sure that if I went to the police that 1) they weren't going to do anything and that 2) they weren't going to protect me."[107] Faced with the distressing fact that speaking out against rape in the Black community risked engaging state actors that were eager to criminalize them, Williams insisted that Black feminists need not retreat into silence. They should build upon the groundwork freshly laid by the predominantly white feminist movement against sexual violence and cut their own course. As she put it, "Black women should capitalize on what has already been accomplished by white women and go on from there . . . We can take that experience and apply it to our needs, make it relevant to our needs."[108] In practice, this meant providing the care assaulted Black women and girls needed but had long been denied by a systemically racist society while gradually changing the structure of that society. Williams envisioned installing victim counseling programs modelled after those piloted by rape crisis centers within Black neighborhood hospitals and broadcasting anti-sexist rape prevention education in Black schools. She added that both measures, neither of which called for extensive collaboration with law enforcement entities, "can be accomplished by work and pressure by Black feminist groups."[109]

Other Black feminist activists in New York expressed varying degrees of skepticism toward law enforcement and constructed their anti-rape activism around it. Hortense Barber explained that the Rape Committee of the NBFO cataloged the many reasons "why Black women failed to report this crime" in the past and present. Chief among them was "the history of police brutality in the Black community," which proved a greater deterrent to Black women's reporting than "society's attitude towards the rape victim and a sense of powerlessness to control our own bodies and lives." Still, the Rape Committee of the NBFO expressed a desire to "encourage Black women to report this crime."[110] Through collaborations with NYC's Women's Anti-Rape Coalition, Black feminists helped to change the corroboration clause of the state's rape law and establish the Sex Crimes Analysis Unit of the NYPD. That mission complemented other projects that were not police dependent, such as staffing the hotline founded by the New York Women Against Rape, sensitizing emergency room personnel to the needs of rape victims, and "educating Black women about rape and its effects on our lives" through workshops, martial arts demonstrations, and personal testimony. Barber contributed to the latter with a presentation on "Rape Prevention and Self Assertion" at the Third Annual New York City Rape Conference organized by NYC WARC in August 1975.[111]

Barber's colleague Elizabeth Bell offered the same explanation for Black women's reluctance to report the crime of rape in a February 1975 interview for *Encore* magazine. After affirming that the majority of rapes consist of a Black offender and Black victim, Bell added that "Black women find that reporting rape is as nonproductive as it is time-consuming" because "law enforcement officials still hold onto a stereotypic view that all Blacks do is 'eat and screw.'"[112] Moreover, "some Black women . . . are trying to protect the Black brother who raped them from the white system." Taken together, the NBFO's most committed advocates opposing the rape of Black women agreed that police cooperation was at best inadequate and at worst actively harmful for Black victims and the communities they lived in. NBFO cofounder Margaret Sloan also attended to the contradiction of helping Black women avoid rape and abuse within their communities without appealing to the overzealous policing of those same communities. During her televised interview with Sandra Elkin in August 1974, Margaret Sloan initially agreed that there should be "stiff penalties for rapists" but immediately clarified that she was "against the prison system" due to its dehumanizing treatment of its disproportionately Black prisoners.[113] She recognized that "Black women [who have been raped] stay away from the police for very real reasons." Sloan smoothed over the paradoxes in her position by strongly endorsing self-defense and assertiveness training for Black women as a means of preventing rape. But clear misgivings about the violent capacities of the state underlaid her statement.

Brenda Eichelberger of the NABF also made public statements in which a Black feminist praxis of care wrestled with carceral assumptions in rape prevention. She collaborated with Pauline Bart, a founding member of Chicago Women Against Rape and feminist sociologist at the Abraham Lincoln School of Medicine of the University of Illinois, on a paper for the annual meeting of the National Women's Studies Association titled "The Empty Cell."[114] At first glance, the title suggests the authors' desire to fill the "Empty Cell" with the men who assaulted Black women with impunity. But the paper actually addressed "the rape of black women by black men and the erasure of this problem by both the political left, the political right, the women's movement and the black movement with the exception of black feminists."[115] Eichelberger and Bart argued that intraracial rape vanished from the discourse through a series of disavowals: white racists disavow Black women as violable victims, and Black leaders and white feminists only avow Black women who have been assaulted by white men, lest they resurrect the myth of the "Black rapist." This left only Black feminists to champion the subset of Black women raped by Black men by meeting their complex needs.

Activists who did not cite Black feminist organizations by name still transmitted their key insight—demanding accountability for violence against Black women while maintaining a safe distance from the most punitive aspects of law enforcement—to the rape crisis center movement. In an open letter printed in the winter 1977 issue of the *Feminist Alliance Against Rape Newsletter*, the Santa Cruz Women Against Rape (WAR) critiqued the anti-rape movement's "attempts at good relations with the criminal justice system" because this strategy often reduced rape crisis centers to referral agencies for the police.[116] In their view, the literature produced by many rape crisis centers was decidedly "biased toward giving women information on how to report a rape," creating a false dichotomy between reporting rape to the police or ignoring rape entirely. CCWWC adhered to this exact dichotomy in their own anti-violence work. Santa Cruz WAR attributed this bias to "the fact that many groups are supported through government funds" and the terms of such grants and contracts encouraged, if not outright demanded, that anti-rape feminists work hand-in-glove with law enforcement entities. The assumption that states should fund feminist anti-rape activities to fortify the criminal justice system's response to rape and advance the "war on crime" gained support among conservative policymakers across the next two decades.[117] Anticipating the argument Angela Davis would make at Sonoma State University in 1977, Santa Cruz WAR recognized that the conflation of feminist revolution with law-and-order goals was adversely impacting women of color. As they surmised, "attempts at good relations with the criminal justice system have served to coopt our movement, and have led to the belief (or hope) that the criminal justice system can solve the problem of rape. Yet, the sexist and racist nature of the criminal justice system only makes the problem worse." They pointed to the disproportionate conviction and sentencing of non-white men and the wrongful imprisonment of women of color who violently defended themselves from sexual assaults. "We must not support a racist process for any end," they concluded.[118] It would fall to Black anti-rape organizers steeped in Black feminist thought to interrogate the feminist movement against sexual violence's acquiescence to "law and order."

While formal Black feminist organizations mostly disintegrated by 1980, their adherents carried their ideas and approaches into the rape crisis centers created by the feminist movement against sexual violence. Growing numbers of Black women joined rape crisis centers as volunteers and paid staffers, spurred to action by the coverage of intraracial rape in local newspapers and the national attention routinely thrust upon causes célèbre like Joan Little.[119] Some could draw a straight line between their membership in Black feminist organizations and their engagement in the anti-rape movement. Beryl Fitzpatrick recalled that during her time with the National Alliance of Black Feminists, Brenda Eichelberger and Michele Gautreaux implored meeting attendees to train as volunteers for Chicago's Rape Victim Advocates. She followed their advice, laying the foundation for her membership in the Chicago Sexual Assault Services Network (CSASN) a decade later.[120] Even those who were not active in formal organizations cited Black feminism as a formative influence on their anti-rape consciousness. Loretta Ross of the Washington D.C. Rape Crisis Center and Wadiyah Nelson of Philadelphia Women Organized Against Rape cited the writings of Black feminists like Toni Cade Bambara, Audre Lorde, and bell hooks as their intellectual basis for anti-rape work.[121] These broad activist and intellectual ecologies linked organized Black feminism to the feminist movement against sexual violence in ways that preserved the distinctive anti-rape politics of the former.

The First National Conference on Third World Women and Violence demonstrated that Black feminist approaches to intraracial sexual violence gained a foothold within the rape crisis centers created by the feminist movement against sexual violence. The first-of-its-kind conference drew over one hundred Black, Latina, Asian, and Native American anti-rape organizers from across the country to the nation's capital in August 1980. African American women comprised 70 percent of attendees, including Nkenge Touré (born Anita Stroud).[122] Six years prior, she joined the Washington D.C. Rape Crisis Center as a volunteer, and quickly ascended to the ranks of administrator and community educator.[123] Touré was deeply concerned about the surging incidence of intraracial rape in her city. But she resisted framing the issue as "Black-on-Black crime" because it foreclosed discussion of systemic oppression and posited law enforcement as the only antidote. "I am of course opposed to black on black crime," she reasoned. "But in order to deal with it, you have to understand how it comes into being and why it exists." Like Essie Mae Williams of the NBFO, Touré explained that "within a racist, capitalistic society, as people are oppressed they become more introverted and strike out at each other."[124]

During Touré's first year as administrator, the DCRCC cast doubts on the efficacy of the prison system in controlling rape by collaborating with William Fuller, an African American inmate and founder of Prisoners Against Rape. Fuller had served fifteen years of his sentence for a rape conviction at the Lorton Correctional Complex in Virginia when he dispatched a letter to the D.C. Rape Crisis Center requesting their help in curbing his desire to commit sexual violence.[125] Touré, Loretta Ross, and another Black feminist volunteer named Yulanda Ward visited Lorton on rotation each Friday to hold study meetings with Fuller and the other Black inmates that he organized.[126] These discussions led Fuller to write a position statement for Prisoners Against Rape, which Touré forwarded to the Feminist Alliance Against Rape (FAAR), a close affiliate of the D.C. Rape Crisis Center. FAAR published Fuller's statement in the September / October 1974 issue of the *Feminist Alliance Against Rape Newsletter*, which circulated to rape crisis centers and anti-rape activists across the nation. Fuller explicated the political understanding of rape that Prisoners Against Rape gleaned from the D.C. Rape Crisis Center, stating that as Black men, "we were culturally, socially, and economically deprived of a proper education, in sexual values, norms, and understanding—as such, we took our tensions, frustrations, and hang ups out on women through the act of RAPE."[127] Pointing to his own experience as a repeat rapist who raped other men while in prison, he deconstructed the arguments made by Ethel Payne and the Coalition of Concerned Women in the War on Crime: "Society in general, and individuals in particular, believe that dehumanizing tactics such as castration, prison, and the like would prevent RAPE . . . Many individuals think that prisons, more time, more convictions are the answer. They are not . . . We must view rape as society would view a cancer. We consider it an epidemic which must be constrained as every man is a potential RAPIST. Incarceration may checkmate it, but not necessarily prevent the symptoms."[128] Even white colleagues within the D.C. Rape Crisis Center were touched by Touré and Fuller's perspective that incarcerating rapists was futile and counterproductive. The D.C. Rape Crisis Center's original policy forbade hotline operators from encouraging callers to report to the police. They simply "offered information so that callers could decide a plan of action appropriate to them."[129] By 1975, the D.C. Rape Crisis Center openly described itself as "an alternative to the police" for the city's rape victims, who were primarily Black women.[130] Nancy McDonald, a white staff member of the D.C. Rape Crisis Center, explained to the *Washington Post* that "there are a lot of good reasons why a woman should not go to the police." Presenting police reporting as the only means of recourse would adversely impact "lower class and minority women" who "have no reason to believe the police will do anything" and have much reason to believe the police will inflict further violence upon them.[131] Nancy McDonald and Lynn Wehrli, another white member of the D.C. Rape Crisis Center, validated Fuller's view of the criminal justice system as an entity that exacerbated rape more than it solved it. "People think [reporting] fixes it," said McDonald. "But I don't think so." Wehrli added, "What good does going to prison do? If anything people get more violent and aggressive in prison society. Rape isn't an individual problem. It is a social problem and the criminal justice system doesn't do anything to get at causes of rape."[132]

Five years later, while organizing the First National Conference on Third World Women and Violence, Tourè and her colleagues banned white women from attending the conference, a decision that triggered grumbling from a few white members of the anti-rape movement and even a short-lived lawsuit from a white policewoman who was denied entry.[133] But Ross, Touré, and the other organizers remained firm that Third World anti-rape activists desperately needed a space removed from the white gaze where they could safely critique the movement's white-centered praxis and envision radical alternatives. The wide-ranging conference touched upon various issues facing women of color working within the anti-rape movement: the difficulties of collaborating with white women who did not share their experience of racism, the resistance they encountered from male community members for confronting the male violence that jeopardized their community's survival, the ambivalence over

First National Conference on Third World Women and Violence

August 21, 22, and 23 Thursday, Friday, and Saturday

The Rape Crisis Center of Washington, D.C. is sponsoring Anti-Rape Week, August 17 to 23. The culminating activity for the week is the First National Conference on Third World Women and Violence.

The conference is for **women and men of color.** We are seeking Third World activists* in women's issues, service providers and community participants.

The purpose of the conference is to analyze, strategize and provide training about the issue of violence against women. The need to assess our past, present and future direction is of utmost importance.

List of Workshops

1. Rape
2. Domestic Violence
3. Medical Abuses (sterilization)
4. Working with men committing violence
5. Media Violence (pornography)
6. Sexual Harrassment

List of Panels

1. Feminism and Third World Women
2. Lesbianism—Third World Perspective
3. International Panel
4. Third World Women and the Family
5. The Criminal Justice System

Technical Seminars

1. Cross-cultural counseling
2. Child Abuse
3. How to run an effective support group

Cultural Festival

Time: 6:00-11:00 p.m. (6:00 Dinner, 8:00 Festival Activities)
Date: August 21, Thursday
Place: All Souls Unitarian Church
Address: 16th and Harvard Streets, N.W.
Washington, D.C.

The cost of the Cultural Festival is $5.00. Activities include a film, poet's readers theater, music, and more. International foods will be on sale. The cultural festival will be open to the general public.

***Third World:** Those nations of people struggling to break the yoke of colonialism and neocolonialism. Principally those nations of Asia, Africa, the Pacific, and Latin America. We include in our definition Native Americans and Black Americans.

Registration

Time: 8:00-9:00 p.m.
Date: August 21, Thursday
August 22, Friday
Place: National Baptist Memorial Church
Address: 1501 Columbia Rd., N.W.
Washington, D.C.

Time: 9:00 a.m.-2:00 p.m.
Date: August 23, Saturday
Place: Calvary United Methodist Church
Address: 1459 Columbia Rd. N.W.
Washington, D.C.

Anti-Rape Week: August 17th to 23rd.

Anti-Rape week will include workshops, guest speakers, films, and a benefit art auction. For further information on these free workshops, locations and times please contact the D.C. Rape Crisis Center (333-RAPE).

• For information on vending space please contact the Rape Crisis Center. • Child care will be provided during the day.

Pre-Registration:

The registration fee is $25.00.*

_______ Yes, I want to attend the First National Conference on Third World Women and Violence.
_______ Enclosed is my registration fee of $25.00.
_______ No, I am unable to attend the Conference but would like to be on your mailing list.
_______ No, I am unable to attend but would like to contribute towards this important event.
_______ I will need child care.

*Note: Due to limited funding, the price of the conference does not include lodging. Participants will be expected to make their own arrangements. However, if this would discourage anyone from attending, the Center can provide places for a few individuals. If you need special consideration please let the Center know as soon as possible.

Name ______________________
Address ______________________
Telephone: Home ____________ Work ____________

Figure 1. Registration form for First National Conference on Third World Women and Violence (1980). Courtesy of the D.C. Rape Crisis Center.

explicitly identifying as feminists, and the ever-present quandary of how to secure funds while preserving their political independence.[134] Unifying these fields of lively discussion was the sense that law enforcement entities actively compounded the violation of non-white rape victims.

The conference reports drafted by Ross and Touré repeatedly called the anti-rape movement's relationship to law enforcement into question. In her report on "Third World Women and Rape," Loretta Ross noted that "the more recent experience revealed that the character of this crime had changed somewhat over the last thirty years."[135] Rape crisis centers across the nation reported that "90 percent of rapes committed are intraracial; that is, confined to racial groups." In Washington, D.C., alone, 60 percent of the victims served in 1980 were Black. Of those, 95 percent were victimized by a Black man. Declining the moralistic explanation offered by the "Black-on-Black crime" narrative, Ross attributed the prevalence of intraracial rape to patterns of residential segregation and the routine emasculation of Black men under racial capitalism. Both factors left the sexual domination of women within their communities as one of the few avenues of control available to them. While rampant sexual violence was "devastating the social and political relationships among Third World women and men," Ross and her fellow conferencegoers countered that turning to the criminal justice system was not a viable solution. Racism manifested in both the disproportionate arrest and jailing of Black men for rape as well as the official scorn and disbelief that dissuaded Black women who wished to press charges from doing so. "The unfair treatment non-white men receive, the police brutality, and the inordinately severe sentences deter Third World women from reporting the crime."

In her second conference report, titled "Working with Minority Men Committing Violence Against Women," Ross echoed the arguments made by the National Black Feminist Organization and the National Alliance of Black Feminists earlier in the decade. Like Margaret Sloan, Brenda Eichelberger, Hortense Barber, and Elizabeth Bell before her, she announced that "rape has become predominately intra-racial over the past seventy years" and "most Third World Women are raped and battered by men of their own race."[136] Like their forebears in organized Black feminism, the conferencegoers "agreed that men needed to become actively involved in the anti-violence-against-women movement because the question of male-perpetrated violence must be seriously addressed by both women and men."

Addressing the systemic roots of gender violence through consciousness-raising and community outreach was crucial for the safety of Third World women because the prevailing criminal justice response of "more prisons, longer sentences, and increased convictions" only exacerbated these systemic issues. As Ross argued, "Many people believe that dehumanizing tactics such as castration, imprisonment, and the like would prevent violence against women. On the contrary, this approach only addresses the symptoms of the problems and leaves untouched its essence."[137] Pointing to the 80 percent recidivism rate and the overrepresentation of African Americans among incarcerated rapists, Ross and fellow conferencegoers concluded that "the criminal justice system is not solving the problem, but simply penalizes the most disadvantaged of the offenders." She encouraged other anti-rape organizations to follow suit by investing their energies in community education programs more so than police referral and court accompaniment.

As the attendees of the First National Conference on Third World Women and Violence concluded, the entanglement of rape crisis centers and anti-rape organizations with the criminal justice system left Black women raped by Black men with "unattractive options" for pursuing redress. Loretta Ross and Nkenge Tourè identified an impasse between Black communities that were "justifiably reluctant to invite greater police intrusion into their affairs" and white-dominated feminist rape crisis centers that sometimes "become so protective of their funding and tax status, they lose their early militancy and become indistinguishable from the government apparatus distrusted by Third World communities."[138] Conferencegoers spotlighted this quandary while also illuminating the possibilities of escaping it. At the end of the conference, attendees compiled a list of long and short-range goals, such as "to learn consciousness-raising and self-defense as a deterrent to sexual assault" and "to change social images and roles by re-evaluating male / female relationships within Third World communities." This list of goals made no mention of law enforcement entities. The companion list of questions intended to guide future research and theorization concluded with, "What alternatives are there to the criminal justice system?"[139] Black feminists active within rape crisis centers and anti-rape organizations had been earnestly asking this question since the early 1970s and would continue to do so in the decades ahead.

* * *

In August 1974, Brenda Eichelberger boldly proclaimed that in the coming years, "the Black woman could be instrumental in getting the government—at the federal, state, and local levels—to pour money into research on the topic [of rape] and develop some viable programs for rape prevention, rape counseling for the victim, and education of society at large."[140] Her statement reflected the urgent calls of a new generation of Black feminists to tackle violence against women head-on, especially the violence enacted by Black men within their own communities. Eichelberger accurately predicted this concern would grip unaffiliated Black women and drive them to rape crisis centers in significant numbers.

The government did not require the provocation of Black women to attend to the issue of rape. In the same year that Eichelberger called upon Black men to interrogate their internalized misogyny and coalesced the soon-to-be National Alliance of Black Feminists, the Law Enforcement Assistance Administration (LEAA) began issuing substantial operational grants to feminist rape crisis centers. The next two decades saw the births of several complementary federal efforts, including the National Center for the Prevention and Control of Rape (NCPCR), tasked with producing state-funded research to inform state actors charged with controlling rape; the Victims of Crime Act of 1984 (VOCA) to facilitate prosecution; and the landmark Violence Against Women Act of 1994 (VAWA).

Black women anti-rape organizers who entered rape crisis centers in the late 1970s owed their anti-rape consciousness to Black feminism, not a moralistic concern about escalating crime rates. Thus, they were cognizant and critical of the perils of state power for Black women that a criminalizing approach to interracial rape overlooked. Their politics compelled them to subordinate the punishment of violators to the project of creating a safer world for Black women at the structural level.[141] This would run contrary to the agendas of many feminist rape crisis centers in the late 1970s, whose institutional legitimacy came at the cost of narrowing their advocacy to actions that served law enforcement. As such, Black anti-rape organizers in the late 1970s decided to act subversively within feminist rape crisis centers. They made use of grant monies intended to knit together the feminist "war on rape" and the federal "war on crime" for the unintended purpose of placing distance between Black victims and a criminal justice apparatus they rightly mistrusted. By acting as space-keepers, they would adapt the praxis of care for assaulted Black women and girls to the post–civil rights era.

CHAPTER 2

Subverting the War on Crime

On a warm June evening in 1978, Lynn Moncrief left her West Philadelphia apartment and headed to the Center City headquarters of Philadelphia Women Organized Against Rape (WOAR). Two years prior, WOAR hired the self-described "Black radical feminist" to serve as "Outreach Coordinator" and tasked her with forging connections between the City of Brotherly Love's premier rape crisis center and its Black neighborhoods.[1] Moncrief took pride in "the connection . . . being made with thousands of Black people" through her outreach efforts.[2] But she still had to explain to her disappointed white colleagues why her relentless outreach did not yield higher numbers of Black volunteers. Moncrief reassured them that "Blacks are definitely interested in the issue [of rape]," in keeping with Black women's tradition of testifying publicly about sexual violence. But she added that "rape is competing with many basic survival issues in the Black community." Specifically, Moncrief pointed to the prominent place of law enforcement in WOAR's advocacy as an obstacle to recruiting Black women who could effectively care for Black victims. "Black women are still primarily concerned with police brutality against their men and boys," she explained.[3] As a result, "they are extremely reluctant to cause Black men or boys to become involved with the police, courts, or jails. This holds true even if Black women are raped or brutalized by Black men." She added that "while this denial of personal self-interest may be difficult for many white women to understand, it is a fact and WOAR must work amid this reality." Working amid this reality was complicated, considering WOAR's financial dependence upon grants issued by the Law Enforcement Assistance Administration (LEAA) and political connections to the self-proclaimed "toughest cop in America," Mayor Frank Rizzo.[4]

Philadelphia Women Organized Against Rape (WOAR) began in 1973 with a hotline in the emergency room of Philadelphia General Hospital

Lynn Moncrief of Women Organized Against Rape

Figure 2. Lynn Moncrief. Source: Temple University Archives.

(PGH). Appalled by the insensitive treatment rape victims received from male doctors and police officers, WOAR's "founding mother" Jody Pinto created a network of women who were regularly on-call to support rape victims and shepherd them through the callous and labyrinthine medical and criminal justice systems. The city designated PGH, its lone public health care institution, to provide cost-free care for victims of sexual assault. By virtue of its location in West Philadelphia and accessibility to the poor and uninsured, PGH was also the city's de facto "Black" hospital.[5] WOAR came to appreciate Black Philadelphia's reliance on PGH through the sheer number of assaulted Black women they encountered in its emergency room. When the city announced the impending closure of PGH in the summer of 1976, WOAR vocally condemned the "racist decision."[6]

Over the next decade, WOAR blossomed into a nationally recognized full-service feminist rape crisis center. A handful of paid full-time staff members coordinated dozens of unpaid volunteers who offered emergency room counseling and court accompaniment to victims of all races from their new Center City headquarters at 1220 Sansom Street. The radical feminist periodical *off our backs* celebrated WOAR as "the first rape crisis center to gain access to a large city hospital emergency room" and secure "an enormous amount of funding."[7] The article attributed WOAR's success to the "strong law and order sentiment from [Mayor Frank] Rizzo."[8] According to *off our backs*, "WOAR inadvertently, though fortunately, may have ridden on the tail of that." Mayor Rizzo was not Philadelphia WOAR's only point of contact with the "law and order sentiment." Between 1975 and 1980, the Law Enforcement Assistance Administration subsidized up to 90 percent of WOAR's operating costs through block grants disbursed by the Governor's Justice Commission of Pennsylvania (GJC).[9]

Congress established the LEAA within the Department of Justice through the Omnibus Safe Streets and Crime Control Act of 1968. As the central agency orchestrating the "war on crime," its purpose was to extend technical and financial support to local law enforcement, as well as to ancillary organizations that supported their mission. Until it disbanded under the Reagan Administration in 1981, the agency oversaw nearly 80,000 crime control projects and awarded more than 150,000 grants.[10] In 1975, the year that Philadelphia WOAR applied for its first LEAA subgrant through the GJC, the federal agency commanded an annual budget of $886 million.[11] Officials within the LEAA funded feminist rape crisis centers in the explicit hope of raising rates of police reporting. As the authors of the LEAA-financed study *Rape and Its Victims* concluded, "One need only consider the influence rape crisis centers may have on a victim's decision to report the crime to the police."[12] The LEAA never devoted the same resources to feminist rape crisis centers that it bestowed upon urban police departments.[13] Yet the LEAA served as the largest reliable source of funding for feminist rape crisis centers like Philadelphia WOAR through the 1970s.[14] Historians of the feminist movement against sexual violence have acknowledged that LEAA funding exerted a conservatizing influence on rape crisis centers that conscripted them into the "war on crime," but have viewed receipt of the funds as a necessary compromise to remain solvent and operational.[15]

As profoundly carceral as the LEAA was, the 1980 First National Conference on Third World Women and Violence noted that the agency "provided a chance for Third World Women to become involved in a conscious antirape effort . . . through programs and centers receiving grants or contracts to sponsor projects or outreach utilizing a Black or Third World woman hired for that purpose."[16] Philadelphia WOAR utilized the LEAA monies acquired through subgrants to the GJC in 1975 and 1976 to hire its first paid Black staff members, including Lynn Moncrief.[17] WOAR's leadership hoped that Moncrief's hire would help to close the gap between WOAR's troublingly "white face" and the overwhelmingly Black women it served.[18] In fact, the role presented an opportunity for Moncrief to act subversively amid the merging of the "war on rape" and the "war on crime." Rather than carry out the LEAA's stated mission of controlling rape through expanded police power, she implemented a praxis of care for Black victims that reflected the values established by Black feminism. Moncrief leveraged her LEAA-funded position to sideline the criminal justice system in WOAR's advocacy and substitute practices that sustained Black victims and volunteers. Her efforts culminated in the birth of the Third World Caucus, a collective of Black volunteers who challenged the forms of racism that festered within WOAR.[19] Thanks to Moncrief's careful subversion, the Third World Caucus reshaped WOAR's anti-rape advocacy from within as the LEAA and other carceral entities endeavored to shape it from the outside.

The LEAA and the Expansion of Police Power over Rape

The LEAA began extending operational grants to feminist rape crisis centers in the mid-1970s, making the control of rape an important aim of the "war on crime." As a transitory agency that straddled the "War on Poverty" and the "war on crime," the LEAA adopted the methodology of the former. Federal policymakers disbursed large block grants to state-level planning agencies in a relatively open-handed manner that allowed local actors to advance the federal agenda as they saw fit.[20] The materials generated by the LEAA about sexual violence laid bare the agency's rationale for funding feminist rape crisis centers. The Law Enforcement Assistance Administration (with the assistance of the Center for Women's Policy Studies) conducted a nationwide survey on the existing rape protocols of police, prosecutors, hospitals, and rape crisis centers. In 1975, they compiled these findings into a "Prescriptive Package" known as *Rape and Its Victims* that would be distributed to interested organizations. Decades later, INCITE! Women of Color Against Violence would describe the production of *Rape and Its Victims* as the opening salvo of the federal government's campaign to "align the anti-violence movement with its criminalization project."[21]

Interpreting increased rates of reported rape in the nation's cities as a symptom of the lawlessness that plagued post-1960s America, *Rape and Its Victims* proclaimed that "rape has emerged as a problem of national dimensions."[22] The publication did not attribute this newfound cultural concern about rape to the emergence of women's liberation but to "the growing anxiety about all forms of violence in our society, which has reached segments of the population heretofore untroubled by the threat of crime." The allusion to "population heretofore untroubled by the threat of crime," presumably white middle-class suburbanites, evoked the state's assumption that Black urban spaces were perpetually violence-ridden and confirmed that the state's response to rape would rely upon policing and incarceration. According to the "Prescriptive Package," rape was primarily a "crime of opportunity," committed with little or no premeditation by perpetrators who seized the chance to commit rape when it presented itself. *Rape and Its Victims* categorized these perpetrators as "career criminals" who repeatedly flout the law in the expectation of not being caught or, if caught, only receiving a trivial sentence. Sex crime investigation units could safely assume that "rapists are likely to be recidivist sex crime offenders."[23] Organizers within the feminist movement against sexual violence basically agreed that rape was a highly recidivist crime, though they questioned whether the LEAA's playbook of policing and prosecution would do much to solve the problem. Nancy McDonald and Loretta Ross of the D.C. Rape Crisis Center and William Fuller of Prisoners Against Rape saw incarceration as *contributing* to rapist recidivism, because caging offenders did nothing to address their socially ingrained urge to rape.

The prevailing wisdom of the LEAA in the mid-1970s held that increased police presence and regular patrolling in crime-stricken areas could serve as effective prevention.[24] Yet the authors of *Rape and Its Victims* acknowledged that "patrol is largely incapable of preventing rape, which is primarily an indoor crime without witnesses."[25] The concealed nature of the crime, combined with the perceived incorrigibility of its perpetrators, led LEAA officials to conclude that the key to controlling rape was incentivizing victims to report their assaults to the authorities. As feminists readily pointed out in the 1970s, the criminal justice system had historically treated women's complaints of rape with contempt and blamed women for their own assaults. This hostility had led generations of women to disavow police reporting as a means of recourse.[26] For African American women, who faced the double burden of racism and sexism in the criminal justice system, reporting their assaults to the police was an especially daunting task.[27] As scholar Beth

Richie has argued, Black women's mistrust of the criminal justice system flows from both the individual impulse for self-preservation and community protection.[28] The LEAA saw this reluctance to report as a direct impediment to crime control.

The LEAA's solutions to rape rested upon expanding police power and convincing victims to entrust themselves to the criminal justice system. In the eyes of LEAA officials, an increase in the rate of reporting for sexual assault would gradually lead to more convictions. A greater likelihood of conviction, in turn, would serve as a strong deterrent to future potential rapists. Rape, like other violent crimes, was surging because offenders supposedly had little to fear from the criminal justice system. Rape could be curbed by convincing potential rapists that capture and conviction for their crimes was certain. With the advent of *Rape and Its Victims*, the LEAA secured a permanent place for rape within the emergent "crime control agenda" of the 1970s, which, in the words of political scientist Kristen Bumiller, purported to discipline "unruly classes of persons" through "certain and severe punishment for crimes against women."[29] Though the title of *Rape and Its Victims* implied a concern with the plight of victims, the LEAA was ultimately committed to improving police performance in the capture and incarceration of offenders.[30]

As the LEAA folded sexual assault prevention into its agenda, the agency's attitude toward rape crisis centers shifted. Previously, law enforcement officials had dismissed rape crisis centers and the feminist volunteers who operated them as overzealous, polemical, and even obstructionist in their criticisms of the criminal justice system's treatment of rape victims.[31] In *Rape and Its Victims*, the LEAA reversed this stance. Negative publicity generated by anti-rape feminists proved instrumental in convincing the LEAA to change course. The authors readily admitted that "where good relations have not been established, the rape crisis center has had to resort to embarrassing law enforcement and medical facilities into compliance, through the political process and the press."[32] LEAA officials realized that publicizing the cavalier attitudes of the criminal justice system toward rape complaints was undermining the agency's mission of shoring up the public's trust in law enforcement.[33] To their great dismay, some feminist rape crisis centers had even gone on the offensive. "Centers in communities where the treatment of victims is particularly bad or where the conviction rate is low . . . believe that a woman who has been sexually assaulted should not be encouraged to subject herself to further abuse at the hands of the criminal justice system. Some groups advise women not to report rape."[34] These groups of concerned and politically engaged women could assist the LEAA in controlling rape by convincing more women to bring their assaults to the attention of local law enforcement. This would ensure the prompt capture and conviction of rapists, thereby preventing future rapes and driving down rates of sex crime overall. LEAA officials concluded that "although many police departments have had quite strained relations with rape crisis centers and similar organizations that have pressed for change in the treatment of rape victims, such groups should be treated as allies in the department's efforts to improve its performance and that of other involved public agencies."[35] They sealed this alliance by offering financial support to rape crisis centers. In 1974, rape crisis centers became eligible for funding under the "comprehensive plan for the reduction of crime" submitted annually by State Planning Agencies to the national office of the LEAA.[36] Under these conditions, the LEAA offered to subsidize feminist anti-rape activity in the expectation that recipient organizations would fulfill the agency's crime control agenda. Specifically, the LEAA expected client feminist rape crisis centers to enthusiastically endorse the criminal justice system for the women it served.

Feminists within the anti-rape movement reacted to LEAA overtures with a mixture of suspicion and curiosity. Pauline Bart, a feminist sociologist at the University of Illinois-Chicago and active member of Chicago Women Against Rape, aired her suspicions in a scathing review of *Rape and Its Victims*. According to Bart, "in order to understand this report, we have to understand why rape has emerged as an important issue . . . The presence of the Women's movement is not enough to explain the emergence . . . But there was another movement emerging in our society-the movement for 'law and order.'"[37] Bart criticized *Rape and Its Victims*—and by extension, the LEAA's interest in supporting anti-rape activity—as a co-optation of the issue by a state agency that was solely concerned with cracking down on crime without addressing the structural sexism that effectively condoned sexual violence. Bart objected to the "law and order" mission of the LEAA, but she also realized that cash-strapped rape crisis centers were hardly able to turn down funding. She uneasily concluded that "whether feminists can or should work or cooperate with agencies of social control and under what conditions is another issue which should be discussed within the women's movement."[38]

The discussions Bart called for were already unfolding across the pages of the *Feminist Alliance Against Rape Newsletter*. One of its earliest issues reprinted the comments of Barbara Allen, a member of the Los Angeles Commission on Assaults Against Women, who questioned the motivation behind the LEAA's interest in rape. She asked, "Are anti-rape groups being used by the government to further strengthen its law and order program?"[39] Allen rejected the LEAA's logic that increased apprehension, prosecution, and conviction of rapists would eliminate sexual violence. She also acknowledged the danger that "law and order" regimes posed to people of color. She wondered: "Is the government using the issue of rape to justify building the power of the police? Will this lead to further oppression of all people, and Third World people in particular?" Allen, like the rest of the anti-rape movement, had no easy answers to these vexed debates. In the September 1974 issue, Mary Ann Largen, head of the National Organization for Women's (NOW) Rape Task Force, revisited the discussion of the LEAA because the agency remained "the only major source of funding at this time."[40] To Allen's point, Largen recognized that the LEAA's "emphasis on law enforcement is contrary to the goals and / or policies of many women's groups." The controversy continued into 1975 when Judy Smith noted that the LEAA was declining to support feminist anti-rape projects that were not anchored in law enforcement operations.[41] In this environment, earlier staples of feminist anti-rape activism, such as speak-outs that challenged rape culture and woman-led self-defense trainings, fell by the wayside.[42]

At the core of white feminist misgivings about LEAA funding was that the agency showed little understanding of the machinations of patriarchy and saw feminist rape crisis centers as a vehicle for achieving "law and order." The LEAA reinforced this message by designating some projects as "exemplary" if they were measurably successful in "reducing crime or improving criminal justice."[43] In 1980, the LEAA bestowed the "exemplary" honor on the Stop Rape Crisis Center of Baton Rouge, Louisiana (SRCC). SRCC earned the favor of the LEAA by providing continuous services to victims of sexual violence "as a subtle incentive to cooperate" with law enforcement officials.[44] The "exemplary" label obscured a contentious power struggle between the original feminist leadership of SRCC and Baton Rouge District Attorney Ossie Davis in 1976. SRCC derived its LEAA funding jointly with the Baton Rouge district attorney's office. When the original director of SRCC disobeyed Davis's order to discontinue supportive services to rape victims who refused to report their assaults to the police, Davis fired her and replaced her with a "law and order" disciple.[45] The debacle in Baton Rouge, which the *Feminist Alliance Against Rape Newsletter* widely publicized in its September / October 1976 issue, sent a clear message to feminist rape crisis centers.[46] The LEAA expected the anti-rape projects it sponsored to encourage victims to report their rapes to the police. Rape crisis centers that did not meet this expectation risked losing their funding and staff. The LEAA administration commented that rape crisis centers like SRCC "have matured over the last few years" and "no longer represent the radical alternative" to the criminal justice response to rape. The financial support of the LEAA had disciplined them into "essential partners in the response to rape."[47] The emphasis on police reporting in the LEAA's response to rape indicated that feminist rape crisis centers were junior partners at best.

Numerous anti-rape feminists recognized that organizing rape crisis centers around reporting in accordance with LEAA priorities could make centers indistinguishable from the police and compel Black victims to avoid rape crisis centers just as they avoided the police. During a Congressional hearing on "Research into Violent Behavior" in January 1978, Nancy McDonald, a white member of the D.C. Rape Crisis Center, complained that "the main thrust of LEAA funding in rape" had thus far been to increase police reporting for sexual assault.[48] This focus was "severely limiting options for women who chose not to prosecute their rapes." McDonald explored the impact of these policies on women of color, arguing that "many Black women have little to gain and much to lose in prosecuting a rape. The racism in the criminal justice system faced by Black rape victims will not be ameliorated by such simple reforms." Black feminists had been issuing the same condemnation of reporting-centric anti-rape advocacy for years, though not before an audience of lawmakers who could determine the priorities of the LEAA.

Anti-rape advocates of all races remained critical of the LEAA's involvement in anti-rape activity, voicing their grievances in the *Feminist Alliance Against Rape Newsletter* and before Congress. Yet, in the absence of other sources of long-term public funding, rape crisis centers regarded the grants offered by the LEAA as their financial lifeline. In a 1980 evaluation of rape crisis centers across the nation, LEAA officials found that nearly one-third counted LEAA grants as the primary source of funding.[49] They knew that refusing LEAA monies would force many centers to close their doors. In a 1982 article for *Aegis* (formerly the *Feminist Alliance Against Rape Newsletter*) titled "A Funny Thing Happened on the Way to Revolution," one feminist anti-rape organizer reflected that "the values and purposes of funding agencies can have a cooptive [*sic*] effect on what work we do and how we do it."[50] "LEAA money" was no exception. As rape crisis centers grew with cash infusions from the "big grants," even indirect criticism of grant-makers could endanger the entire operation. "We can now see some of the destructive impact on the movement that this development method has had," *Aegis* reflected. "When those funds have been cut, some groups have not been able to survive." The non-feminist press verified the movement's unhealthy dependence on LEAA monies. The *New York Times* reported in 1981 that the number of operational rape crisis centers in the United States had fallen by half in the wake of the LEAA's disbandment.[51]

In an article written in 1980 for *No More Cages*, a radical feminist publication that condemned racist state violence and repudiated police as a protector of women, Janet Howard declared that the government agencies that fund anti-violence projects "exist primarily to strengthen the state."[52] She took particular umbrage with "the Law Enforcement Assistance Administration, which mostly provides weapons for law enforcement." Still, Howard conceded that without these funds rape crisis centers would disappear altogether. Howard also entertained the possibility that state funding would not automatically compel all rape crisis centers to adhere to the criminalizing model of rape control. She explained that "all money is dirty; whether the dirt creeps into the work or not depends to a great extent on the politics of the people using the money." Philadelphia WOAR, with its signature "empowerment model" for victims and access to LEAA monies, was vulnerable to this "creep." It also positioned individuals hired with this "dirty" money to limit the "creep."

The "Law and Order" Entanglements of Philadelphia WOAR

During the rape crisis center's formative years, Philadelphia WOAR received considerable financial support from the LEAA. Between 1975 and 1980, the GJC awarded WOAR over half a million dollars of LEAA money in support of its Crisis Center Project and the Statewide Outreach Project. These funds subsidized the salaries of directors, administrators, coordinators, and secretaries at WOAR.[53] Although the LEAA required Philadelphia WOAR to match these funds with donations from private charities and membership dues, WOAR remained financially beholden to the agency. When LEAA funds dried up in 1980, WOAR seriously considered laying off its staff and suspending hospital service.[54]

Before the first check arrived from the Governor's Justice Commission, WOAR's early leaders tactically presented themselves to Philadelphia law enforcement as reliable allies in the struggle to control crime. In January 1974,

WOAR's Jody Pinto wrote directly to Mayor Frank Rizzo praising "the concern over crime and compassion for its victims that you have always demonstrated."[55] A former police commissioner, Rizzo was already a national icon for "tough on crime" governance with little patience for left-leaning activists.[56] Rizzo also enjoyed support from legions of the white working-class women of Philadelphia, who saw his overlapping crackdowns on crime and leftist protest as the key to the city's salvation.[57] Though Jody Pinto did not share Mayor Rizzo's hardline politics, she identified them as a potential inroad for tapping the city's coffers in the struggle to end rape. Anticipating the LEAA's rhetoric, Pinto conveyed to Mayor Rizzo the reluctance of rape victims to report and promised that WOAR's services "will encourage more women to report and prosecute this crime while at the same time making it easier for the police to investigate and apprehend the offender." Pinto continued, "Mr. Mayor, this is your city and its potential as a leader in the fight against crime has barely been tapped . . . We want to work with you Mr. Mayor to develop a completely humane system for the prosecution of rape cases because without such a system, women will continue to not report the crime of rape."[58]

Some WOAR members bristled at this coziness with law enforcement. Like Pauline Bart, Barbara Allen, and Nancy McDonald, they saw the criminal justice system as a target of feminist criticism and not a suitable collaborator. One anonymous volunteer sarcastically suggested that the group rebrand themselves as "Good Girls Organized Against Rape" because they were "getting caught up in trying to please the patriarchy—the male grant-givers, the judges, the D.A.s."[59] Former volunteer Glenavie Norton remembered that many WOAR members viewed the police with hostility, and vigorously debated "how to deal with the police and law enforcement in general."[60] Letty Thall, a white policewoman turned social worker who penned the original LEAA grants, served as Executive Director between 1976 and 1977. She also recalled that cooperation with the criminal justice system was a consistent source of tension within the rape crisis center during her tenure. "How do you do advocacy?" she wondered retrospectively. "Do you want to shut down the place, or are we going to kill people with kindness and try to negotiate?"[61]

According to Thall, Philadelphia WOAR never withheld services if a woman desired not to report and the GJC did not press the issue. However, reporting was an important component of WOAR's "empowerment model" for victims. Because rape was "a crime taking away your control," Thall felt that prosecuting their attack placed victims "in the driver's seat" and on the path to reclaiming control over their lives.[62] Thall, like most white leaders of feminist rape crisis centers in the 1970s, operated within a compromised position. She took seriously the criticisms of volunteers that catering their advocacy to the desires of law enforcement entities would blunt WOAR's radical edge. At the same time, Thall believed that the criminal justice system was amenable to reform. Through sustained contact with WOAR, the Philadelphia Police Department would gradually relinquish its racist and sexist assumptions about rape victims and become an effective tool of women's empowerment. WOAR's conditional alliance with law enforcement, forged with Mayor Rizzo since early 1974, primed them to accept LEAA funding as a net positive. Continued LEAA funding would forestall any criticisms of their alliance going forward.

From 1975 to 1979, WOAR applied for LEAA support for its Crisis Center Project with the goal of retaining full-time staff who would recruit, train, and coordinate volunteers. This would ensure complete twenty-four-hour coverage of the rape hotline and more consistent coverage of the emergency room counseling and court accompaniment program.[63] The second LEAA-funded venture, the Statewide Outreach Project, paid two full-time consultants between 1975 and 1977 to travel to Pennsylvanian communities outside Philadelphia to develop their systems of support services for rape victims.[64] On paper, the grant applications submitted by Philadelphia WOAR to the GJC affirmed the LEAA's view that increased reporting and vigorous prosecution would curb the rate of sexual violence. Each year, their narratives lamented the rising rate of sexual violence in Philadelphia while promising that their various services, made possible by the generous support of the LEAA, would convince more women to trust the criminal justice system to adjudicate their assaults. Hitching the services of Philadelphia WOAR to the Philadelphia Police Department could lead Black victims, who were loath to subject themselves to the worst abuses of the criminal justice system and invite greater police intrusion into their communities, to avoid the former as they did the latter.[65] Former WOAR volunteer Wadiyah Nelson recalls, "That was one of the issues that came up all the time, about Black women's reluctance to press charges and engage the criminal justice system."[66] Any reservations Philadelphia WOAR held about the crime control response to rape vanished from the language of their LEAA applications in the service of securing funds from state actors who could not conceive of a response to rape that did not revolve around law enforcement.

In their first application to fund the Crisis Center Project in March 1975, Philadelphia WOAR warned that "according to FBI projections, there may be nearly 10,000 rapes occurring in Philadelphia each year, yet this crime goes unreported nine times out of ten."[67] WOAR promised that "if victims of rape receive legal information, are encouraged to cooperate with police, and are offered court accompaniment, an increase in the number of women who prosecute is likely."[68] WOAR's application to the GJC succeeded in 1975, securing $56,750 in LEAA funds to support the Crisis Center Project from July 1975 to July 1976.[69] WOAR subsequently secured LEAA funds to continue the Crisis Center Project annually, from 1976 through 1979. Each application reaffirmed the place of police reporting in WOAR's philosophy. The 1977 application opened with the distressing FBI statistic that while the overall incidence of "serious crime" in Philadelphia had dropped by 8.5 percent in 1976, the rate of rape in the city had increased by 7 percent.[70] WOAR clarified that the rape crisis center "encourages women to report rapes and other crimes of sexual abuse and expects to make in the future an even greater impact upon the City of Philadelphia as it deals with all aspects of the crime of rape." The following year, WOAR assured the GJC that their direct services would "ultimately result in an increase in the reporting of rape and decrease in the crime of rape."[71] WOAR's understanding of sexual violence ran deeper than mechanistically controlling crime. But its leadership also understood that reciting frightening crime statistics was a dependable method for prying open state coffers during the "war on crime." These references to surging crime rates, however tactical, activated violent anti-Black state functions that had historically answered accusations of widespread criminality.

Philadelphia WOAR argued that the Statewide Outreach Project, though more educationally oriented than the Crisis Center Project, would also "lead to greater willingness on the part of women to report cases of rape to the police and to cooperate with them in the apprehension of rapists." WOAR's 1977 application to fund the Statewide Outreach Project recapitulated the logic of the LEAA. They reasoned that "if arrest, conviction, and incarceration are a deterrent then we should expect a reduction in the incidence of this crime" should the project be funded.[72] The Statewide Outreach Project fit so snugly with the principles of the LEAA that in 1977 the GJC nominated it to be an "exemplary project."[73] The LEAA declined to award them the coveted "exemplary" label because the project had not resulted in a measurable reduction in the crime of rape.[74] The subsequent application to extend the Statewide Outreach Project into 1978 proved unsuccessful, with the GJC citing the LEAA's preference to directly fund law enforcement officers and not their helpers.[75] The LEAA's support for Philadelphia WOAR evaporated shortly thereafter. They rejected WOAR's application to fund the Crisis Center Project into 1980, sending the rape crisis center into a financial tailspin. The LEAA itself would fold the following year.

Even after the GJC suspended its financial support in 1980, WOAR remained in the orbit of Philadelphia institutions that championed rape control through police power. In 1980, Berit Lakey (who had recently been promoted to executive director) appealed directly to Mayor Frank Rizzo—in his eighth consecutive year as mayor—to secure municipal funding for WOAR. In a private meeting with Mayor Rizzo and Police Commissioner Joseph O'Neill, Lakey cited WOAR's record of public service for victims of rape who would be lost to the criminal justice system entirely if WOAR ceased to exist due to lack of funds.[76] Commissioner O'Neill vouched for WOAR's effectiveness in increasing rates of reporting among rape victims, and Mayor Rizzo pledged $50,000 of the city budget to subsidize WOAR. When the LEAA failed, WOAR appealed to Mayor Rizzo, the personification of "tough on crime" thought in American politics, to weather the financial storm. Like Jody Pinto years prior, Lakey presented WOAR's law-and-order credentials to Mayor Rizzo out of political expediency more so than sincere belief. Yet her ability to penetrate Mayor Rizzo's inner circle and win his support indicated Lakey's racial privilege and the stickiness of criminalizing rhetoric within the feminist anti-rape movement.

WOAR's collaboration with local law enforcement entities continued into the 1980s. In 1981, Lakey applauded the newly established sixty-member sex crimes unit on the Philadelphia police force as "one more positive example of how seriously the city views the crime of rape."[77] In March 1982, District Attorney Edward G. Rendell gave graphic testimony before Congress about violent rapes that had taken place on the streets of Philadelphia in the previous month as a "typical example" of the crime that was ravaging the city.[78] He clamored for the restoration of the LEAA. As late as 1984, Rendell remained a faithful adherent of the LEAA's approach to rape control. He proclaimed that the "very existence" of Philadelphia WOAR held "tremendous symbolic value in helping to correct to the psychological climate that makes victims of the crime of rape more likely to report the offense to law enforcement authorities."[79] According to former Black volunteer Samia Cherry, WOAR continued to work closely with the Philadelphia Police Department well into the 1980s to implement rape kits and impart sensitivity training to officers.[80]

Philadelphia WOAR's financial relationship with the LEAA lasted five years. Though a relatively brief chapter in the center's organizational history, the infusion of LEAA monies through the GJC catalyzed the growth and development of Philadelphia's premier rape crisis center. Through its grant-making practices, the LEAA concentrated the diffuse "tough on crime" ethos that was already percolating in Philadelphia under Mayor Rizzo. By pursuing and accepting those grants, Philadelphia WOAR, which had already forged alliances with City Hall and the Philadelphia Police Department, formalized their commitment to expanding police power over rape. While some members expressed concerns that closely partnering with the criminal justice system would compromise their radical feminist politics, few pondered the impact that LEAA funding would have on the Black women they served.

A "Black Radical Feminist" Approach to Anti-Rape Advocacy: Subversion

Philadelphia WOAR allocated a portion of the funds it received from the LEAA to hire its first paid Black staff members.[81] Deborah Johnson arrived at WOAR as a consultant for its Statewide Outreach Project in August 1975. Lynn Moncrief joined as the outreach coordinator for the Philadelphia area the following October. A native Philadelphian, Johnson was trained to be a guidance counselor at Temple University. Aside from tutoring GED students under the auspices of the Model Cities Program of the "War on Poverty," Johnson's life before WOAR had little activist content. She accepted the position of Statewide Outreach Consultant from WOAR "knowing women in my community that had experienced those kinds of issues, [and] wanting to do what I could to be supportive of them."[82] Moncrief, by contrast, cut her political teeth in North Philadelphia as both a community organizer in the busing controversy and an administrator within the Model Cities Program of the "War on Poverty."[83] Her background in community organizing and service provision prepared her well for the role of outreach coordinator at WOAR, which required her to "establish and expand [WOAR's] volunteer network and support system with increased minority participation."[84]

WOAR's leadership constantly fretted over the near-uniform whiteness of its staff and volunteer pool. The city of Philadelphia remained sharply racially segregated during the 1970s with virtually all Black residents confined to its North and West corners.[85] Philadelphia WOAR's respective headquarters in Philadelphia General Hospital in West Philadelphia and Jefferson Hospital in Center City were among the few genuinely integrated spaces in the city. For many white women, volunteering with WOAR was their first opportunity to interact with Black women in a significant way. This bright spot of integration did not offset the troubling racial imbalance between volunteers and victims. As of February 1976, only 21 of WOAR's 153 trained volunteers were Black women and there were no women of color on the paid staff.[86] But most of the women who received WOAR's services were women of color, specifically Black women. Of the nearly 1,500 rape victims WOAR assisted between March 1974 and April 1976, 72 percent were Black.[87] Like the broader "second wave" feminist movement that birthed it, Philadelphia WOAR was eager to shed its reputation as an organization created by and for middle-class white women.[88] Executive director Letty Thall specifically hired Johnson and Moncrief to militate against "the community skepticism toward WOAR as primarily a white middle-class women's group centered around one issue."[89] Despite this reputation, according to internal statistics collected by WOAR, more than 70 percent of the adult victims they intercepted in the emergency room in 1980 were Black women.[90]

Though her salary was directly subsidized by the LEAA, Moncrief did not follow the agency's guidelines for "exemplary" anti-rape advocacy. She did not prioritize raising rates of reporting and convictions for sexual violence. This refusal was consistent with her professed "Black radical feminist" politics, which historically attended to the simultaneity of interpersonal and state violence in the lives of Black women and regarded law enforcement skeptically at best.[91] While LEAA funding positioned her on the "hostile terrain of the state," Moncrief saw no contradiction between the source of her salary and her radical Black feminist identity.[92] Instead, she saw an opportunity to apply a Black feminist praxis of care through the tactic of subversion. She would repurpose resources provided to control rape through a violent law enforcement apparatus toward projects that supported and sustained Black people. Moncrief's background in the "War on Poverty" left her with more than a lengthy list of Black community contacts. It imparted a crucial skill: appropriating the inadequate resources offered by the state on unfavorable terms and applying them to projects that spoke to the needs of Philadelphia's Black community. Moncrief was brought onboard for the purposes of outreach, a task that required her to build trust between Black Philadelphia and feminist rape crisis centers.[93] In practice, this meant adjusting WOAR's model of advocacy to reflect the needs of Black women. Among these needs was preserving the space separating Philadelphia WOAR from the Philadelphia Police Department. The goal of Moncrief's outreach was not to convince assaulted Black women and girls to entrust themselves to the Philadelphia Police Department, as the subsidizers of her position might have hoped. Instead, she used her position of influence within WOAR to criticize practices that alienated Black victims and volunteers and instigate changes in the structure of the organization to amend those practices.

Moncrief wasted no time seeking recruits among the congregants of North and West Philadelphia's Black churches, such as Pinn Memorial Baptist Church, Mount Olive, Mount Carmel, and Whiterock, as well as the members of community organizations like the Coalition of 1,000 Black Women and the Tioga Welfare Rights Organization.[94] Moncrief introduced herself to Mattie McDaniels of Tioga WRO "as a Black woman" with "a commitment to seeing that Black women are made aware of the full scope of the services provided by WOAR."[95] She identified "common ground" with McDaniels based on their shared commitment to "the advocacy of oppressed women," broadcasting an understanding of the interconnectedness of the racial, sexual, and economic oppression acutely felt by Black women in Philadelphia. By her own calculation, in her first year at WOAR Moncrief had written 73 letters and made 174 phone contacts to community groups regarding outreach activities, represented WOAR at 47 community meetings, fielded 157 phone calls requesting a speaking engagement, personally conducted 34 speaking engagements, gave 35 print and electronic interviews, and wrote 13 press releases and letters to the editor of Philadelphian newspapers.[96] When she wasn't conducting outreach to Philadelphia, Moncrief busied herself forging connections with other Black anti-rape organizers around the country, including Ruth Hall of the Boston-based Community Programs Against Sexual Assault (C-PASA) and Nkenge Tourè of the Washington, D.C. Rape Crisis Center (DCRCC).[97] She wrote to Deb Friedman applauding her article in the nationally-circulated *Feminist Alliance Against Rape Newsletter* titled "Rape, Racism and Reality." The article connected the interrelated histories of Black women's sexual exploitation under slavery and Jim Crow and the weaponization of false rape charges in the lynching of Black men, while foregrounding how these histories allowed the contemporary feminist movement against sexual violence to feed into anti-Black racism. Moncrief was thrilled to see the "development of a perspective on race and rape" that "not only included race and economics, but had the courage to take it beyond that."[98]

Throughout her tenure as outreach coordinator, Moncrief communicated to her white colleagues that her political commitment to empowering Black women preempted her professional duty to expand police power over rape. In her view, preventative education about sexual violence was a necessary alternative to referring Black victims to the criminal justice system and an indispensable component of a Black feminist praxis of care. In her April 1977 piece for *HOTLINE*, WOAR's newsletter, entitled "Before the Fact of the Crime," Moncrief reminded her colleagues that "if we carry our concern about rape to its logical conclusion, we should find ourselves deeply involved in rape prevention."[99] Moncrief's rape prevention programs contrasted with the LEAA's vision of rape prevention. According to the LEAA, consistent reporting by victims and lengthy incarceration of offenders was the only feasible method for preventing rape. According to Moncrief, community education programs that taught the concepts of rape culture, consent, and self-defense were preferable to facilitating the prosecution of rapists. This strategy reflected the anti-rape programs piloted by the NBFO and NABF during the 1970s.[100] Moncrief reported that the requests for programming she received as outreach coordinator "invariably" called for rape prevention. "If we are to be responsive to the needs of the community, to the terrified women living in Fairhill and Cambridge housing projects, anywhere in Philadelphia," she concluded, "it is IMPERATIVE that we give rape prevention equal import with our direct service and advocacy programs."[101] A poster Moncrief created advertising a seminar she planned to give at the Wilson Park Housing Project Community Center in September 1977 hinted at the content of her rape prevention education. She titled the talk "Rape: Can It Be Prevented?" and answered the titular question with an illustration of a woman's fist assertively clutching a set of keys. The poster broadcasted Moncrief's preference that women (and Black women in particular) learn to defend themselves from assault, rather than appeal to law enforcement as the chief arbiter of their safety. This preference, rooted in the Black feminist tradition of self-help, stood athwart an LEAA that preserved law enforcement's monopoly on violent defense.[102]

Like her Black feminist contemporaries, Moncrief did not reject the criminal justice system as an option for assaulted Black women seeking recourse.[103] In March 1978, Moncrief sat for an interview with *Drummer*, an underground leftist Philadelphia newspaper. When asked if WOAR cooperated with law enforcement entities in the city, she answered that they were actively "trying to work closer with police," thanks to the infusion of crime-fighting monies from the Governor's Justice Commission that paid her salary.[104] But for Moncrief, the cornerstone of her anti-rape advocacy was the prevention of rape through education, not the deterrence of rapists through punishment. "I don't think rape can be eliminated unless sexism is eliminated," she opined. She defined success in community outreach as "preventing men from becoming rapists in the first place," not raising rates of reporting, prosecution, and conviction for rape. Moncrief also did not share the LEAA's certainty that prisons served as effective deterrents to rape. In the same month that she spoke with *Drummer*, she gave a second interview to a local gay newspaper discussing the unchecked sexual violence within the American prison system that afflicted incarcerated men and women alike.[105] She also corresponded approvingly with William Fuller, the incarcerated founder of Prisoners Against Rape (PAR) who decried the prison system as promoting rape.[106] As a Black woman used to working within broken systems, Moncrief was willing to accept police reporting as an option for victims seeking to reassert control over their lives. But she did not enthusiastically embrace the criminal justice system as a panacea, as the LEAA would have had her do. Even as they collaborated with state entities to control rape, Black feminist anti-rape organizers like Moncrief retained a critique of its violent capacities. This selective collaboration should not be read as contradiction or hypocrisy, but as a kind of practical politics whereby marginalized people occupied the available niches within fundamentally broken and repressive systems to extract social goods for themselves and their communities.

The Third World Caucus of Philadelphia WOAR

In August 1979, Lynn Moncrief resigned from her position as outreach coordinator. Over three years of full-time anti-rape work had made her "see the world solely in terms of aggressor-victim," to the detriment of her physical and mental health.[107] She would continue to serve Philadelphia WOAR as a volunteer. Her resignation was well-timed. The Governor's Justice Commission declined to continue funding Philadelphia WOAR's Crisis Center Project past 1980, eliminating her salary. Two years prior, the GJC had withdrawn support for the Statewide Outreach Project, forcing Deborah Johnson to resign and take a paid community organizing position with Planned Parenthood.[108] The withdrawal came after the LEAA declined to award the Statewide Outreach Project the coveted "exemplary" label since "the Project has not demonstrated a reduction in crime."[109]

Moncrief's interventions on behalf of Black women in Philadelphia WOAR did not expire with her LEAA-funded position. During the summer of 1977, twenty-three non-white members of WOAR formed the Third

World Caucus (TWC), what the Board of Directors described as a "special interest group . . . devoted to dealing with race and other minority issues in the organization."[110] In fact, the Third World Caucus was a network for non-white volunteers and staff members in Philadelphia WOAR united in criticism of the racism that permeated the rape crisis center.[111] Moncrief played a vital role in instituting and sustaining the TWC. During her stint as the paid outreach coordinator and later as an unpaid volunteer, Moncrief oversaw the birth of the caucus, served as its first chair, and even offered her apartment as a meeting space.

Black women who volunteered for WOAR formed the core of the Third World Caucus. Generally, the white majority of Philadelphia WOAR's volunteers joined the rape crisis center as an extension of their activism within the women's liberation movement or their professional backgrounds in social work.[112] Many of WOAR's Black volunteers were survivors of male violence. Joan Ashton first encountered Philadelphia WOAR as a victim of rape on the receiving end of the center's services.[113] In 1976, Ashton arrived in the emergency room of Philadelphia General Hospital seeking prophylactic treatment. Like most Black women served by WOAR, Ashton elected not to report her assault to the police. The only people who learned of her rape were the WOAR emergency room volunteer who assisted her, her future husband, and the friends she found within the Third World Caucus. Ashton joined WOAR shortly after her assault, hoping to emotionally process her rape by assisting other women who found themselves in the same situation.[114] In 1977, Wadiyah Nelson had just returned to her native West Philadelphia after a three-year stint as a kindergarten teacher in Jamaica where she suffered extensive abuse at the hands of her ex-husband, a Pan-Africanist teacher. Eager to work on "issues related solely to women," Nelson signed up to be an emergency room counselor after learning about Philadelphia WOAR in the student union building of Temple University. Samia Cherry's trajectory into WOAR resembled that of Wadiyah Nelson. A founding member of the Atlantic City Chapter of the Black Panther Party, Cherry organized the Party's signature Free Breakfast Program for Black children in the community.[115] She relocated to North Philadelphia with her children in 1970 to escape an abusive husband. Although she never formally joined the Philadelphia chapter of the Black Panther Party, she shared their outrage over unchecked police brutality toward Black citizens. At first, Cherry rejected feminism because her "struggle wasn't just about women."[116] She was compelled to join Philadelphia WOAR after taking a job as a Child Advocate in the Philadelphia court system. One of her Black adolescent clients gave birth to her father's child after the court dismissed her allegations of abuse.

Whichever way they arrived at the rape crisis center, all of WOAR's Black volunteers were driven by their concern over "how extensive rape was in the Black community."[117] All aimed to provide the comprehensive care that Black victims needed and "question[ed] the ability of [white] volunteers to effectively counsel third world rape victims."[118] The training Wadiyah Nelson underwent to become an emergency room counselor made no mention of race.[119] While WOAR's training for emergency room counselors ignored race, the training for court accompanists compacted the Black experience into stereotypes. Court accompanist trainees engaged in scripted roleplays meant to replicate the experience of assisting a victim. The only scenario that addressed Black victims requested that prospective volunteers imagine themselves as "a streetwise 19 year old who lives alone in a Housing Project" with "highly developed slang" who had been raped by her gang member ex-boyfriend.[120] The guide omitted any reference to Black women's reasoned skepticism of the criminal justice system and presented prosecution of offenders as a successful outcome for volunteers. Johnetta Miller, a Black volunteer and Third World Caucus member, complained that such inadequate training led well-meaning white volunteers to "speak condescendingly to Black victims" and "seek out white victims to give support to but not Black ones."[121] Black women in Philadelphia arguably required WOAR's supportive services more than any other population. Yet white volunteers' unease serving Black women, combined with the dearth of Black volunteers, seriously compromised the care WOAR offered to Black victims.

The racism baked into WOAR's model of anti-rape advocacy also impacted the performance of Black volunteers. White staff members frequently confused Black volunteers with each other and called them by the wrong names. Black trainees routinely received negative evaluations from the staff for failing to "open up" emotionally during training sessions. In response, Black volunteers took to the pages of *HOTLINE* to explain that "being Black is a daily lesson in emotional control if one is to stay alive, out of jail, and employed. Therefore, it is a severe cultural shock for many of us to walk into WOAR after 20 or 30 years of this selectivity and suddenly be expected to lay bare our very innards to a group of mostly white strangers."[122] These racial blind spots in WOAR's praxis were evident in the concentration of Black women in the volunteer ranks and exclusion from paid positions. This imbalance was systemic in origin. For the positions it subsidized, the LEAA required the selected candidate to hold a master's degree.[123] While Deborah Johnson and Lynn Moncrief made the cut, most Black women in WOAR's "target community" did not. Wadiyah Nelson noticed when she joined in 1977 that only two out of thirteen of WOAR's staff members were Black women: one was Lynn Moncrief, the other was a secretary.[124] In July 1977, WOAR's Black volunteers channeled their frustrations with the multifaceted racism of the rape crisis center into the formation of the Third World Caucus.

White members of WOAR agreed that the Third World Caucus was a necessary intervention. One month prior to the formation of the Third World Caucus, WOAR's staff had completed an "introspective look at our volunteers" and confirmed that Black women comprised only 16 percent of the volunteer pool.[125] In response to the questionnaire that accompanied the study, one volunteer lamented "it's a disgrace to me that we serve mostly Black women but cannot attract Black volunteers." She asserted to the white feminist leadership that "if we are racist, we need to confront this." Retrospectively, white WOAR members confirmed that race relations were strained. The relocation of WOAR's headquarters to Sansom Street in Center City after the closure of Philadelphia General Hospital in 1977 reduced a somewhat diverse group that had served an overwhelmingly Black clientele into "a very white crew."[126] Letty Thall reported "feelings of helplessness" over WOAR's inability to bridge racial difference. Lee Nelson seconded that the racial imbalance was "really uncomfortable."[127] She added that the white feminist leadership of WOAR "really didn't have any tools for dealing with [racial difference]" at the time. Glenavie Norton similarly recalled that "there was always a point of tension with the Third World Caucus, the white and Black."[128] This discomfort and tension was a consequence of a vicious cycle. Black women's underrepresentation within WOAR allowed the overwhelmingly white leadership to discount Black women's experiences in the construction of their reporting-centric "empowerment model." The dominance of this model discouraged Black women whose experience refuted the model from joining WOAR in sufficient numbers to challenge it.

The Third World Caucus created a seat of power for Black women within WOAR to continue Moncrief's subversive work by adjusting the rape crisis center's policies away from controlling rape and toward caring for Black victims. Its members shared Moncrief's concern that WOAR's programs did not incorporate the lived realities of Black women, which discouraged Black women from joining the organization. The caucus pressed further that WOAR would continue to marginalize Black victims and alienate Black volunteers until white women within the rape crisis center grappled with their own racism. The Third World Caucus articulated this view in the July 1977 edition of *HOTLINE*, insisting that "working together on these issues can only make us a stronger and more effective organization in the struggle for the equality of *all women* and the fight against rape."[129] They proposed recruitment drives in target communities, sensitivity training on matters of race for current volunteers and staff members, and even committees to screen and potentially expel undesirable volunteers.[130] During their first year, the caucus composed an Attitude Exploration Questionnaire designed to root out "hidden prejudices or misunderstandings concerning third world people" among prospective volunteers and hosted internal seminars on such topics as "Race Relations" and "Rape and Racism."[131] Berit Lakey remembered the Third World Caucus as an "important consciousness raiser" for WOAR's white members who previously had few opportunities to learn from women of color.[132] Additionally, the caucus held public-facing community workshops intended to "emphasize the role of WOAR in Black and Hispanic communities, provide pertinent information to those who attend, and encourage community members to join and participate in the Caucus." The Third World Caucus's participation in community workshops built upon the community outreach already piloted by Lynn Moncrief, prioritizing community-based care ahead of police-based control.

Over the next two years, the Third World Caucus continued to gather monthly in the homes of its members to discuss the racism they experienced within WOAR and the necessary internal changes for uplifting Black women both as victims of sexual violence and activists within the feminist movement against sexual violence. They spearheaded a "Big Sister" program designed to "stem the rate of attrition for Third World volunteers."[133] They also suggested eliminating the $10 training fee for new volunteers, arguing that it constituted a "major stumbling block" in the caucus's effort to recruit non-white women "from all socioeconomic strata, including women on welfare." In a speech before the Third World Caucus, which was printed in the October 1979 edition of *HOTLINE* and circulated to the general membership, Moncrief accused WOAR of "fraudulent advertising and mislabeling" themselves as a feminist organization because a "so-called radical feminist" on WOAR's paid staff regularly called her by the name of another Black member. [134] Her anecdote corroborated an internal report released by WOAR that revealed the non-white volunteer proportion had slipped to 12 percent by late 1979.[135]

The TWC's critique of WOAR's racial climate intersected with the rape crisis center's ongoing financial relationship with the LEAA. In the final year of the Crisis Center Project, Philadelphia WOAR allotted dollars to hire a new volunteer training coordinator. After some deliberation, the Hiring Committee settled on a white woman. The caucus had demanded that the Hiring Committee allocate paid positions to non-white women, believing that this would bolster the recruitment of non-white volunteers and lead to improved treatment of non-white rape victims.[136] Anticipating the backlash, the Hiring Committee circulated an internal memorandum defending their decision. Alleging "a great deal of concern about the overwhelmingly white 'face' of WOAR," they approached more than twenty organizations for minority recruiting. Nevertheless, their search did not yield any non-white women "qualified" to be trainers.[137] The LEAA's imposed criteria for a "qualified" trainer, which included a master's degree in social work or a related field, advantaged white middle-class women and overlooked non-white women who lacked such credentials.[138] Dissatisfied with this explanation, Moncrief rebuked the Hiring Committee on behalf of the Third World Caucus. "Too often," she wrote, "Third World people have been told that, 'we'd be willing to hire a (fill in the appropriate minority) but we haven't been able to find one that was 'qualified.'"[139] By pointing to the ways in which employers cudgeled "qualification" against non-white people, Moncrief alerted her white colleagues that WOAR was replicating institutional racism. The blowback from the TWC in the hiring incident also demarcated the limits of the subversive mode of Black-led anti-rape advocacy. Although the LEAA grants provided a vehicle for Black women like Moncrief to obtain paid positions within the feminist movement against sexual violence, and those positions could be leveraged to introduce a Black feminist praxis of care contrary to the desires of their funders, the LEAA itself circumscribed these positions through the exclusionary logic of "qualification."

Just as the white leadership with WOAR maintained its relationships with Philadelphia's "law-and-order" advocates after the LEAA withdrew financial support, the TWC kept fighting to empower Black women within WOAR and preserve a Black feminist praxis of care. In the wake of the hiring incident, the Board of Directors heeded the demands of the Third World Caucus and installed a Task Force on Racism to investigate WOAR's racial dynamics.[140] The Task Force on Racism sent out a questionnaire to the volunteer membership of WOAR, which garnered an impressive 45 percent response rate.[141] The published summary recapitulated the complaints the Third World Caucus had originally made in July 1977, but this time their accusations were bolstered by statistical evidence: 77 percent of Black respondents felt that racism affected the services delivered by WOAR, compared to 44 percent of white respondents; Black respondents acknowledged "the unconsciousness of much of the racist behavior and attitudes they observed and experienced"; 91 percent of Black respondents (as opposed to 37 percent of white respondents) claimed that racism was expressed through the organizational structures and practices as well as individual behavior; and Black respondents elaborated on the "cultural views or definitions of rape" that deterred Black women from volunteering, including "differing historical experiences with rape and the societal roles of women."[142]

To rectify these issues, the Task Force on Racism recommended that WOAR redouble its recruitment efforts within Philadelphia's Black community. Following the logic of Lynn Moncrief, the Task Force on Racism concluded that an increased concentration of Black volunteers in WOAR's ranks would ease the anxieties of Black victims and convince them that WOAR was not a feminized extension of the Philadelphia police force. Speaking to Wadiyah Nelson's concerns, the Task Force instructed trainers to "address Third World Women's fears and concerns during training and integrate their experiences into the training program."[143] The Training Team agreed to adopt supervisory double-staffing to ensure Black counselors and victims would make contact, and overhaul the volunteer training manual to incorporate materials written by Black feminists by March 1981.[144] The new manual included an article by Audre Lorde that addressed the simultaneity of racism, sexism, classism, and homophobia in women's lives. The manual also featured a second piece that elucidated how "the anti-rape movement has suffered from the failure to recognize how the charge of rape and the practice of rape have been used to perpetuate racism in our country."[145]

The influence of the Third World Caucus could also be detected in the revised seminar on "Black Women and Rape" offered during in-service training and staff development workshops. The script of the seminar explained that "Third World participation in the anti-rape movement has always been low" due to a combination of limited outreach efforts and the anti-rape movement's affiliation with police and judicial systems, as "this affiliation can be interpreted by some to mean that it is policy to urge victims to become involved with them."[146] Trainees were instructed to "reiterate the fact that rape crisis centers do not cajole or force victims to do anything against their will." The Third World Caucus also called for WOAR's white members to form anti-racist study groups and for all standing WOAR committees to actively seek the advice and input of Third World Caucus members.

While the white feminist leadership of WOAR worked to amend its racism internally, the Third World Caucus cemented healthy relations with Philadelphia's Black community. In April 1981, the Third World Caucus hosted an open house at WOAR's offices on Sansom Street on the theme of "Rape in the Black Community." The event educated political, social, and medical professionals who worked in Philadelphia's Black community while facilitating the recruitment of Black volunteers.[147] That June, an editorial by Black journalist Sandra Long in the *Philadelphia Bulletin* indicated that "Rape in the Black Community" hit its mark. Long argued that "too many Black women think rape happens to other women, not to them" and cited the alarming overrepresentation of Black women and girls among the victims WOAR served.[148] She decried the fact that "only 20 of 100 WOAR volunteers are Black women" and endorsed the Third World Caucus's recruitment efforts, urging her Black women readers to consider volunteering with Philadelphia WOAR.

The Task Force on Racism did not achieve all the Third World Caucus hoped it would. Third World Caucus member Johnetta Miller submitted "An Open Letter to All My Black Sisters in WOAR" to the spring 1981 edition of *WOARpath*, the center's quarterly newsletter, in which she lamented the persistence of "the unbalanced racial make-up of the organization" and "training techniques which assume a common white experience," as well as the loneliness of being "the only Black woman in a committee meeting."[149] Denise Pressley, also a Caucus member, spoke to WOAR's continued difficulties in recruiting sufficient numbers of Black women volunteers. She placed the blame for these difficulties partly on "Black women being too busy with jobs, children, and other family obligations," echoing Lynn Moncrief's analysis from 1978. But she also implicated the sexual politics of Black Philadelphia. "Although Black women are aware of sexual assault, they are too embarrassed or reluctant to talk about it," she argued. "Society has conditioned us to accept forms of sexual abuse, dating back to slavery." Invoking Richie's "trap of loyalty" paradigm, Pressley explained that "many Black women are absorbing their rage against males . . . in hopes that Black men will turn their rage against our oppressors and not against our women."[150] Apparently, the public education and outreach efforts of Lynn Moncrief and the Third World Caucus did not entirely dislodge Black women's apprehensions about frankly discussing the sexual violence within their communities. Black feminism had made limited inroads among the denizens of Philadelphia.

Both Miller and Pressley defended the Third World Caucus as an essential locus for Black feminist organizing against rape in Philadelphia. Miller asserted that "the women of the Third World Caucus have given me support without which I could not continue to struggle at WOAR." She steeled herself and her Black sisters against the stubborn cultural racism of WOAR with her sense of humor. In jest, she instructed her Black colleagues to "never sit with a Black woman in a meeting . . . white folks think we are planning a revolution." Pressley optimistically forecasted that given sufficient encouragement by the caucus, Black women in Philadelphia would gradually come to the defense of other Black women. "The reality is that rape and sexual assault deeply impact the Black community," she reasoned. "In order to fight rape and help their Black sisters, Black women are joining WOAR." By 1983, Third World Caucus chair Valarie Oulds confidently asserted that the caucus had grown steadily from twenty-three in 1977 to nearly fifty.[151] Oulds credited the continued existence of the caucus with allowing WOAR's Black members "to support and strengthen each other as Women of Color, and to bring that strong sense of ourselves, without fear of confrontation, to WOAR as a whole."

* * *

In November 1978, Ms. Shirley Jackson penned a letter expressing her gratitude to Philadelphia WOAR for assisting her after her rape. She explained, "I have an older sister somewhere I've never seen, and never will. But if I knew my big sister, I would hope and pray she would be as loving and caring as you and WOAR have been to me and my children . . . You've been our single life line, without that life line we would have sunk and died."[152] After stating her desire to serve WOAR as a volunteer in the future, she concluded that WOAR's services were vital resources for Black women in Philadelphia: "There are a lot of people out there in my situation, who need you, and will not be turned away because of race or color and THIS in today's world is beautiful! God bless and keep fighting!"

Ms. Jackson's letter affirms that, for all their setbacks, WOAR's Third World Caucus succeeded in establishing responsive care for non-white rape victims in Philadelphia. The Black women who comprised the Third World Caucus could trace their success to Lynn Moncrief's subversion. Moncrief retained her identity as a "Black radical feminist" while drawing her salary from the LEAA. By prioritizing preventative education ahead of police cooperation and forcing the white feminist leadership to incorporate Black women's experience into their anti-rape praxis, Moncrief and her colleagues in the Third World Caucus subverted the LEAA and its mission of controlling rape through extended police power. By reformulating Philadelphia WOAR's praxis to account for Black women's experience, Lynn Moncrief and the Third World Caucus effectively changed the structure of the feminist rape crisis center. This restructuring eventually enabled Vanessa Grant Jackson, a Black woman, to rise to the executive director's seat in 1990.[153]

The tactic of subversion functioned best for Black anti-rape organizers in the second half of the 1970s, when the federal government still adhered to the "War on Poverty" convention of issuing sizable federal grants for grassroots actors to carry out national aims. The National Center for the Prevention and Control of Rape (NCPCR) would succeed the LEAA as "the focal point for Federal activities related to the social problem of sexual assault."[154] Though smaller and less explicitly carceral than its predecessor, the NCPCR provided another opportunity for Black women to act subversively in the merging of the war on rape and the "war on crime." Just as the LEAA provided a path into the predominantly white feminist movement against sexual violence for Black women who could subsequently undermine its mandates, NCPCR funds connected Black anti-rape organizers to a body of white researchers operating in tandem with the federal government. There, they could deliver the same message: that "police reporting was not necessarily effective as a prevention strategy for Black women" and any anti-rape advocacy that was premised on police reporting was destined to fail them.[155]

CHAPTER 3

"Special Populations" Contest Official Knowledge

In April 1977, Nkenge Touré crossed the Potomac River from Washington, D.C. to Arlington, Virginia, to attend a conference sponsored by the National Center for the Prevention and Control of Rape (NCPCR, sometimes shortened to the National Rape Center). The NCPCR had been established as a division of the National Institute of Mental Health under the Health Revenue Sharing and Services Act of 1975.[1] It arrived on the heels of the Law Enforcement Assistance Administration as the second major federal intervention to control the crime of rape. The NCPCR broadly followed the formula set by the LEAA in which a large federal agency allocated grants to jumpstart anti-crime programming in the grassroots, but with two significant differences. First, unlike the LEAA, the NCPCR did not funnel its monies through state-level planning agencies. Second, the NCPCR was never authorized to fund direct service provision, much to the chagrin of feminist anti-rape organizers eager for federal funding that would not directly link them to law enforcement operations.[2] Rather, the NCPCR aimed to become a "national clearinghouse," disseminating scientifically vetted knowledge about sexual violence "to both the general public and the professional community."[3] It parceled out its modest $10 million budget as grants to professional researchers who investigated the causes and occurrence of sexual violence in the United States and, based on that research, recommended policy changes.[4] The NCPCR, which commanded a much smaller budget than the LEAA, would outlive the embattled crime control agency by five years.[5] By that time, the NCPCR had funded more than sixty individual projects proposed by researchers committed to preventing and controlling rape.[6] The NCPCR awarded half of those projects during its first two years of operation, selecting from over 250 applicants.[7]

The purpose of the April 1977 NCPCR conference was to place grassroots anti-rape activists in conversation with the researchers it funded. Its thematic focus was "Special Populations."[8] The NCPCR designated African Americans—alongside the disabled, the elderly, and children—as a "special population" whose experience of rape urgently demanded research. Touré recognized the importance of rigorous research for advancing a Black feminist praxis of care within rape crisis centers. She observed that, as late as 1977, "no research has been done . . . that would provide a realistic, rational, and proper perspective with which to view this phenomenon in the Black community."[9] In her view, "existing research, if it can be so called, has been conceived on the basis of racism, sexual stereotypes, dogmatism, a compiled wealth of assumptions, and is characteristic of that element in research which operates beyond the realm of ethics." Upon her arrival in Arlington, Touré discovered that there were no people of color among the first cohort of researchers funded by the National Rape Center. Only a handful of white feminist social scientists had received grants to conduct research that was directly applicable to African American women.[10] Touré expressed "deep concern" over the fact that "so few or no Black proposals [were] being funded."[11] She was already concerned that the research-oriented NCPCR was diverting federal funds away from supporting organizations that actually delivered services to Black victims. But the agency's disregard for Black knowledge producers further marginalized Black women's care work within the feminist movement against sexual violence. Tourè would later cite her dissatisfaction with the "Special Populations" conference of April 1977 as part of the inspiration for organizing the First National Conference on Third World Women and Violence in Washington, D.C. three years later.[12]

As representatives of a "special population," Touré and her colleagues had reason to criticize the politics of knowledge production at the National Center for the Prevention and Control of Rape. Since the early twentieth century, professional researchers had explained the violent criminal behavior of African Americans as a uniquely intractable cultural pathology that required punitive intervention.[13] Touré and her colleagues feared that the "official knowledge" sanctioned by and produced under the auspices of the National Rape Center would displace the knowledge Black women acquired through caring for Black victims.[14] This "unofficial knowledge" consisted of Black victims' experience-based understanding of the social forces that made them vulnerable to rape, their reasoned recommendations on what should be done to rectify these forces, and how the extant systems that responded to rape had failed them. Their "unofficial knowledge" frequently challenged the conclusions reached by the NCPCR, namely the promotion of law enforcement as the arbiter of women's safety. By dismissing "unofficial knowledge," the National Rape Center declared Black women's caring labor irrelevant to the prevention and control of rape.

Black anti-rape organizers answered the NCPCR's attempted erasure of their care work by insisting on its importance. In doing so, they performed another act of subversion against the state's pro-policing rape control initiatives. In Philadelphia, Lynn Moncrief had practiced subversion by repurposing the carceral resources of the LEAA for Black women's care work within WOAR. Black anti-rape organizers who attended the National Rape Center's "Special Populations" conferences practiced subversion by championing their "unofficial knowledge" and practice of care before the credentialed white researchers. The NCPCR ultimately rejected the "unofficial knowledge" of Black grassroots anti-rape organizers and the caring labor that produced it as the basis for policymaking. But the practice of subversion continued among non-activist Black women who participated in a study conducted by white feminist sociologist Diana E. H. Russell under the auspices of the NCPCR. Their "unofficial knowledge" survives in the unpublished survey responses collected by Russell. Their responses demonstrated a widespread mistrust of law enforcement and distaste for reporting among Black Bay Area women, undermining the NCPCR's published assertions that greater police involvement would broadly reduce rates of sexual violence for "special populations." Their responses also affirmed the centrality of Black women's caring labor to their short-term safety and long-term survival.

The Creation of the National Rape Center

In late 1974, the *Feminist Alliance Against Rape Newsletter* alerted its readership that Charles Mathias Jr., a Republican Senator from Maryland, was sponsoring a piece of legislation that might be of interest to rape crisis centers. The Mathias Bill, as it was known, would establish a National Center for the Prevention and Control of Rape within the National Institute of Mental Health in what was then the Department of Health, Education, and Welfare, and endow it to the tune of $5 million. The Feminist Alliance Against Rape immediately identified the proposed center as "a potential source of funding for feminist anti-rape projects."[15] It hoped that a well-funded National

Rape Center "could serve as an alternative for groups wary of LEAA (Law Enforcement Assistance Agency) funding." When the bill finally passed over President Gerald Ford's veto in July 1975, the Alliance rejoiced that the long-awaited National Center for the Prevention and Control of Rape would "consider [rape] as a health or social problem rather than a criminal problem."[16] It also warned rape crisis centers that were eager to extract themselves from law-and-order entanglements that although "the bill may be generally liberal, this by no means guarantees that it will serve the interests of feminists." Mathias framed the NCPCR in protectionist terms, professing a need to "care for our women" who were threatened by gender violence.[17] In the end, the bill was "worded so vaguely that it gives NIMH complete freedom to determine the priorities of the Center."

Early materials publicizing the National Center for the Prevention and Control of Rape presented the Center as a less carceral alternative to the Law Enforcement Assistance Administration. Unlike LEAA officials, the NCPCR did not see rape victims as merely a means to more efficiently capturing and incarcerating serial sex offenders. In the words of Nancy Gager and Cathleen Schurr, authors of the influential 1976 book *Sexual Assault: Confronting Rape in America*, the creation of the NCPCR marked the first time the federal government invited "serious considerations of the victims along with the other aspects of sexual assaults."[18] The center would achieve this by "apply[ing] the best of our scientific knowledge to the prevention of this crime and total rehabilitation of its victims."[19] To that end, the National Rape Center committed to funding empirical research on various aspects of rape victims' experience, including their treatment by law enforcement agencies and the courts, the prevalence of sexual violence beyond incidences reported to the police, the "root causes" of rape, and the "effectiveness of existing programs of rape control." The National Center credited the feminist movement against sexual violence with fixing public attention on the prevalence of rape and the myriad problems facing rape victims. At the same time, Elizabeth Kutzke, chief of the NCPCR, insisted that rape crisis centers alone were insufficient to end rape. Despite the anti-rape movement "generating ideas and lines of inquiry into what is needed to help understand and combat the problem of rape . . . a great deal is unknown" and "the need for sophisticated studies is imperative."[20] Kutzke reminded them that the amendment to the Health Services Act that created the NCPCR prohibited its funds from supporting direct service provision. Research projects funded by the Center were intended to improve the medical and criminal justice systems' response to rape, not replace them with a feminist third party.

The NCPCR's inability to fund direct service provision indicated policymakers' disinterest in the caring labor performed by lay women on behalf of victims. The omission suggested that the agency interpreted the prevention and control of rape as the duties of law enforcement professionals. When the newly minted National Center for the Prevention and Control of Rape solicited her for a research proposal in 1975, Pauline Bart was initially apprehensive. Bart had received her doctorate in sociology from the University of California, Los Angeles in 1967 and served as professor at the Abraham Lincoln School of Medicine within the University of Illinois Chicago.[21] She also claimed membership in the Chicago Women Against Rape and headed the Hospital Subcommittee of the Citizens Advisory Committee on Rape in Chicago. Bart had already excoriated the Law Enforcement Assistance Administration's forays into anti-rape organizing as a cynical co-optation of feminist institutions motivated solely by the "law and order" politics of the day. Bart attributed the creation of the National Center for the Prevention and Control of Rape to the same "concerns with rape felt by the law-and-order anti-crime-in-the-streets constituency."[22] Reluctant to contribute to a federal agency that, as she saw it, existed primarily to further the "war on crime," she left the proposal packet unopened on her desk for nearly a month. She finally relented at the urging of Susan Brownmiller, a nationally recognized voice within the feminist movement against sexual violence, recently triumphant in the publication of *Against Our Will: Men, Women, and Rape.*[23] Though Bart suspected from the outset that the NCPCR was furnishing research that reinforced the narrow crime-control response to rape, she pursued NCPCR funding as an opportunity to embed genuinely feminist ideas into state-subsidized rape research.

In 1976, the National Center for the Prevention and Control of Rape issued its first round of approved research grants. It divided $3 million among more than a dozen researchers. Among the cohort was Diana E. H. Russell, whose study on "The Prevalence of Sexual Assault and Rape in San Francisco" received $150,635 to support two years of research.[24] Russell, a native of Cape Town, South Africa, arrived in the United States in 1963, earned her doctorate at Harvard University, and took a sociology post at Mills College in San Francisco, California.[25] Like Bart, Russell was an unapologetic feminist active within the U.S. women's liberation movement. In the same year that she secured National Rape Center funding, Russell helped to found Women Against Violence in Media and Pornography, a precursor to Women Against Pornography.[26] By the time she received her grant, Russell was already an internationally recognized expert on gender violence. Her groundbreaking 1974 study *The Politics of Rape* validated what would become a mainstream feminist truism: that men who raped were not pathological sexual deviants but generally normal men acting upon societally inscribed ideas of masculinity.[27] Although Russell was a white woman, Black women's experience of sexual violence was an integral focus of *The Politics of Rape*. Not all readers approved of Russell's engagement with race as an analytic category. Angela Davis and Robert Staples bristled at the "seeming obsession with the Black rapist" that flowed through *The Politics of Rape* and took issue with the "disproportionately large number of cases [that] deal with Black men—raping white women."[28] Davis did commend Russell for acknowledging that "black females are far more subject to rape by black men than are white females."

For the NCPCR, Russell designed an interview-based study of the greater San Francisco metropolitan area. To ensure significant numbers of African American women respondents, she and her research assistants would engage in door-to-door canvassing that targeted Black neighborhoods in the Bay Area. She even wrote to the Berkeley headquarters of the Third World Women's Alliance requesting to place an advertisement in their newspaper *Triple Jeopardy* to reach more Third World women who might be willing to participate in the study.[29] Between 1977 and 1979, Russell conducted 930 interviews, nearly 10 percent of which were with women who identified as Black. This aligned roughly with the proportion of African Americans in the population of San Francisco, which hovered around 11 percent.[30] Russell aimed to measure rates of sexual abuse across a diverse group of women in San Francisco to determine which demographic factors put women at risk. She was particularly interested in rapes that had not been reported to the police and therefore did not appear in the victimization surveys compiled by the Law Enforcement Assistance Administration.[31] Russell explicitly hoped that the "official knowledge" she produced as a researcher funded by the National Rape Center would inform state policy. Her findings on the prevalence of sexual assault in San Francisco was of immediate interest to policymakers within the "war on crime." In 1981, the California Commission on Crime Control and Violence Prevention tapped Russell to be their expert consultant on sexual violence. The Commission had been convened through the Law Enforcement Assistance Administration's National Institute of Justice to investigate the "root causes of crime" and Russell, as an expert consultant, would "guide their formulation of recommendations aimed at preventing these crimes in California."[32]

Anti-rape organizers voiced their disappointment that the NCPCR was subsidizing feminist researchers like Russell and not feminist rape crisis centers. Although service providers could apply for NCPCR grants by presenting rape crisis centers as "research demonstrations," the *Feminist Alliance Against Rape Newsletter* cautioned that "community organizations may have difficulty in obtaining funding except in collaboration with professional researchers."[33] By late 1976, the Alliance's newsletter regretted that "the establishment of the National Center has proved not to be a windfall for rape crisis centers."[34] Some frustrated anti-rape organizers suggested that the movement would do well to "ignore the National Center altogether," lest the "promise of grant money for research . . . divert us from our real priorities."[35] The direction of the National Center for the Prevention and Control of Rape seemed to confirm the Alliance's prediction that deputizing federal agencies to address rape would mean that "those of us who have been responsible for the increased 'concern' for rape victims may be squeezed out of the picture."[36] In 1977, Black anti-rape organizers joined the surging chorus of criticism of the National Rape Center.

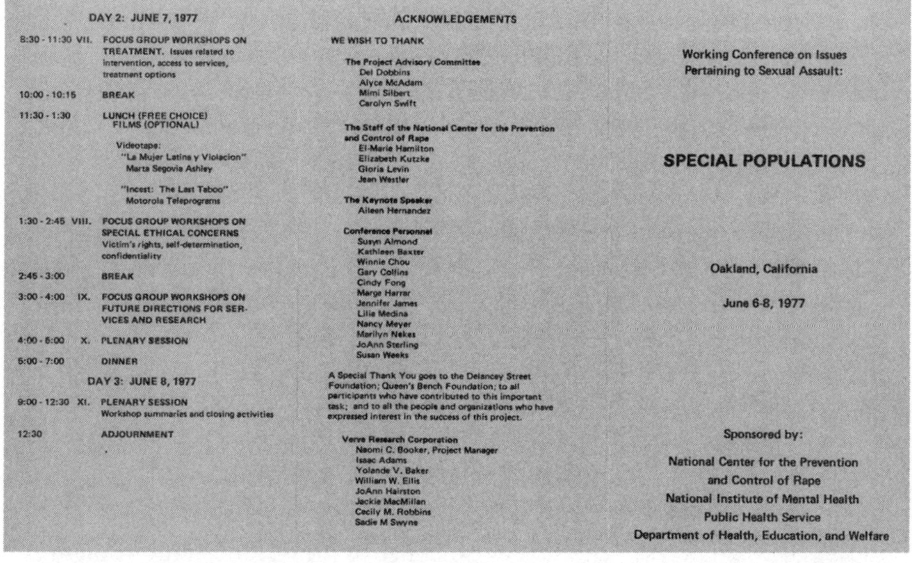

DAY 2: JUNE 7, 1977

8:30 - 11:30	VII.	FOCUS GROUP WORKSHOPS ON TREATMENT. Issues related to intervention, access to services, treatment options
10:00 - 10:15		BREAK
11:30 - 1:30		LUNCH (FREE CHOICE) FILMS (OPTIONAL) Videotape: "La Mujer Latina y Violacion" Marta Segovia Ashley "Incest: The Last Taboo" Motorola Teleprograms
1:30 - 2:45	VIII.	FOCUS GROUP WORKSHOPS ON SPECIAL ETHICAL CONCERNS Victim's rights, self-determination, confidentiality
2:45 - 3:00		BREAK
3:00 - 4:00	IX.	FOCUS GROUP WORKSHOPS ON FUTURE DIRECTIONS FOR SERVICES AND RESEARCH
4:00 - 5:00	X.	PLENARY SESSION
5:00 - 7:00		DINNER

DAY 3: JUNE 8, 1977

9:00 - 12:30	XI.	PLENARY SESSION Workshop summaries and closing activities
12:30		ADJOURNMENT

ACKNOWLEDGEMENTS

WE WISH TO THANK

The Project Advisory Committee
Del Dobbins
Alyce McAdam
Mimi Silbert
Carolyn Swift

The Staff of the National Center for the Prevention and Control of Rape
El-Marie Hamilton
Elizabeth Kutzke
Gloria Levin
Jean Westler

The Keynote Speaker
Aileen Hernandez

Conference Personnel
Susyn Almond
Kathleen Baxter
Winnie Chou
Gary Collins
Cindy Fong
Marge Harrar
Jennifer James
Lilie Medina
Nancy Meyer
Marilyn Nekes
JoAnn Sterling
Susan Weeks

A Special Thank You goes to the Delancey Street Foundation; Queen's Bench Foundation; to all participants who have contributed to this important task; and to all the people and organizations who have expressed interest in the success of this project.

Verve Research Corporation
Naomi C. Booker, Project Manager
Isaac Adams
Yolande V. Baker
William W. Ellis
JoAnn Hairston
Jackie MacMillan
Cecily M. Robbins
Sadie M Swyne

Working Conference on Issues Pertaining to Sexual Assault:

SPECIAL POPULATIONS

Oakland, California

June 6-8, 1977

Sponsored by:
National Center for the Prevention and Control of Rape
National Institute of Mental Health
Public Health Service
Department of Health, Education, and Welfare

Figure 3. NCPCR Special Populations Conference in Oakland, California (June 1977). Courtesy of the Schlesinger Library on the History of Women in America.

As they saw it, the NCPCR's research agenda was not merely depriving them of the funds needed to continue their care for victims. It was creating biased and incomplete data sets, particularly for "special populations," and skewing the policies that drew upon this data.

The "Special Populations" Conference Series and Its Discontents

In 1977, the NCPCR announced four regional conferences dedicated to what they deemed to be "Special Populations." These were groups at high risk of sexual assault but whose experience of rape was under-researched. The NCPCR identified Black women as a "special population" alongside Spanish-speaking women, the disabled, the elderly, children and adolescents, gay men, sex workers, and prisoners.[37] The Arlington "Special Populations" Conference, the first in the series, attempted to "define the issues of sexual assault as they pertain to special population groups, articulate new research questions, generate ideas for new service models, and share information and perspectives between researchers and practitioners."[38] Black women anti-rape organizers agreed that a state-sponsored conference that focused squarely on the issues facing Black rape victims was urgent. They complained that as late as 1977, there was "no accurate research available on Blacks in relationship to rape" that they could utilize in advocacy.[39] But they did not attend to pitch novel inquiries to a crowd of white credentialed researchers. They attended to subvert the NCPCR and its scientific rationalization of controlling rape instead of caring for victims.

During a workshop designated for Black service providers, Tourè and her colleagues drafted a proposal to amend the National Rape Center to better accommodate a Black feminist praxis of care. They called for the creation of a Special Populations Advisory Council that would ensure non-white representation during the grant review process and more expansive criteria for fundable projects.[40] Touré and her colleagues insisted that their experiential knowledge about the struggles of Black rape survivors, acquired from their care work within rape crisis centers, was just as valuable as the research the NCPCR solicited from white social scientists. In fact, their unofficial, experiential knowledge exposed the inadequacies of the "official knowledge" produced by NCPCR researchers. They explained to the researchers at Arlington that "reporting was not necessarily effective as a prevention strategy for Black women due to racism." They rejected the rationale advanced by some

NCPCR researchers that "if more rapists were caught, fewer rapes would occur." Citing their experiential knowledge of the "distrust built up over the years between Black communities and the police departments" and Black women's chronic mistreatment by law enforcement officials, Touré and her allies conveyed to NCPCR officials and their client researchers that "reporting should be an option open to the victim if desired, but would not be considered the focal point of a prevention plan." In lieu of "reporting as a means of prevention," they urged the NCPCR to redirect its efforts and funds to projects that supported Black women's care work. Like other Black feminists, Touré and her colleagues specifically recommended community education as "an important and far-reaching prevention strategy" that encompassed activities from writing curricula for grade schoolers to hosting seminars for neighborhood groups.[41]

Touré and her colleagues also subverted the National Rape Center by questioning the racial dynamics of its research model. Traditionally, research on race and rape consisted of white researchers collecting knowledge about Black subjects, oftentimes without securing their informed consent regarding how they would use the information. Too often, the results failed to account for how systemic racism shaped Black women's experience of and response to sexual violence. Arlington conference attendees complained to the conveners of the "glaring lack of grants for research designed by members of the special population groups (and service providers and activists in general)."[42] The only remedy to this was to include Black women, both credentialed professional researchers and grassroots rape crisis center workers, in the production of "official knowledge" about race and rape. The NCPCR could achieve this by diversifying its review panel and extending technical assistance grants to rape crisis centers. NCPCR chief Elizabeth Kutzke expressed sympathy with the proposal, but claimed she was not positioned to implement it. Black conferencegoers' calls for the diversification of the NCPCR's review panel and direct financial support for service providers had fallen on deaf ears, leaving Nkenge Touré to conclude that the National Rape Center was actively hostile toward Black women's care work.[43]

With frustration mounting, the Black conferencegoers resolved to gather again independently "to develop particular approaches to rape and its implications within the Black community."[44] They felt that the Special Populations Conference had neither "identified nor articulated the special concerns of Blacks based upon the culture and historical experiences of ourselves as a people."[45] Black women anti-rape organizers would create this space in

August 1980 with the First National Conference on Third World Women and Violence in Washington, D.C.[46] The National Center for the Prevention and Control of Rape, like the Law Enforcement Assistance Administration, was sympathetic to law-and-order solutions and wedded to a racialized professional hierarchy. Consequently, the tactic of subversion had limited utility for Black anti-rape organizers hoping to create the conditions for care under agencies premised on rape control.

Black women's criticisms of the structure and politics of the National Center for the Prevention and Control of Rape intensified during the subsequent "Special Populations" conferences of 1977. Deb Friedman, who attended the Midwestern Conference in Ann Arbor, Michigan, reported with dismay in the *Feminist Alliance Against Rape Newsletter* that only seven of one hundred attendees of the Ann Arbor Special Populations conference were Black women.[47] The facilitators of the "Black Workshop" wondered aloud how Black women's attendance at the conference could be so meager given Ann Arbor's proximity to Detroit, "an activist city with many Black organizations that should have been contacted in order to facilitate recruitment and participation in this conference."[48] The frustrated facilitators devoted their scheduled time block to drafting a resolution that decried the lack of recruitment for non-white participants. Beyond their recruitment complaints, their listed objections echoed the arguments originally made by Touré and her colleagues during the first Special Populations Conference in Arlington. They, too, faulted the National Rape Center for "overlooking the value of Third World peoples' and special population groups' perspectives based on their unique experiences."[49] They worried that "the proceedings of the conference could be used to support a position that would not be in the real interests of the special populations that the workshops were expected to address."[50] The NCPCR could emerge from the Special Populations conferences with an endorsement of police reporting as a deterrent to rape and claim that Black women supported this policy, omitting their subversive objections. The remaining conferences were just as liable to fossilize the Black marginalization witnessed at Arlington and Ann Arbor.

Black women anti-rape organizers' criticisms reached the ears of NCPCR officials but did not render the desired effect. Instead of addressing their concerns, the National Rape Center abruptly cancelled all future Special Populations conferences. The *Feminist Alliance Against Rape Newsletter* speculated that "the conferences are being cancelled because the National Rape Center does not wish to accept the criticisms that were made at the first series of conferences."[51] Black anti-rape organizers' subversion triggered a defensive response from the NCPCR that kept them from even indirectly accessing the agency's resources. Suspending the Special Populations conference series did not stifle the criticism. In January 1978, Nancy McDonald of the D.C. Rape Crisis Center commented on the performance of the NCPCR during the Congressional hearing on "Research into Violent Behavior: Overview and Sexual Assaults." She described the 1977 Special Populations conference series as "the most visible effort of the National Rape Center for Black and Hispanic people."[52] However, it was organized primarily to serve the interests of white researchers. According to McDonald, this power imbalance reflected the structure of the NCPCR, which privileged the scientific knowledge about rape produced by credentialed professionals and discredited the care work of women of color organizing in the grassroots. "By the third conference in Ann Arbor," she explained, "it was clear that the conferences themselves were a prime example of the problem being addressed: the failure of institutional programs to address the needs of special populations."[53] McDonald argued that the NCPCR still held "considerable potential for future impact on the relationship between racism and rape, and on the needs of Black women," but that potential would only be unlocked pending structural changes to the research agency.[54] These changes included proactive outreach to Third World women's groups to keep them abreast of NCPCR findings, funding for technical assistance in rape crisis centers that served large numbers of women of color, improved representation of non-white women on the National Advisory Committee, and, crucially, "direct solicitation from Third World women active in anti-rape organizing of ideas for priorities for research and demonstration funding."[55]

Nancy McDonald called for the NCPCR to entrust Black women currently operating within rape crisis centers with knowledge production about Black women's experience of sexual violence. She knew that Black women anti-rape organizers were acutely aware of the unmet needs of Black women survivors from their daily work within rape crisis centers and that their experiential knowledge was just as legitimate as the formal studies produced by white social scientists endowed by the National Rape Center. McDonald insisted that "there is nothing magical or mystical about scientifically precise or statistically significant research" and Black women anti-rape organizers could easily translate their grassroots observations into widely applicable policies and practices "given adequate program development assistance and funds for consultation" from the National Rape Center.[56] McDonald encouraged the National Center for the Prevention and Control of Rape to recognize the valuable "unofficial knowledge" of Black women anti-rape organizers and elevate it to the status of "official knowledge" by offering them technical assistance grants. With the help of these grants, Black women working within rape crisis centers could disseminate crucial insights on the discriminatory treatment of non-white women by medical and law enforcement personnel, the differential conviction and sentencing patterns for Black and white defendants accused of rape, and the specific counseling techniques that best served Black women.[57]

As Black women anti-rape organizers like Tourè repeatedly pointed out, the National Center for the Prevention and Control of Rape's purported concern over Black women and girls conflicted with their continued reliance upon white professional researchers to investigate this "special population." If the NCPCR wished to institute meaningful care for Black victims, they first needed to recognize Black women working within rape crisis centers as legitimate producers of knowledge worthy of direct federal monies. Each day they spent counseling and caring for Black rape victims educated them about the material conditions that exposed Black women to violence and the social, cultural, and financial obstacles that blocked them from recourse and recovery. Black women anti-rape organizers hoped to install a Black feminist epistemology of sexual violence within the NCPCR whereby Black women, from their interested standpoint, could harness their everyday knowledge of intersecting oppressions to make uniquely informed claims about race and rape.[58] The National Rape Center remained unresponsive to their overtures for recognition as intellectual producers. The agency's emphasis on professional credentials and institutional connections as preconditions for funding sidelined the care work of Black anti-rape organizers.

"I See the Police and Get as Far Away as I Can"

The controversy that swirled around the 1977 Special Populations conference series did not interfere with Diana E. H. Russell's research agenda. As a grantee of the National Rape Center and an active member of the feminist movement against sexual violence, she was possibly aware of the debacle but never commented on it. On paper, Russell's project on "The Prevalence of Sexual Assault in San Francisco" was sensitive to the grievances voiced by Black anti-rape organizers who attended the "Special Populations" conferences. She pledged to contribute to the production of knowledge about Black women's experience of rape and drew heavily upon interviews with Black women rape survivors to do so.

The Bay Area neighborhoods that Diana E. H. Russell canvassed between 1977 and 1979 were already served by two feminist anti-rape organizations: the San Francisco Women Against Rape (SFWAR) and the Bay Area Women Against Rape (BAWAR).[59] Both groups were founded by local feminists in the early 1970s who abhorred climbing rates of sexual violence within their communities and the dismissal of rape complaints by the medical and criminal justice systems. Their activism encompassed the trademark services of the nationwide feminist movement against sexual violence: a twenty-four-hour hotline for rape victims, consciousness-raising sessions, self-defense training, and pressuring hospitals and law enforcement officials to improve their responses to rape victims. BAWAR also distributed their signature "Street Sheets" around Berkeley and Oakland to alert women to known rapists in the area.[60] The racial composition of both groups was mixed, though BAWAR served a substantially higher number of women of color than SFWAR.[61] BAWAR initially sought funding from the Law Enforcement Assistance Administration but withdrew their application after they "realized that our goals and principles could be easily coopted by such a law-enforcement oriented agency."[62] Executive Director Robin Welles elected instead to selectively cobble together county and municipal funds to support the group's community education endeavors while precluding any potential pressure from the federal government to push police reporting on victims. BAWAR readily acknowledged that reporting rape was not only undesirable for Black women who did not wish to invite police attention into their lives and communities, but also posed direct dangers for Black women. Marsha Blackstock, who joined BAWAR in 1977 and eventually succeeded Robin Welles as director, confirmed that Black women regularly contacted her claiming they had been sexually assaulted by police.[63] By contrast, SFWAR was more comfortable with police collaboration in their service provision. A majority of their members declined to publicly participate in the defense campaign of Inez Garcia, a Latina woman tried for murdering her assailant in 1974, out of fear that doing so would sour their working relationship with the San Francisco Police Department.[64]

The feminist anti-rape organizations that served the Bay Area were conversant in Black women's experience of sexual assault. But this offered little comfort as a Black serial rapist dubbed "Stinky" by the press assaulted dozens of women in Oakland and Berkeley between 1973 and 1978.[65] In September

1978, *Ebony* syndicated the story of Carolyn Craven, an African American television news reporter, whom "Stinky" assaulted in her Berkeley home in January of that year.[66] Craven retraced each step of the terrifying encounter, from the moment she awoke in the middle of the night to find a foul-smelling, knife-wielding Black stranger in her bed to her assailant's flight after three excruciating hours. She immediately identified her assailant as "Stinky" given his repugnant odor.[67] Craven reported that she was paralyzed by fear and did nothing to physically resist "Stinky," who threatened to murder her and her five-year-old son if she made any noise. After "Stinky" departed, she woke up her son, scrambled to collect some personal items, and fled to a neighbor's home where she immediately contacted the police. Craven closed out her article with a ringing endorsement of the feminist movement against sexual violence, particularly the Bay Area Women Against Rape, and charged the magazine's national readership to uproot the patriarchally sanctioned rape culture that created "Stinky" in the first place. "Women alone cannot stop a crime we don't commit," Craven said. "Men, too, must learn why other men commit rape and must do it before it's too late, must do it before the next victims are their mothers, sisters, wives, and daughters."[68] Departing from its historical reluctance to discuss the rape of Black women, *Ebony* concluded the article with a directory of over forty rape crisis centers across the United States.[69]

Despite the national attention garnered by "Stinky" in Carolyn Craven's *Ebony* article and BAWAR's relentless informational campaign charting his every move, the serial rapist proved elusive for Berkeley police. Police captured a suspect in October 1978, but the case unraveled after the District Attorney declined to prosecute due to circumstantial evidence.[70] Carolyn Craven's rape in January 1978 was the last one attributed to "Stinky."[71] The bungled police response and anticlimactic conclusion meant that his reign of terror was fresh in the minds of the Black Bay Area women interviewed by Diana E. H. Russell between 1977 and 1979. The feeling of vulnerability to sexual assault that had long accompanied Black women sharpened acutely as law enforcement proved themselves unable or unwilling to intervene. Making matters worse, both BAWAR and SFWAR nearly collapsed in the summer of 1979 due to an exodus of volunteers, infighting over racial representation and policies within the organizations, the discontinuation of funding sources, and a series of expensive lawsuits.[72] Though both organizations survived their ordeals, their instability inspired little confidence from agonized Black women in the Bay Area. The apparent dysfunction of local feminist anti-rape organizations who presented themselves as an alternative to the police for assaulted women left law enforcement standing as the only available, if woefully inadequate, option.

This desperate yearning for any resources or recourse that the state might offer pervaded the narratives of the ninety Black women Russell encountered, forty of whom disclosed that they had personally experienced some form of sexual assault in their lives. In calling up traumatic stories of violation, many offered their own commentary on the nature of sexual violence against Black women and what ought to be done to stop it. By transforming their "unofficial knowledge" into "official knowledge" to be consumed by professional researchers and policymakers, Russell abstracted their anecdotes and life histories into quantifiable data. Some Black women actively resisted abstraction. One of Diana Russell's research assistants recorded that she was turned away by a prospective Black woman interviewee who took umbrage with the government's overriding interest in researching Black people and crime, which from her point of view came at the expense of extending material resources.[73] Zidar (identified in the record as Case #217–024), a twenty-seven-year-old single mother and "a Black woman on AFDC in a neighborhood with almost no other Blacks," initially refused to participate in the interview out of fear that discussing her income with the interviewer might jeopardize her public assistance payments.[74] Zidar did not disclose any sexual abuse in her life, but her anxiety surrounding the interview process painfully illustrated the precariousness of Black women in the Bay Area that exposed them to inordinate levels of violence.

The detailed stories and commentary of those who agreed to participate did not appear in the final published version of *Sexual Exploitation* (1984). However, a close reading of the archived interview transcripts reveals their "unofficial knowledge" production regarding the root causes of gender violence and how it might be stopped. Occasionally, respondents interpreted intraracial violence within the moralistic "Black-on-Black crime" framework and made the same recommendations as the Coalition of Concerned Women in the War on Crime. Their calls for invigorated law enforcement responses to rape are understandable considering the unstable feminist rape crisis centers and unchecked serial rape that surrounded them. Even more interviewees rejected greater police presence as an effective deterrent to rape. Replicating the complaints of the frustrated Black anti-rape organizers who attended the NCPCR's Special Populations conferences, these non-activist Black women research subjects acted subversively. Though the NCPCR funded research for the purposes of validating law enforcement responses to rape, the "unofficial knowledge" of Black women undermined these intentions by shattering the illusion of consensus. They knew that the care and support provided by anti-rape organizers sustained their lives and communities in ways that police-centric rape control never could.

Several of Russell's subjects offered their own theories about the root causes of Black women's vulnerability to sexual violence in San Francisco. Juanida (identified in the records as Case #101–013) was forty years old, separated from her husband, and working as a breakfast shop cook. She saw rape as a "big problem" in San Francisco, whereas crime itself was only "some problem" in the city, and implicated the urban environment in exacerbating violence between Black men and women.[75] "In the country there wasn't any rapes of Black women by Black men," she said. "We respected each other. Sometimes white men caught Black women in the wrong place at the wrong time and raped them, but Black men respected us."[76] Ela (Case #230–002), a fifty-year-old former waitress collecting disability, agreed with Juanida that rape was a "big problem" in San Francisco. She tied the issue of sexual assault to issues of racial oppression, arguing against the "misconception" that Black men were especially keen on raping white women and professing that "the majority of rape is committed by white men" against women of their own race.[77] Others attributed the prevalence of sexual violence among African American women in San Francisco to the unchecked sexism of Black men. Gwen (Case #320–001), a twenty-eight-year-old divorcee who worked as a coordinator for a community anti-crime organization, reported that she personally knew at least twenty Black women who had recently been raped. She herself had been sexually abused by her ex-husband. Gwen maintained that a rape epidemic was gripping the Bay Area because "men in general, regardless of their age, are creatures composed of mass insecurities" who "want women to be educated and intelligent, but [also] want them to be barefoot in the kitchen."[78]

Other interviewees did not offer insights on the origins of Black women's vulnerability to rape but did elucidate the grievous impact of that violence on their mental health. The most prominent themes connecting Black women's responses to Russell's survey were their reported feelings of depression and anxiety that persisted long after the initial assault. Barbara, a thirty-seven-year-old unmarried legal secretary (Case #145–013) told Russell's research assistant that she had been molested by her father and raped by several boyfriends. She refused to "view rape as a sin" or a source of shame for Black women. Instead, she argued that the repeated incidents "shows how little

[Black men] thought of me as a Black female" and subsequently "contributed to my low self esteem [and] lack of self-worthiness."[79] For some subjects, like fifty-eight-year-old housekeeper Dorothy (Case #421–163), the interview marked the first time they ever divulged their assaults and the lifelong pain they concealed. Dorothy tearfully recounted to Russell's research assistant how her adoptive father sexually abused her throughout her childhood. Upon learning of the abuse, her adoptive mother warned her that she "wasn't supposed to tell anybody or they'd put him in jail."[80] Dorothy's mother's admonition that incarceration would further harm the family underscores the problematic equation of fighting rape with police reporting. Because she "really didn't have no help in dealing with it" in her native Louisiana, she fled across the country to San Francisco in her early twenties. Unfortunately, Dorothy's flight from her abuser and his enabler did not resolve her repressed trauma, which manifested as paranoia. Collectively, Barbara and Dorothy's responses indicated that Black feminist sexual politics and mistrust of criminal justice solutions had popular purchase beyond activist spaces in the late 1970s. Their unresolved mental health issues also underscored the importance of supportive counseling for Black sexual assault survivors, a staple of the Black anti-rape organizers' care work.

Some of Russell's Black interview subjects voiced conservative opinions about sexual violence and its impact on African American women. Margaret (Case #200–037), a thirty-four-year-old head attendant in surgery living apart from her husband, expressed her belief that "most of the rapes are invited" because "women carry themselves in a poor manner."[81] A few explicitly called for punitive solutions to the epidemic of sexual violence in the Bay Area. Elmira (Case #181–019), a married forty-seven-year-old nurse's assistant, declared that Black women "aren't safe on the street" and called upon the police to "clean up this crime that's going on."[82] Juanita (Case #235–050), a single twenty-five-year-old former clerk typist with the U.S. Navy, similarly endorsed harsh punishment in defense of Black women. "When they catch rapists, they need to put them up under the jail," she asserted.[83] She recommended establishing regular police patrols in areas where rapes had occurred. Invigorated police presence would not have prevented the attempted rapes that Elmira and Juanita reported from their childhoods, which occurred at the hands of male family members behind closed doors. Still, their endorsement of law enforcement showed that the non-feminist perspective of Chicago's Coalition of Concerned Women in the War on Crime had some adherents.[84] With no overhauls of social structure immediately forthcoming, they looked to incarceration as offering speedy short-term protection from physical threat that would allow them to navigate the streets free of fear.

Other Black interviewees did not endorse punishment as the ultimate solution to rape, even as they invoked the obligation of police to shield them from violence. Jacquelyn (Case #197–014), a thirty-four-year-old divorcee and clerk for San Francisco Water, shared Elmira's belief that "the police department should be more aware of these crimes against women" but balanced it with a call for expanded economic opportunity for Black Bay Area residents, arguing that "they should keep these young boys employed so they won't get into so much trouble."[85] Along similar lines, an anonymous fifty-year-old respondent who worked as a psychiatric nurse (Case #401–008) suggested that "if the government is going to make a survey, they should provide free self-defense classes for girls starting from 7th or 8th grade and to all women in general" that would allow them to protect themselves from rape without relying on the police.[86] Ernestine (Case #235–051), a fifty-year-old domestic worker, proclaimed that rape afflicted as much as 80 percent of the Bay Area's female residents, including herself. She asserted that "if the police would be a little better to the woman when they report a rape, more of them would come forward."[87] Jazelle (Case #246–011), a single twenty-five-year-old part-time nurse, seconded Ernestine.[88] She drew upon a frightening personal experience in building her critique. A few years prior to the interview, a man stalked her as she walked home from work and attempted to rape her in a vacant public parking lot on Fell Street. She managed to escape and file a police report, but struggled to identify her assailant in the police station line-up, after which the police inspector in attendance "implied that [she] was making it all up."[89] Lacking closure over her own assault, she refused to venture outside by herself after dark. Still reeling from her betrayal by the police force, she voiced "hope that [research] would help change police attitudes towards victims."

Even if they did not propose a solution to rape, many of the Black women who participated in Russell's study drew upon their everyday experiences and life histories to assert that the expansion of police power would not serve them well. A twenty-four-year-old nursing student named Gail (Case #420–024) cast doubt on the concept of incarceration as a deterrent to rape since "rapists are put in jail but they get out and they continue doing it."[90] Because "jail won't do anything," Gail insisted that "boys must be taught differently," underscoring the idea advanced by Black feminists that effective community education would lead young men to relinquish their sexual power over women and girls.[91] Juanita (Case #307–017) was a forty-three-year-old clerk typist who earnestly believed that 100 percent of women would experience sexual assault in their lives.[92] She had an extremely compelling reason to reject the expansion of police power over rape: she was one of the unfortunate Black women alluded to by Marsha Blackstock. At age eighteen, Juanita was standing at a bus stop waiting to go to work when a passing white police officer demanded that she enter his vehicle. He removed her clothing and forcibly "searched" her, only ceasing when a Black man, who happened to be driving by, saw her struggling and approached the police car. The incident left Juanita with severe emotional scars and permanently destroyed any faith she had in law enforcement to protect her. "I see police now and I get as far away as I can," she concluded.[93]

The interviews collected by Russell and her research assistants in San Francisco cataloged the complicated and varied attitudes that Black women held regarding the relationship between policing and rape. Some, like Elmira and Juanita (#235–050), openly demanded more stringent enforcement of rape law, perhaps anticipating that increased police presence was the only gesture the state would conceivably make for Black women's safety. Others like Jacqueline, Ernestine, and Jazelle looked to local law enforcement as a potential protector of Black women, pending significant reforms. The most consistent throughline in these interviews, exemplified by the statements of Gwen, Dorothy, Gail, and Juanita (#307–017), was that controlling rape through policing was at best a superficial solution and at worst a consistent source of violence against Black women. Their acquired distaste for the criminal justice system informed the Black anti-rape organizers who attended the NCPCR's Special Populations conference series in 1977. Their lived experience called for a multifaceted anti-rape advocacy that cared comprehensively for Black victims in the present and prevented sexual assault in the future by correcting the social dynamics of patriarchy, poverty, and racism. The NCPCR called for easily quantifiable and replicable data sets that could not capture these subjective nuances but served the known entities of policing and prosecution well enough.

While Russell continued to collect and process the "unofficial knowledge" of Black women, the National Center for the Prevention and Control of Rape garnered even more criticism from frustrated feminists. At the end of 1978, Mary Ann Largen resumed Black anti-rape organizers' campaign to amend Bill S.2565 to grant the NCPCR authority to administer grants and contracts that would directly support services for victims. Largen acknowledged in the pages of the *Feminist Alliance Against Rape Newsletter* that the "fashionable fiscal conservatism" of the 95th Congress endangered the funding of all social service programs not immediately attached to law enforcement.[94] The proposed service amendment fell out as S.2565 lurched its way through Congress in 1979. Just as the Feminist Alliance Against Rape feared, the NCPCR was free to set its own priorities with little accountability toward feminist victim service providers despite their deep knowledge about the issues facing rape victims. According to Jane BenDor, a psychologist and counselor with the Southeast Michigan Anti-Rape Network, "the Rape Center has failed to meet both its research and clearing house responsibilities," miscarrying its research mandate by not communicating findings with local victim service programs already underway.[95] To these accusations of an out-of-touch and ineffective federal agency, Elizabeth Kutzke rebutted that the National Rape Center could and did inform myriad policies and procedures for the treatment of rape victims in institutional settings as well as rape crisis centers.[96] She recited a litany of ongoing research projects, including "studies of high-risk groups potentially vulnerable to sexual assaults," whose findings contained policy implications that promised to "make important contributions toward the ultimate goal of controlling and eliminating rape in our society."[97]

As she defended the NCPCR, Kutzke struggled to separate the National Rape Center from the crime control ethos that infused all state activity around rape. During the third session of the Congressional hearing on "Research into Violent Behavior," Robert S. Walker, a Republican Representative from Pennsylvania, grilled Kutzke as to why the Center was housed under the National Institute of Mental Health as opposed to the Department of Justice.[98] Walker, like other conservative representatives, felt that rape should be recognized primarily as a violent crime and be dealt with in the same manner as murder, assault, and burglary. Walker warned that a National Rape Center divorced from crime control apparatuses would "lead us astray in terms of the final solution" to sexual violence.[99] Kutzke resisted Walker's insinuation, countering that Congress "could have made the decision to put [the NCPCR] in the LEAA" but wished to keep the NCPCR responsive to multiple aspects of sexual violence, especially the difficulties facing victims.[100] Unconvinced, Representative Walker pointed out that the agency's title—The National Center for the Prevention and *Control* of Rape—required the research it funded to directly serve the interests of crime control. Recycling the punitive logic of the LEAA, Representative Walker asserted that "you don't prevent rape by helping the victims afterwards . . . you prevent rape by putting offenders behind bars."[101] On this point, Kutzke demurred, only offering that "we ask ourselves what it means to 'control' rape. That's a very difficult issue to deal with, and I don't think we really do address that one."[102] Kutzke insisted that placement within the National Institute of Mental Health allowed the National Rape Center to attend to the many facets of rape that fell outside the criminal justice response. Still, the NCPCR's research mandate overlapped with the crime control mission of the LEAA. In 1979, Kutzke returned to Congress on behalf of the National Center to once again answer accusations of "too much research and too little assistance to [rape crisis] centers."[103] Kutzke counted law enforcement and criminal justice personnel among those reaping the benefits of research projects funded by the NCPCR.[104] She avowed that the NCPCR, unlike the LEAA, remained committed primarily to "addressing the impact and trauma to victims and potential victims." But in practice, the National Rape Center consistently dedicated its resources to projects that aimed to expand the criminal justice system's capacity to incarcerate rapists. In this way, the NCPCR served the same purpose as the LEAA.

By 1980, feminists active within rape crisis centers had abandoned all hope that the National Center for the Prevention and Control of Rape would grow beyond its preoccupation with funding rape research. In the next decade, Russell would complete the final step of translating the "unofficial knowledge" of a vulnerable "special population" into "official knowledge" by publishing a book that transmitted her findings to fellow academics, medical professionals, law enforcement personnel, and policymakers. Much was lost in the translation of wrenching anecdotes and personal confessions into a polished, professional manuscript. This partial translation affirmed the crime control response to rape with scant attention to the caring labor of Black women anti-rape organizers.

From Narrative to Numbers Game: Russell Publishes Her Findings

Diana E. H. Russell published her findings from "The Prevalence of Sexual Assault and Rape in San Francisco" under the title *Sexual Exploitation: Rape, Child Sexual Abuse, and Workplace Harassment* in October 1984. She did not include quotations from any of her research subjects in the text. Her quantitative focus in *Sexual Exploitation* marked a departure from her earlier methods. In her career-launching study *The Politics of Rape* (1974), Russell quoted rape survivors at length to substantiate her claims. Russell's original preference for stories over statistics was an extension of her feminist politics. She intentionally sought out "the victim's perspective" to contest the perspectives of mostly male clinicians that downplayed the extent and severity of sexual violence.[105] The early feminist movement against sexual violence gained momentum through the practice of consciousness-raising, which relied on ordinary women sharing their personal experiences to develop a political basis for organizing against rape.[106] Russell shifted to a statistical mode of analysis in *Sexual Exploitation* (1984) in keeping with the preferences of the National Center for the Prevention and Control of Rape and the goals of the California Commission on Crime and Violence. Both entities were primarily interested in determining the causes of sexual abuse to devise policy solutions.[107] They favored digestible and unambiguous statistics over the subjective and often contradictory stories of survivors.

The NCPCR, like the LEAA, was engaged in a lively "numbers game" to advance rape control efforts. Both feminist anti-rape organizers and the state agencies that subsidized them eagerly furnished statistics that showed climbing rates of sexual assault in the United States to justify the receipt and expenditure of funds. Whether sexual violence was surging through the 1970s as the feminist anti-rape movement and law enforcement agencies claimed is difficult to ascertain. Reported sexual assaults increased markedly as the feminist movement against sexual violence encouraged victims to come forward and legal reforms made rape convictions easier to sustain. At the same time, feminists and law enforcement officials concurred that reported assaults still represented only a small fraction of the total incidence of the crime.[108] Debate continues over whether more rapes were being committed or rapes were simply receiving more public attention. In either case, the *claim* that there was more rape in the United States than previously thought served as a powerful catalyst for investment in the feminist movement against sexual violence. The more pernicious consequences of playing the "numbers game" are apparent when examining the longer historical context. Sounding the alarm over soaring rates of crime—including the crime of rape—consistently animated violently anti-Black thought and action during Reconstruction, the Great Migration, and the civil rights movement.

Diana E. H. Russell participated in this "numbers game" through her NCPCR study on "The Prevalence of Sexual Assault and Rape in San Francisco." As she conducted interviews and interpreted her data, she translated Black women's stories of suffering and survival into "official knowledge" that was legible to other researchers, professionals who encountered rape victims, and policymakers. In some respects, Russell amplified the ideas introduced by the Black women anti-rape organizers who flocked to the Special Populations conference series. Her final report and published work condemned the discriminatory treatment Black women survivors received from the criminal justice system and rejected theories of Black urban cultural pathology as an explanation for Black women's vulnerability to rape. Still, Russell harnessed the experiences of Black rape survivors to justify aggressive policing and harsh punishment as a rape prevention strategy. In keeping with the NCPCR's "numbers game," Russell collapsed the messy lived experiences of Black women that she collected into a neat set of statistics suitable for policy recommendations. The policy suggestions extrapolated from Russell's work did not countenance Black women's lived experience or their persistent calls for care. Her "official knowledge," in the hands of bureaucrats seated within the National Center for the Prevention and Control of Rape, rationalized the crime control response to rape.

As she unpacked her data on the prevalence and patterns of rape among African Americans in *Sexual Exploitation* (1984), Russell qualified her findings to avoid assigning scientific legitimacy to longstanding racist notions that Black men were animalistically prone to rape and Black women were sexually loose and unaffected by sexual assault. Her main strategies for achieving this were presenting Black women as regular reporters of their assaults and explaining the overrepresentation of Black rapists as a function of their class status more than their race. Russell determined that forty out of the ninety African American women (44 percent) who participated in her study had encountered some kind of forced sex at one or more points in their lives. This placed Black women's vulnerability to rape slightly above that of all women. According to Russell, 379 of her 930 interviewees (roughly 41 percent) reported rape or attempted rape. This confirmed for Russell that sexual violence was far more widespread in the Bay Area than officially acknowledged. Based on her data, Russell inferred that the actual rate of rape incidence in the Bay Area was 3,548 per 100,000 females, nearly seven times higher than that reported by the 1973 National Crime Survey conducted by the Law Enforcement Assistance Administration.[109] The basically proportional representation of Black women among rape victims gave Russell pause, "given the considerable agreement in the literature about the overrepresentation of Black women among rape victims."[110] Russell attributed this incongruence to the fact that previous studies had focused exclusively on rapes perpetrated by strangers or acquaintances, whereas her study incorporated sexual abuse inflicted by family members, romantic partners, and spouses.[111] When accounting for these variables, white women's sexual vulnerability increased and Black women appeared less vulnerable by comparison. A second surprising finding of Russell's study was that non-white women who were raped by non-white men reported their rapes more consistently than any other combination of victim and assailant.[112] Of the rapes committed against Black women, 17 percent were reported to the police, a significantly higher proportion than those committed upon any other group.[113] The conclusion that African American women were comparatively consistent reporters of rape, which Russell presented to the NCPPCR and to her colleagues as "official knowledge," concealed the complicated attitudes toward law enforcement that her Black research subjects mentioned at length during their interviews.

Russell also used her interviews to compile statistics on the racial composition of rapists in San Francisco. Russell stated that for every Black victim who appeared in her study there were four Black rapists. When presented alongside the more modest victim / rapist ratios for whites (1:2) and Latinos (1:3), Russell's statistical discourse veered dangerously close to confirming the myth of the Black rapist. However, she quickly assured her readers that "these ratios changed significantly when a distinction is made between rape / attempted rape by strangers and nonstrangers."[114] When the data set was narrowed solely to non-stranger rapes (meaning rapes perpetuated by someone the victim knew intimately) these stark ratios evened to 1:2.7 for Blacks, 1:1.3 for whites, and 1:2.5 for Latinos.[115] Russell further contextualized the overrepresentation of Black rapists in her study as an overrepresentation of the poor- and working-class in crime-related surveys.[116] She revisited this point as she explained why nearly a quarter of the Black rapists in her study (24 percent) were reported to the police, when only 7 percent of the Latino rapists and 5 percent of the white rapists were subject to police reports. Russell asserted that Black rapists were most likely to be reported because they were more likely to engage in rape practices that would sufficiently embolden victims to file a report, such as completing the assault, verbally abusing the victim, and attacking in a public place. Russell noted that "because the data on the race and ethnicities of perpetrators are unavoidably better than the data on their social class, there is a danger of conveying the erroneous impression that race and ethnicity are more important determinants of some aspects of rape than social class."[117] She worked to dispel this "incorrect notion" by repeatedly pointing out "the significant correlation between race and social class in this society."

The "official knowledge" of rape produced by Diana E. H. Russell resisted racist conclusions about the Black community's propensity for crime. But because the final product eliminated the voices of her Black interview subjects, it failed to fully convey their "unofficial knowledge" about the adversarial function of the police. *Sexual Exploitation* never questioned the criminal justice system's role as women's first line of defense, ignoring testimonies like those of Gail (Case #420–024) and Juanita (Case #307–017). Instead, Russell dedicated space to discrediting responses to rape that did not directly engage law enforcement. She specifically criticized other researchers who "see rape as one crime of violence among many (homicide, aggravated assault, and robbery), all of them caused by unemployment, poverty, and marginality" and consequently recommend programs that addressed economic inequality.[118] Although several of her Black research subjects recommended the expansion of economic opportunity and social welfare to prevent rape, Russell rejected the "faulty theory" on the grounds that if it were true "Black women should then be the most overrepresented group among criminals" since they enjoyed the least economic security.[119] Russell's primary issue with welfare measures as a deterrent to rape was that it failed to interrogate "the dangerous consequences of this culture's concept of masculine behavior."[120] As a feminist, Russell believed that a patriarchal culture that objectified women was the root cause of sexual violence. Measures to reduce socioeconomic inequality would not control rape because they would inevitably leave patriarchy untouched. Her objections, while not incorrect, allowed the state's preferred police-centric response to rape to stand uncontested. They also further displaced the caring labor performed by Black anti-rape organizers.

* * *

Gail E. Wyatt, a clinical psychologist, sex therapist, and professor in the Department of Psychiatry and Biobehavioral Sciences at the University of California, Los Angeles, was among the few members of a "special population" to receive funding from the National Center for the Prevention and Control of Rape. She received a modest one-year grant from the National Rape Center in 1983—seven years after Diana E.H. Russell received hers—for her project titled "Experiences of Afro-American Women."[121] Wyatt and her team interviewed 248 African American and white women between the ages of eighteen and thirty-six recruited from 11,000 phone numbers listed in Los Angeles County.[122] The research project spawned a series of articles

Wyatt penned between 1985 and 1994 that compared Black and white women's experience of sexual violence, from sexual abuse in childhood to their encounters with sexual harassment as adults.[123]

Wyatt presented the findings from her NCPCR-funded research during the June 1990 Congressional hearing on "Victims of Rape." Though the National Center for the Prevention and Control of Rape had been defunct for years, Wyatt cited the National Rape Center as the benefactor that enabled her, as a professional Black woman researcher, to generate statistics about prevalence, effects, and reporting patterns among Black women rape survivors.[124] For example, she reported that one in four African American women reported at least one incident of attempted or completed rape since the age of eighteen, compared to one in five white women. While this was not a significant difference across race, Wyatt clarified that of her interviewees "African American women were most likely to disclose their sexual assault to no one."[125]

Only 25 percent of Wyatt's respondents reported their assaults to the police, substantially below the 34 percent of white respondents who did.[126] To explain to Congress why "disclosure of rape is unlikely, particularly among African American women," Wyatt directly cited her Black women respondents who "described a lack of trust in police and other agencies because of past treatment which discriminated against them due to their racial or ethnic background."[127] Wyatt located the origins of Black women's mistreatment by law enforcement in history. "For over 250 years of slavery and the years beyond, African American women have been stereotyped as sexual objects and I think they still are today," she explained. "This may be part of the reason why some African American victim survivors feel there is really no reason for disclosing their experiences. They are sometimes more apt to be misunderstood by the legal and the mental health agencies that attempt to help them."[128] Echoing Juanita's statement to Diana E. H. Russell in San Francisco, Wyatt further elaborated that several Black women in her study could not turn to the police for protection because the police were their assailants. "More than one person called the police, the police came to their home or apartment, saw that they were in a very vulnerable situation, and raped them again," she declared. "It made absolutely no sense for that person to go back to the police."[129]

Gail Wyatt's Congressional testimony on the findings of "Experiences of Afro-American Women" stood in contrast to the published scholarship of Diana E. H. Russell. Though similarly credentialed, Wyatt incorporated the unedited perspectives of her Black research subjects into her process of "official knowledge" production. This allowed the experiential knowledge of Black rape victims, particularly their reasoned reluctance to report to the police and learned mistrust of law enforcement, to appear unmodified in a public statement before state officials. Though she was not a grassroots anti-rape organizer or service provider, Wyatt was closer culturally and geographically to the community she studied than the scores of white researchers funded by the National Rape Center. Consequently, Wyatt better fulfilled the vision articulated by the Black attendees of the Special Populations Conference series hosted by the National Center for the Prevention and Control of Rape in 1977. She too could practice subversion, appearing before Congress to play the "numbers game" in a way that contradicted its core assumptions.

The creation of the National Center for the Prevention and Control of Rape began the state's investment in producing research about sexual violence outside the domain of the Law Enforcement Assistance Administration. However, the boundary between the Law Enforcement Assistance Administration and the National Center for the Prevention and Control of Rape was blurred, with many subsidized researchers gearing their research projects to inform state policy. By declining to fund direct service provisions, the NCPCR raised the question as to who within the feminist movement against sexual violence had the right to produce knowledge about the sexual violation of Black women. The white professional researchers who received the bulk of NCPCR funds genuinely hoped their research would improve Black women's lives. But their methods for producing "official knowledge," which were shaped by their standpoint as white feminist academics who hoped to influence state policy, did not fully incorporate the "unofficial knowledge" gleaned from their Black female subjects. Because their research and interpretive strategies did not convey the full weight of Black women's experience, the "official knowledge" they produced uncritically reinforced the state's methods of controlling rape through criminalization. While the NCPCR's leadership overlooked the practice of care championed by Black anti-rape activists like Nkenge Tourè, it resurfaced in the words of Black women surveyed by Diana E. H. Russell.

The National Center for the Prevention and Control of Rape was the last gasp of large federal grantmaking with regards to the feminist movement against sexual violence. The austerity of the 1980s, undergirded by a disdain for social service provision and preference for individualized market-oriented solutions to social problems, decimated federal funding streams that were not explicitly carceral. Those sources that remained, like the National Center on Child Abuse and Neglect (NCCAN) and the Office for Victims of Crime, were even more committed to invigorating the criminal justice system's response and disavowed the partial reciprocity shown by the LEAA and NCPCR to grassroots organizers. In this funding landscape, feminist rape crisis centers that had become habituated to federal funds either worked hand-in-glove with law enforcement or simply perished. The tactic of subversion developed by Black anti-rape organizers in the late 1970s, though always limited, was no longer functional in this shifting landscape. To continue pressing for the care of Black victims and obstructing carceral co-optation, Black anti-rape organizers would increasingly divert their advocacy into other institutions beyond feminist rape crisis centers. Nkenge Touré, fresh off her searing critique of the racial politics of knowledge production within the NCPCR, would turn to a different tactic: diversion. She could build a more care-oriented and racially conscious response to child sexual abuse by institutionalizing it outside of the feminist movement against sexual violence. The public school system of Washington, D.C. stood ready to receive.

CHAPTER 4

Not Race Neutral: Addressing Child Sexual Abuse

Between attending the Arlington "Special Populations" Conference and organizing the First National Conference on Third World Women and Violence, Nkenge Touré (born Anita Stroud in 1951) was a dauntless representative for Black women within the feminist movement against sexual violence. She contributed to the movement most consistently in her daily work at the Washington, D.C. Rape Crisis Center, where she served as general administrator from 1975 to 1978 and as the director of community education from 1978 to 1988.[1] Perhaps the most impactful part of her tenure at DCRCC was the child sexual abuse prevention program she developed and delivered to the public schools of the District of Columbia under a substantive government contract.[2] This state-funded program endured for decades despite the fiscal conservatism of the 1980s that choked federal funds for anti-rape activism and stifled the LEAA and NCPCR. By Touré's reckoning, the program she launched "had never been done before." As she recalled, "when the rape crisis center did our education and prevention program in the schools . . . we were the first center around that topic, the first organization to be in the school system."[3]

Touré made Black children the subject of her Child Assault Safety Awareness and Prevention Program (CASAPP). As a former member of the Baltimore chapter of the Black Panther Party and an active participant in D.C.'s Black nationalist scene during the 1970s, race had always been an indelible dimension of Touré's activism. CASAPP was no exception. "Since the majority of pupils in public schools in DC are Black," she wrote, "this program has always strived to develop a Third World perspective around prevention and assault."[4] The demographics of Washington, D.C. encouraged this choice. In the same year that she assumed leadership of the CASAPP, the population of the "Chocolate City" reached 70 percent Black and civil rights veteran Marion Barry entered the newly created mayor's office. This ushered in an era of practical "Black Power" politics.[5] Touré recounted that her colleagues at the D.C. Rape Crisis Center supported the approach and her stewardship over the program. "They really felt that going into the schools for education should be a Black woman, because that's mainly who was going to be in those schools."[6] Even as Mayor Barry's political fortunes declined, CASAPP reached hundreds (if not thousands) of Black Washingtonian families during the 1980s. Years after departing from the D.C. Rape Crisis Center, Touré would frequently "run into people who say, I remember when you came to my school . . . You came to Charles Drew [Elementary School]. You came to my school. And that was really good."[7]

Touré's program was doubly revolutionary for speaking directly to Black children about the dangers of sexual assault. For most of the twentieth century, medical and legal authorities had dismissed incest and the sexual abuse of children as extraordinarily rare phenomena, despite ample evidence to the contrary, and relegated the "disorder" to poor African American families.[8] Black families combatted the cultural assumption that they sexually abused their children more often than their white middle-class counterparts by forcefully silencing all discussions of child rape and incest. Black feminist writers like Ntozake Shange, Alice Walker, and Michele Wallace were harshly censured when they wrote openly about sexual abuse within the Black community.[9] Loretta Ross, a colleague of Nkenge Touré and longtime administrator at the D.C. Rape Crisis Center, agreed that incest has always been "a great untold secret in the Black community."[10] This code of silence served as an imperfect survival strategy to prevent "airing dirty laundry in public"— that is, giving racists any ammunition to use against them.[11]

Organizing a child sexual abuse prevention program around Black children was also a crucial intervention for the feminist movement against sexual violence, but for different reasons. Since the early 1970s, anti-rape feminists had been shattering the silence that surrounded child sexual abuse and incest by loudly insisting that within a patriarchal society sexual abuse could and did occur in all families irrespective of race and class.[12] Nancy Gager and Cathleen Schurr, authors of *Sexual Assault: Confronting Rape in America*, insisted that "contrary to popular opinion," incest and child rape "are not confined to the ghetto."[13] Their race-neutral analyses of child sexual abuse tipped off a "child abuse revolution" and eventually a "child sexual abuse panic" that reigned in American media from the late 1970s through the 1980s.[14]

But this race-neutrality proved double-edged, as it led feminists to endorse punitive solutions like child removal that were far from race-neutral in their application.

Nkenge Touré did not attempt a race-neutral approach to child sex abuse prevention. Through CASAPP, she adapted Black women's tradition of caring for the assaulted and introduced a new tool to the arsenal of practices: diversion. The conservative "turn" of the late 1970s and 1980s had rendered federal funding sources for anti-rape activities scarcer and more rigidly carceral than before. This left the surviving feminist rape crisis centers with little political flexibility outside of connecting victims to law enforcement. Touré responded by diverting her advocacy outside of the D.C. Rape Crisis Center and into the District of Columbia's public school system, where she could center Black children and families while keeping law enforcement at arm's length.[15] Historically, Black women approached education as a vehicle for racial uplift that could address community needs that the white supremacist state had neglected.[16] The child sexual abuse prevention curriculum developed by Touré built upon this foundational caring labor, with the Black feminist intervention of eschewing punitive state intervention in the Black community. CASAPP emphasized Black children's sexual sovereignty, even sanctioning physical resistance against their abusers. The program respectfully engaged Black parents in the prevention of child sexual abuse, effectively deconstructing stereotypes of Black sexual depravity and familial dysfunction. In sum, Tourè institutionalized the self-defense training and culturally competent community education that Black anti-rape organizers were already performing in the new context of a majority-Black public school system. This diversion preserved these practices as state funders who were invested in rape control squelched them of feminist rape crisis centers.

"Not Confined to the Ghetto": The Feminist Race-Neutral Analysis of Child Sexual Abuse

Concerns about child sexual abuse had long concerned reformers and lawmakers. At the turn of the century, Progressive Era moral reformers counted sexual dangers among the brutal conditions of modern industrial life that threatened children.[17] The same desire to protect children animated the "sexual psychopath" laws of the 1930s and 1940s.[18] Cultural concern over the sexual abuse of children in the United States collapsed after the Second World

War as psychoanalysis came into vogue and trivialized instances of sexual contact between adults and minors. The issue remained largely dormant until the women's liberation movement of the 1970s breathed new life into it. Florence Rush, a psychiatric social worker, issued the first extensive feminist analysis of child sexual abuse at the April 1971 "Rape Conference" sponsored by the New York Radical Feminists.[19] She expanded her presentation, titled "The Sexual Abuse of Children: A Feminist Point of View," in the New York Radical Feminists' 1974 anthology *Rape: The First Sourcebook for Women.* Drawing upon her professional experience intervening in abusive homes, Rush declared that "the sexual abuse of children, who are overwhelmingly female, by sexual offenders, who are overwhelmingly male adults, is part and parcel of the male-dominated society which overtly and covertly subjugates women."[20] In her view, dismantling patriarchy was the only surefire way to eliminate sexual threats to children. As the feminist movement against sexual violence expanded rapidly in the late 1970s, Rush's colleagues amplified her message. Their experience as service providers substantiated her argument that child sexual abuse was insidious. In 1975, for example, Women Organized Against Rape reported that a full half of the victims they served were under the age of eighteen.[21]

Anti-rape feminists frequently asserted that child sexual abuse occurred in otherwise normative families outside the racialized space of urban ghettoes. To combat the prevalence of this abuse, in the late 1970s, feminists stationed within grassroots rape crisis centers launched Child Assault Prevention Projects (CAPs) in which they modified their prevention outreach and counseling methods to better suit young victims and distraught parents.[22] In the fall of 1978, *Aegis* (formerly the *Feminist Alliance Against Rape Newsletter*) profiled Christopher Street Inc., a prominent CAP based in Minneapolis, through an interview with codirector Barbara Meyers. Christopher Street Inc. was a program for all victims of child sexual abuse that specialized in cases of father-daughter incest. Christopher Street Inc. built the peer counseling they offered to abused children and adult survivors on the premise that children were most frequently abused by their fathers or older male relatives acting on their social permission as men to coerce the vulnerable members of their households. Heavily influenced by the work of Florence Rush, Meyer articulated incest as a product of patriarchal oppression. According to Meyers, "ninety-eight percent of the sexual assault on kids is done by men and 90 percent of the victims are female. I really see it as a crime against women primarily."[23] Like most CAPs, the analysis of child sexual abuse that informed Christopher Street Inc. was gender-specific but race-neutral. When asked by *Aegis* contributor Deb Friedman if incest occurred in all families, Meyers replied that the problem of child sexual abuse did not observe race and class divisions. "Many people would like to think that it happens in the ghettos, or it happens in Black families or it happens anywhere but in their own families," she stated. "That's part of trying to keep it away from themselves and not looking at it realistically."[24]

By insisting upon the race neutrality of child sexual abuse, feminists pushed back on deeply entrenched racial stereotypes. As scholar Lynn Sacco has argued, Americans historically understood incest and molestation to be rare transgressions that only thrived in the most depraved corners of American society, namely poor African American families.[25] Feminist insistence to the contrary highlighted the anti-racist aspirations of their movement. The National Center for the Prevention and Control of Rape endowed Judith Lewis Herman, a renowned feminist psychiatrist, with the funds to conduct the requisite research for "Father-Daughter Incest: A Clinical Study" between May 1, 1977 and April 30, 1978.[26] The conclusions of her study, as expressed in her classic 1981 publication *Father-Daughter Incest*, vindicated feminists' claims about the shocking pervasiveness of child sex abuse in the United States and its roots in the same systemic sexism that enabled adult rape.[27] Herman's study proclaimed race-neutrality by purposefully excluding African American women as research subjects "in order to avoid even the possibility that the information gathered might be used to fuel idle speculation about racial differences."[28] She agreed that "there is no question . . . that incest is a problem in Black families, as it is in white families," but reasoned that "white people have indulged for too long in discussion about the sexual capacities, behaviors, and misbehaviors of Black people."[29] Fellow NCPCR grantee Gail Wyatt confirmed through her own body of research that although Black girlhood contained slightly more risk factors for sexual abuse, such as living with stepfathers or other older male relatives, "sexual abuse in childhood appears to be of equal concern today for Afro-American and white women alike."[30]

Though well intentioned, the feminist race-neutral analysis of child sex abuse had drawbacks. The feminist movement against sexual violence indicted the patriarchal family, rather than the Black family, as the main source of sexual violence toward children, and insisted that overturning the patriarchal family would effectively prevent children from being raped and molested. However, their goal was not to exonerate Black families; it was to subject the white middle-class family to the same level of scrutiny. In this respect, feminist agitation against child sexual abuse in the 1970s was firmly rooted in the "everywoman analysis," a disposition that scholars have since identified within the broader feminist movement against sexual violence. The "everywoman analysis" proclaims all women and girls everywhere are at constant risk of sexual assault and decisive action to protect them is urgently needed.[31] Though they lacked the specific terminology, contemporaneous activists and scholars expressed concern over analyzing child sexual abuse through the lens of the "everywoman analysis." In a 1984 article, researchers L. H. and R. L. Pierce worried that a "color-blind" or race-neutral approach to child sexual abuse elided important distinctions between racial groups on attitudes toward sexuality and family.[32] In 1991, Black feminist legal scholar Kimberlè Crenshaw warned that the argument that gender violence afflicts stereotyped and nonstereotyped groups equally often led to the erasure of the stereotyped group while theorizing on how to confront gender violence.[33]

Despite the consensus about its patriarchal roots, disagreement proliferated within the feminist movement against sexual violence about the role the criminal justice system should play in responding to child sexual abuse. Barbara Meyers averred that, at Christopher Street Inc., it was policy "to work with kids to report to the police. It's a crime and there needs to be a police report."[34] She posited that child sexual abuse could be prevented "if more offenders are brought through the court system" because "it will let our society know that we are taking it seriously that kids shouldn't be sexually abused."[35] Meyers saw this solution as equally viable for white and non-white child victims, asserting that "A lot more children of different classes and races have got to get into the [criminal justice] system." Deb Friedman of the Feminist Alliance Against Rape challenged Meyers's endorsement of criminal justice as a deterrent to child rape and molestation. She noted: "The way I feel about increasing reporting is that eventually we'll get to a point where more rapes—more abusive situations—are being reported and there will be more convictions. But we'll still have a distinction being made that one class of people in particular are the perpetrators. It won't necessarily be seen as something that hits all classes of society."[36] Friedman feared that the punishment of the criminal justice system would fall disproportionately on poor African Americans, cementing the impression that Black families were particularly prone to child sexual abuse and undoing the efforts of race-neutral analysis.

Friedman's fears were prescient. The race-neutral analysis of child sexual abuse transformed the feminist statement that child sexual abuse *could* strike families beyond the confines of "the ghetto" to one in which *all children everywhere* faced unprecedented risk of abuse from sex offenders lurking in their midst and demanded heroic intervention. Activists who stripped their analyses of the nuances of race regularly embraced solutions that appeared race-neutral on their surface but disproportionately harmed Black families in practice. This included the indefinite removal of children from homes where sexual abuse was alleged. For most of the twentieth century, "child saving" professionals treated the removal of children from abusive homes as a last resort, appropriate only for households that proved impervious to reform.[37] Feminists steeped in the race-neutral analysis of child sexual abuse decried this hesitancy. Barbara Meyers of Christopher Street Inc. strongly encouraged removal as a necessary action for halting the cycle of child sexual abuse. "Leaving a child in a home where she has been raped is like sending a woman to live with a rapist," she asserted. "Children should be removed from the home . . . and they should not be placed back in that home."[38]

As a proponent of the feminist race-neutral analysis of child sexual abuse, Meyers overlooked how African American families historically experienced child removal as a discriminatory and punitive state intervention. Since the 1970s, child protective services have removed Black children from their parents' care at twice the rate of their white peers for a wide array of offenses, including sexual abuse, and their stays in state custody are longer by an order of magnitude.[39] This is not because Black families are inherently more abusive than their white counterparts, but because poor non-white families are more frequently observed and scrutinized by public agencies than affluent white ones. This hypervisibility and unequal surveillance results in a greater number of overall reports and creates the inaccurate impression that abuse is particularly prevalent among African Americans.[40] The idea that Black families were inherently deleterious and impervious to reform, as opposed to white families whose dysfunctions were environmental in origin and could be corrected, has informed the white-dominated field of social work since its inception.[41] The publication of Secretary of Labor Daniel Patrick Moynihan's infamous report *The Negro Family: The Case for National Action* (commonly shortened to the *Moynihan Report*) in 1965 shored up the stereotype that dysfunctional Black families led by "pathological" Black matriarchs were raising a generation of criminals and abusers.[42] When feminists began demanding serious attention and resources toward combatting child sexual abuse in the late 1970s and 1980s, their movement collided with this still-living stereotype.

Black survivors of child sexual abuse and the Black press corroborated the unequal impact of child removal policies on the Black community in the wake of the "child abuse revolution" of the 1970s and 1980s. In *No Secrets, No Lies:*

How Black Families Can Heal from Abuse (2004), Robin D. Stone included the firsthand accounts of Black women and girls who survived sexual abuse, and their families. One of the documented survivors, Karla, appeared to be a success story for dealing with child sexual abuse. Karla's stepfather Charles molested her for over four years before she disclosed the abuse to her sister, who in turn told Karla's mother, Brenda. Upon learning of the abuse, Brenda immediately sprang into action. She moved herself and her children out of the home and contacted an attorney, who directed her to county children's services. Charles was arrested, confessed to the abuse, and served fifteen years in prison, far longer than the national average of three to six years for sex offenses.[43] The saga of Karla's disclosure and Charles's prosecution brought punitive state interventions into Brenda's life in unexpected ways. The first blow came when the lawyer advising Brenda suggested that she may also be charged in connection to her daughter's assault, since she failed to prevent it. "I was floored," Brenda explained. "I thought that if I went to an agency for help, I would get help. This was so unfair."[44] Brenda's real punishment came when the two white social workers assigned to her case ordered Karla and her other two children out of her care. Though they were eventually reunited, a distraught Brenda contemplated suicide during the indeterminate period of forced separation from her children. In her words, "I try to fix this and have my kids separated from me? I just plummeted."[45] Brenda sought a divorce from Charles during his incarceration but admitted that the bonds of familial attachment were harder to sever. She and her children—including Karla—maintained regular correspondence with Charles while he was imprisoned. Brenda was neither enthusiastic nor vengeful about the prospect of Charles's incarceration. "I wasn't saying 'Hang him, castrate him.' I was saying 'Yes, I want him to be incarcerated, but just don't throw him in there. Get him some help.' . . . I still love him . . . It's not easy to admit, but it's the truth . . . I don't think that I'm betraying Karla by feeling that way."[46] Karla herself was "glad that Charles went to jail" but hoped for an early release so that he could be a part of her younger brother's life, though an early release seemed unlikely. After Charles was denied parole, one officer made no secret of their contempt for him, telling him that "When you do get out, I hope [Karla] blows your brains out."[47]

The stories of Karla and Brenda illustrate how the push to swiftly remove children from households where abuse was alleged caught Black families in an ever-widening web of punishments that further destabilized them. Their stories also help to explain why African American women were far less likely than white women to seek help in situations of child sexual abuse. Dr. Jeanne Hartsfield of the Rosa Parks Sexual Assault Crisis Center in Los Angeles reported that Black mothers frequently turned to the center when they discovered the sexual abuse of their children only to retreat when they learned that the abuse will be reported and the offender will be arrested.[48] Janet Davis, who served as a senior clinical social worker at the Northside Center for Children in Harlem throughout the 1980s, recalled that nearly half of her clients disclosed some form of child sexual abuse. Yet none pressed charges, fearing lengthy incarceration of the offender and permanent family disruption.[49] This mistrust was reinforced in the Black press. For example, an article in the November 1986 issue of *Ebony* titled "How to Protect Your Children from People They Trust" warned readers that "in cases of incest the offender or the abused child may be permanently or temporarily removed from the home."[50] Similar disclaimers about the prospect of child seizure do not appear in mainstream press coverage of child sexual abuse during the same period. *Ebony*'s editorial staff may have realized that family dispersal was a much more likely outcome for Black families than for white families. As scholar activist Tashmica Torok has more recently asserted, "Much of what happens after disclosure is controlled by laws, requirements, and processes that have little flexibility in allowing for a survivor-led approach to addressing child sexual abuse within a family structure," particularly when the family in question is Black.[51] This reluctance to report sexual violence and activate violent state machinery was well understood by Black anti-rape organizers.

Feminist support for the removal of children from sexually abusive families was reinforced structurally by the new funding priorities of the National Center for Child Abuse and Neglect (NCCAN). The NCCAN, like the LEAA, predated the feminist movement against sexual violence. The Child Abuse Prevention and Treatment Act (CAPTA) of 1974 created the agency well before feminist attention to child rape and molestation reached the mainstream. Otherwise known as the "Mondale Act," CAPTA fulfilled the aims of the "War on Poverty" of extending social services to neglected children whose parents, for one reason or another, failed to provide for their needs. NCCAN initially spent its $20 million budget funding the demonstration projects of child welfare programs. In 1980, NCCAN disbursed $2 million of grant money to four regional treatment centers and six elementary education programs that focused on child sexual abuse.[52] NCCAN funding for child sexual abuse prevention and treatment projects peaked at $10.7 million in 1985, eclipsing the funds the agency allocated toward preventing and treating physical abuse and neglect. According to scholar Nancy Whittier, the NCCAN framed child sexual abuse "as a crime to be prevented or prosecuted, rather than a psychological or political problem" and steadily favored "criminal approaches over feminist ones" in its funding priorities.[53] The scant budget of the NCCAN compared to the more richly endowed LEAA and NCPCR was symptomatic of the conservative governance of the 1980s that disdained social service provision while esteeming crime control. What funds the agency did command by the mid-1980s went toward law enforcement, collaboration between law enforcement and other agencies, and direct intervention by child protective services.[54] Beyond the projects it chose to fund, CAPTA accelerated child removal by mandating that all social service workers report any suspected instances of child abuse among their clients.[55] Between 1976 and 1985, police reports of child sexual abuse rose eighteenfold across the United States.[56] In April 1983, former NCCAN director Douglas J. Besharov announced that the 1.3 million children reported annually to authorities as suspected victims of physical abuse, sexual exploitation, physical neglect, and emotional mistreatment resulted in 400,000 families under the supervision of child protection agencies.[57] This, in turn, constituted a dramatic increase in the number of children seized from their parents, from about 75,000 in 1963 to more than 300,000 in 1980. In true race-neutral fashion, Besharov failed to mention what portion of families under supervision were Black. Scholars have since confirmed that they were (and are) significantly overrepresented.[58]

The National Center on Child Abuse and Neglect's preference for projects that hinged on law enforcement furthered the merger of the war on rape and the "war on crime." It also reflected the national mood of moral panic over "stranger danger" and the sexual vulnerability of children in the late 1970s.[59] Shortly after child sexual abuse captured the attention of grassroots feminists, a rash of articles erupted in the mainstream press and the Black press.[60] Selectively paraphrasing feminist anti-rape organizers, these articles speculated on the causes of rising rates of reporting for child sexual abuse and advised anxious parents on how best to protect their children from assault.[61] Legal scholar Aya Gruber pinpoints the moral panic of child sexual abuse in the American press "at the intersection of brutality and ubiquity," where journalists combine "images of brutal child murders committed by deviant strangers together with statistics about the frequency of child sexual assault writ large."[62] The juxtaposition obscured the fact that the majority of child assaults were lower-order sexual touching by family members. Under this dissonance of framing, readers could easily conclude that the epidemic of child sexual assaults consisted entirely of the obscene mutilation depicted in mass media.[63] In 1984, *Newsweek* decried child sexual abuse as "A Hidden Epidemic" that was "all at once . . . as ubiquitous as it once was unmentionable."[64] "It is no longer sufficient for parents to warn their children against accepting candy or rides from strangers," they announced. *Newsweek*'s suggested tactics for parents included teaching "stranger danger" instincts to children and screaming techniques that would draw the attention of bystanders. These recommendations presupposed that children would be attacked in public places by unknown men, a departure from feminist analysis.

Some Black press outlets replicated the moral panic coverage that proliferated in the mainstream press. In May 1981, *Ebony* instructed Black parents on "How to Protect Your Child From Molesters."[65] Given its historical baggage, the fact that *Ebony* broached the subject at all was remarkable.[66] It took the Atlanta Child Murders, a year-and-a-half-long reign of terror by a sex offender and serial killer who targeted Black children, as its point of departure. The piece aimed to horrify Black parents with stories of Black children in the affected neighborhoods. *Ebony* ominously cautioned that "if parents don't carefully supervise their children's activities and make them aware that some person may harm them, one of the children could represent the next statistic in a police report." To be sure, the mutilation of Black youth did not command the same public sympathy as their white counterparts. The Atlanta Child Murders received scant attention beyond the local and Black press and were seldom cited by name in the discourse of "stranger danger."[67] But the coverage of the abductions in *Ebony* followed many conventions of the "stranger danger" genre, namely the insistence that sexual abuse of children, both Black and white, was spiraling out of control. Playing the "numbers game" with child sexual abuse yielded the same results it did with adult rape. The moral panic over child sexual abuse that simmered in American media instilled in parents, police, and politicians the belief that child rape and molestation had reached "epidemic proportions."[68] This belief sanctioned punitive responses to the emotionally jarring crime, enabling a state agency originally created to ensure children's welfare to become a carceral actor.

Debates over the merits of punishing sexually abusive families bubbled up through the decade. In 1987, Jane Roberts Chapman and Barbara Smith of the Center for Women's Policy Studies evaluated the responses of criminal justice agencies and social service agencies to child sexual abuse complaints.[69] Chapman and Smith considered 388 closed child sexual abuse cases from

Fairfax County, Virginia, and Santa Cruz County, California. Of those, 183 had been closed by social service agencies, while 205 had been closed by the police, though most cases jointly engaged law enforcement and social service workers. Slightly more than half (51 percent) of all accused child sexual abusers in the study faced arrest, though 63 percent of those arrested faced prosecution and 75 percent of those prosecuted either pled or were found guilty. Of those found guilty, 60 percent were incarcerated, typically for less than a year, and the remaining 40 percent of convicted child sexual abusers served no jail time. Chapman and Smith argued that the criminal justice response to child sexual abuse "could be considered inadequate given the dimensions of the problem and the severity of the abuse." They refrained from endorsing an invigorated criminal justice response, acknowledging that "controversy over whether or not to prosecute intrafamily sexual abuse remains alive."[70] Their study did not attend to the racial demographics of those abusers who were incarcerated or otherwise punished, abiding by the feminist race-neutral analysis that concealed the discriminatory interventions of the state.

Chapman and Smith found that child welfare agencies had supplanted "the only source of protection, prevention, or supervision of the abuser," though this should not suggest their interventions were any less punitive.[71] Their most frequently utilized method of protection was court-backed removal of the abused child from the family, which occurred in 71 percent of cases in which a child welfare agency took official action. Chapman and Smith found it "surprising" that child welfare agencies did not pursue court-ordered child removal more often. In their view, such an intervention "does not sufficiently guarantee protection for child victims . . . particularly in view of the fact that in many instances the social service response will be the only official action taken, because relatively few cases will be passed on to the criminal justice system."[72] Chapman and Smith conceded that "there is continuing debate about what the scope of [child welfare] agency intervention should be, as well as the proper relationship between social service agencies and the criminal justice system." The authors ultimately threw their support behind the removal of abused children by child welfare agencies as the correct response to the sexual abuse of children, in the hope that this would lead to the incarceration of abusers by the criminal justice system. The racially discriminatory potential of child seizure and incarceration did not factor into Chapman and Smith's analysis.

Other activists within and outside the feminist movement against sexual violence more pointedly questioned the punitive bent of responses to child sexual abuse. In 1980, the National Legal Resource Center for Child Advocacy and Protection of the American Bar Association cautioned that the "zealous pursuit" of sanctions against alleged abuse meant to "meet the public clamor for retribution" and "protect the child often results in the automatic and sometimes unwarranted removal of the child from the supportive mother."[73] In 1989, *Aegis* raised alarm over proposed legislation recommended by the American Bar Association that would include provisions for prosecuting the "non-offending parents" in abusive families for failure to intervene in defense of their children, a trap Brenda nearly fell into.[74] *Aegis* interpreted the proposed legislation as punishing mothers and "holding women responsible for men's violence" when they too suffer under the violent patriarchal domination of abusive husbands and fathers. They also anticipated the consequences of such measures for Black mothers, warning of "the racism and class oppression endemic to that [criminal justice] system." They asked, "What assurances will Third World and poor women have that such laws won't be used against them disproportionately and in order to take their children away from them?"[75] Nkenge Touré was acutely aware of the anti-Blackness that afflicted the adjudication of child sexual abuse and shaped her own education and prevention program accordingly. The conditions were right for constructing such a program in the predominantly Black public school system of the District of Columbia.

"Teach Your Child They Have the Right to Say NO"

By the 1980s, concern with the sexual vulnerability of children had reached a fever-pitch in the District of Columbia. Attendant commentary was stripped of the condemnation of patriarchy, suspicious of Black families, and uncritical of child removal. In 1983, the *Washington Post* alerted parents in the Metro area that Children's National Hospital was treating an "alarming number of victims of childhood sex abuse," over three hundred in the past calendar year.[76] Joyce Thomas, director of the hospital's Child Sexual Abuse Victim Assistance Project, repeated the feminist race-neutral analysis of child sexual abuse line for line. She reported that the sexual abuse of children "affects many families regardless of ethnic and financial background" and "the largest offender in these cases is generally a person known to the family." On June 8, 1984, the *Washington Post* relinquished all restraint. In "Child Sexual Abuse: Hidden Crimes Come Out of the Closet," Detective

Stephen R. Mathews, a fifteen-year veteran of the Sex Offense Branch of the District of Columbia's police force, alerted parents to an "epidemic" of child sexual abuse in the nation's capital.[77] In just two years' time, Det. Mathews witnessed police reports of child rape and molestation jump by 39 percent. He knew from social workers and feminist activists who worked on the issue that this surge in reporting represented only a tiny fraction of all instances of child rape and molestation in the city. Mathews claimed that the epidemic did not observe lines of race and class and was engulfing ghettoes and suburbs alike. "No community," he stated, "is immune from child molestation."[78] However, his speculation on the cause of the epidemic—the proliferation of "female-headed households" that relied upon relatives and neighbors to supervise children—carried unmistakable racial undertones in a city that had been majority Black since 1960. Though African American mothers have historically depended on cooperative networks of extended relatives and neighbors for childcare so they could work for a living, the *Post* recommended that mothers abstain from unvetted daycare and dating to keep their children safe, an impossible demand for many Black women to meet.[79] Mathews demonstrated in microcosm how repetition of crime statistics without reference to the patriarchal underpinnings of family violence—a form of the "numbers game"—misled the public about the reality of sexual violence and advanced punitive approaches to rape control.[80]

The D.C. Rape Crisis Center, where Nkenge Tourè first stepped into antirape advocacy, had a decade-long lead on the *Washington Post* in showing concern for the sexual vulnerability of children. A group of feminists affiliated with the Washington Area Women's Center founded the D.C. Rape Crisis Center in 1972 to offer telephone counseling to rape victims.[81] DCRCC quickly secured permanent office space just north of DuPont Circle in the Northwest quadrant of the District of Columbia and offered more extensive services, such as group counseling. According to historian Anne Valk, the novice rape crisis center struggled to fulfill its commitment to bringing Black and working-class women into the collective and as a result "the demographics of the center's clientele mirrored that of the women who ran it."[82] Change swept the DCRCC on both fronts in 1974, when they hired Nkenge Touré to replace Nancy McDonald as general administrator and Michelle Hudson, another African American woman, to coordinate community education projects.[83] With Touré's appointment to general administrator, DCRCC began to build bridges with the city's Black residents and organizations in earnest. A March 1975 internal study recorded that "as part of a predominately black city the [D.C.] rape crisis center has always been concerned with how it related to black women" but it was only after hiring Tourè and Hudson in a "self-conscious attempt by the center to reach the black and Hispanic communities" that the DCRCC became a credible fixture of its target community.[84] Hudson, for her part, eagerly forged connections with the public school system of Washington, D.C.[85] Touré's tenure as the first Black woman to lead a nationally recognized rape crisis center lasted about four years. In 1978, she was succeeded by Loretta Ross, another Black woman whom she had recruited as a volunteer. That year, Hudson departed from DCRCC to take a post at My Sister's Place, the District of Columbia's flagship shelter for battered women.[86] Touré assumed Hudson's vacated position as community education director and took charge of the fledgling Child Assault Safety, Awareness, and Prevention Program (CASAPP) until her resignation in 1988.[87]

Nkenge Touré acutely understood the importance of educating young children about the reality of child sexual abuse. Her formative sexual experience was an assault from an older man in the Baltimore public housing complex where she grew up.[88] Touré's colleague, successor, comrade, and friend Loretta Ross also suffered through a childhood riddled with sexual violence. At the age of eleven, she was beaten and raped by a stranger who offered her a ride home in his car in her hometown of Temple, Texas. Four years later in 1969, she gave birth to her son, Howard, after falling victim to incest at the hands of a male relative.[89] For both Touré and Ross, their lived experience of childhood sexual abuse was refracted through their identities as Black women. They acutely felt "the institutional silencing in both race and gender terms" of Black child victims.[90] The first time Touré and Ross disclosed their childhood assaults was within the relatively safe space afforded by the D.C. Rape Crisis Center. Even that space did not shield them entirely from community censure. Ross recalled that "when [Black women at the D.C. Rape Crisis Center] started being active and fighting . . . child sexual assault and abuse in the Black community . . . we got pilloried for it and we got attacked for it because we were airing the dirty laundry and in some ways being told that we were cooperating with our oppression."[91] This harsh silencing held firm even after Black feminists shattered the silence surrounding intracommunal violence against Black women and girls.

Nkenge Touré also carried Black Power and Black feminist politics to her post at DCRCC. Initially, Touré more closely identified with Black Power than with Black feminism. In 1968, seventeen-year-old Anita Stroud led a student walk-out at Eastern High School in Baltimore against the administration's failure to remove a teacher who regularly used racial slurs against the students.[92] She previously dabbled in some Black Power demonstrations in school, such as raising her fist during the morning flag salute.[93] Though she had been disciplined during previous incidents by the school administration, the police answered the walk-out by beating her, spraying her with mace, and arresting her.[94] As a consequence of her early activism, Nkenge Touré would never earn her high school diploma. The incident demonstrated to her that the main purpose of the police was to terrorize Black people and squash Black protest. After her expulsion from Eastern High School, she took refuge in the safe house of the Baltimore Chapter of the Black Panther Party. Amongst the Panthers, she took the name Nkenge and oversaw the free breakfast program. This would be her first introduction to care work as an extension of radical Black politics. Relentless police surveillance of the Baltimore Panther safe house, which culminated in a raid on the free breakfast program, nurtured Touré's emergent mistrust of law enforcement.[95]

In 1972, Nkenge Touré relocated to Washington, D.C., with her husband Patrice and their infant daughter, where they quickly submerged themselves in the capital's Black radical networks. In addition to distributing the Black Panther newspaper, they opened the Education for Liberation Bookstore at the corner of 9th and H Streets, which also served as a meeting space for their own Black nationalist group called Save the People.[96] Touré split her time between Save the People and an assortment of other Black liberation groups, such as the National Black United Front, the Marxist-inspired D.C. Area Study Group, and the Citywide Housing Coalition. When she branched out from Black liberation networks to join the D.C. Rape Crisis Center in late 1974, she couched her anti-rape activism in the Black nationalist language of community survival. In an interview for the *Feminist Alliance Against Rape Newsletter* in late 1976, Touré announced that she "felt a genuine responsibility to serve my sisters through the vehicle of the Rape Crisis Center."[97] By conceptualizing anti-rape advocacy as service to other Black women, Tourè also aligned herself with Black women's tradition of caring labor for the assaulted.

Nkenge Touré's access to Black Washington did not just improve the public image of the D.C. Rape Crisis Center. She saw the relationship as an opportunity to educate the white feminists that operated DCRCC. "Among the many things Third World women would contribute [to white-dominated anti-rape groups] is knowledge concerning the special problems they face when confronting institutions."[98] Among these institutions was the criminal justice system. According to Touré, the police were "going to give Black women the same treatment they've always given historically." Even in the District of Columbia, where African Americans made up a large segment of law enforcement officials, Touré warned that Black women could expect "very unsatisfactory treatment, very humiliating treatment . . . [and] very dehumanizing treatment" that positioned them as perpetrators more so than victims.[99] Touré's mistrust of law enforcement manifested most acutely in 1980 after the death of Yulanda Ward, a DCRCC volunteer and member of the Citywide Housing Coalition. Police insisted that Ward died in a botched robbery.[100] Touré was "immediately suspicious" of the police's account of the murder, arguing instead that the bizarre circumstances of Ward's death more closely resembled the assassination of other revolutionary Black figures.[101] The refusal by the police to thoroughly investigate Ward's death only deepened Touré's suspicions. Decades later, Touré maintained that Ward's death was, if not politically motivated, politically determined by the systemic inequalities in which she lived.[102]

By 1980, Touré was engrossed in developing curriculum and delivering in school-presentations for the DCRCC's Child Assault Safety Awareness and Prevention Program (CASAPP). Touré's mistrust of law enforcement informed the child sexual abuse prevention education she crafted. This swam against the current of the "child abuse revolution" of the late 1970s and 1980s driven by media outlets peddling moral panic and state ventures like the National Center on Child Abuse and Neglect that promoted family dispersal. These entities called upon social service agencies and the criminal justice system to intervene in suspected cases of child sexual abuse swiftly and punitively. In 1977, just before seizing the reins of CASAPP from Michelle Hudson, Touré outlined the "short and long term processes" that she believed were necessary to eliminate rape and sexual abuse. In the long term, the prevention of rape and sexual abuse required no less than "the elimination of this society as it presently stands, with its promotion of racism, classism, sexism, capitalism, and imperialism."[103] On this point, she was of an accord with other Black feminists like Brenda Eichelberger, Margaret Sloan, and Lynn Moncrief. To prevent rape in the short term, Touré called for community education that modeled healthful family dynamics and imparted self-defense skills. This approach redoubled the care work that safeguarded Black communities from punitive systems bent on disrupting them. Tourè continued this care work while crafting CASAPP's curriculum.

During the late 1970s and early 1980s, the white staff of the D.C. Rape Crisis Center proved receptive to Nkenge Touré's vision of anti-rape advocacy and child sexual abuse prevention. Though the white founders did not share Touré's radical Black tutelage, they recognized early on that immediately referring victims to the criminal justice system was an ineffective strategy for eliminating rape.[104] An "Orientation Packet" from a training session for volunteers in 1975 established "the rights of rape victims . . . to not report the rape to the police" and affirmed that "The Rape Crisis Center does not view prison sentences as a deterrent to crimes, including rape."[105] This disavowal of incarceration made the DCRCC an outlier within the feminist movement against sexual violence, especially by the 1980s. In the same packet, DCRCC advocated for women to practice self-defense to shield themselves from sexual violence rather than rely upon fickle law enforcement officials to avenge them after the fact. They called for self-defense classes for women and girls to be "integrated into existing physical education programs" in public high and junior high schools. DCRCC staff members even offered to share self-defense training modules with high school physical education teachers.

Self-defense training remained a priority of the D.C. Rape Crisis Center in the 1980s. The center issued a statement of purpose ahead of the 1981 Take Back the Night March that tied self-defense training to the prevention of child sexual abuse. The specific goals laid out by the DCRCC were "to raise the public's consciousness about the amount of sexual abuse of children, effects and functions of child sex abuse."[106] They punctuated the statement of purpose with a demand for further funding of self-defense courses for women in the community and children in the schools. They called upon attendees to write to their school board members demanding self-defense classes as a regular part of school curriculum.[107] Through the early 1980s, the D.C. Rape Crisis Center accepted self-defense training as a legitimate deterrent to rape and abuse and separated their advocacy from the criminal justice system. These conditions enabled a publicly funded child sexual abuse prevention education program for the District of Columbia's Black schoolchildren that embraced self-sovereignty while eschewing punitive state intervention.

In late 1974, the DCRCC applied to the Department of Health, Education, and Welfare (HEW) for a $29,000 grant to cover the costs of expanding their community education program.[108] Crucially, these funds would not support the daily operating costs of the DCRCC. This allowed the center to nominally preserve some of its independence from the state that regularly leveraged anti-rape funding to extend the reach of law enforcement. Hotline callers, for example, would never be pressured to report their assaults to the police in exchange for supportive services.[109] Instead, the HEW grant extracted Hudson and Tourè from the DCRCC headquarters and placed them in the public schools of the District of Columbia solely for the purpose of providing sexual abuse prevention education. This grant was paltry compared to those issued by the LEAA and NCPCR in the 1970s. Touré recalled that "even in 1975, $29,000 was not a lot of money to run a program."[110] But it was sufficient for a Black anti-rape organizer like Tourè to divert her anti-rape advocacy into a new venue that could accommodate her politics. HEW restructured the DCRCC's grant application as a government contract. The first contract went into effect in March 1975 with the possibility of annual renewal. The contract's tentative status suggests that HEW expected the parental backlash that typically followed any attempt to discuss sex in the classroom in the late twentieth century.[111] The anticipated backlash never arrived. Indeed, by 1977, the D.C. City Council thought it prudent to extend the DCRCC's rape prevention education to all the District's elementary schools.[112]

The DCRCC welcomed its expanded responsibilities as the newly appointed Touré set about adapting a program designed for high schoolers to the grade school set. Touré and Ross recollect that holding onto the contract was a constant struggle that required the regular intercession of the City Council.[113] The tug-of-war over funding the program reflected what Nancy Whittier has called the "contradictory dictates" of child sexual abuse prevention in the early 1980s, when conservative slashing of social programs collided with "the political unpalatability of appearing to be 'soft' on child abuse."[114] In 1981, the recently renamed Department of Health and Human Services suggested cutting the D.C. Rape Crisis Center's annual contract almost in half from $64,000 to only $35,000.[115] An outraged letter to the editor of the *Washington Post* decried the "incredible insensitivity" of the proposal. Nearly 7,000 women and children were sexually assaulted in the District of Columbia each year, and the 250 school presentations performed annually by the rape crisis center were the only meaningful gestures made by the District government to combat the problem. "There is no excuse . . . even to propose this kind of budget cut when we are facing escalating violence at home and on the street," the letter writer concluded. Vocal support from the public and the D.C. City Council eventually spared the program from the fiscal chopping block. Though funds were never guaranteed, Loretta Ross gratefully recalled how "that contract sustained the Rape Crisis Center for its first twenty years."[116] At the time of Nkenge Touré's departure in 1988, the state paid the D.C. Rape Crisis Center $97,000 each year to perform child sexual abuse prevention education in schools. This payment comprised nearly 40 percent of the center's annual budget.[117]

Diversion was possible because the political landscape of the District of Columbia from the late 1970s through the 1980s was receptive to building a Black-centered child sexual abuse prevention program in public schools. Prior to 1973, commissioners appointed by the sitting President of the United States governed the District of Columbia. The only elected government body at the time was the school board, which Black Power advocates targeted as a site for enacting community control of schools.[118] Under the D.C. Home Rule Act of 1973, Washington, D.C. residents could finally elect their own mayor and City Council. In a city that had been majority Black since 1960, home rule "was justly celebrated as both a major achievement of the civil rights movement and an exciting opportunity to wield Black Power."[119] In 1978, Black Power reached the highest echelons of D.C. politics with the election of Mayor Marion Barry. A former Chairman of the Student Non-Violent Coordinating Committee and District of Columbia City Council Member, Mayor Barry positioned himself as a champion of the city's radical grassroots and a challenger to the respectable political elite. He handily won reelection in 1982 and 1986, though his political career collapsed in 1990 after a sting operation publicized his crack cocaine addiction. Barry dedicated his mayoralty to dismantling the distant and ineffectual bureaucracy that had long governed the District of Columbia and replacing it with what historians Chris Myers Asch and George Derek Musgrove have termed "functional Black Power politics."[120] This primarily took the form of issuing city contracts to Black-owned businesses and firms. Though stymied by funding shortfalls, official corruption, and an aggressive federal campaign to clamp down on the flow of illegal drugs, the Barry administration modeled how a city that was 70 percent Black could be governed by a Black mayor without appealing to traditional white power structures.

The Barry administration and the majority-Black D.C. City Council provided a comparatively flexible funding stream that allowed Nkenge Tourè to perform child sexual abuse prevention outside the formal channels of the feminist rape crisis center. More importantly, they allowed her to build a program that spoke directly to Black children and their families. Treating race as a relevant category in dealing with child sexual abuse flew in the face of the race-neutral analysis that dominated feminist and popular discourse. Retaining racial specificity also spotlighted challenges that the Black community faced in combatting child sexual abuse, leading Touré to develop a prevention curriculum that excluded the state and its punitive responses. Touré's takeover of the prevention program in the schools spawned a new curriculum aimed at students from second through sixth grades and an accompanying booklet titled "Staying Safe," which encapsulated this curriculum.[121] Concerned adults across the country could purchase "Staying Safe" for a nominal fee of $3 sent to the D.C. Rape Crisis Center's P.O. Box.[122] Touré recalled that through CASAPP "we were systematically working our way through the city."[123] She maintained a demanding schedule, stationing herself in D.C. public schools at least three weeks out of a given month. Depending on the size of the school, delivering presentations to each class and grade level could take up to one week.[124] Touré designed both the in-school CASAPP presentation and the "Staying Safe" booklet to speak directly to Black children. *Aegis* alerted its readership that "Staying Safe has a multi-racial, multicultural perspective with emphasis on children in urban areas."[125]

As community education director for the D.C. Rape Crisis Center, Touré still believed that punitive state intervention posed a threat to assaulted Black women and girls, even if the state itself contained more Black faces. Touré looked to the Black family rather than the state as "a key site to the function of prevention and rape education."[126] Historically, state actors from police officers to social workers viewed Black families as likely sites of dysfunction that required punitive correction. Black Power activists in the late twentieth century recognized how the criminal justice and child welfare systems teamed up to disperse Black families and disintegrate Black communities, going so far as to call for an alternative Black-run child welfare system as a means of self-determination.[127] Nkenge Touré, in keeping with her Black Power politics, positively assessed the Black family. She described them as spaces of potential where values that warded off sexual abuse could be successfully cultivated. Touré argued that Black parents could protect their children from sexual abuse "by directly teaching children the ability to be positive about one's self without the need or desire to oppress another person" and "constantly demonstrating these values by the example of their own actions." But she knew that these values had to be taught. Tourè committed to educating Black families as a kind of care work that promised to spare them from unforgiving state control. In another speech, Touré pinpointed incest and rape as a "priority issue" that must be addressed within the community to ensure "the survival of the family and the working interaction between Black women and men" as well as the continued existence of the Black nation.[128]

Tourè built the CASAPP curriculum on three main principles: informing children of their sexual self-sovereignty, sanctioning physical self-defense when necessary, and respectfully engaging the parents of Black children in the work of prevention. Born out of Black women's care work, these principles contradicted the imperatives of family dispersal and child seizure endorsed by the National Center on Child Abuse and Neglect and encouraged by panic-stricken newspapers. State actors like police officers and social workers were peripheral figures in the CASAPP curriculum and the "Staying Safe" booklet. Touré only referenced them obliquely as one of the many trusted adults in whom they might confide their abuse. Like other Black feminist anti-rape organizers, Touré could not entirely avoid law enforcement officials and social workers within the field of child sex abuse prevention. The parental foreword of the "Staying Safe" booklet listed the phone number of the Children's Hospital of the District of Columbia and Child Protective Services.[129] However, her curriculum positioned them as secondary to the project of Black youth defending themselves from would-be authority figures who disregarded their bodily integrity.

For the Child Assault Safety Awareness and Prevention Program, Touré slightly modified her lesson plans based on the grade level she addressed. For example, she simplified the language and assumed less prior knowledge when she spoke to second graders as opposed to sixth graders. Conceptual simplification did not mean muting the political principle of sexual self-sovereignty. Irrespective of grade level, Nkenge Touré began each lesson with the same handout entitled "Inappropriate Behaviors from Others Towards You," which the instructor encouraged the students to read at home with their parents. The sheet included a catalog of abusive sexual behaviors and described them in graphic detail. For instance, it instructed children that "no one should be allowed to hug or kiss you in a grown-up way." In lieu of patronizing euphemisms for genitalia, the "Inappropriate Behaviors" guide only used medically accurate terms. For example, it advised children that "nothing should be inserted into the vaginal or rectal area, such as objects, fingers, or penis."[130] It further advised children that "no one should ask you to be in an isolated place alone with them for the purpose of touching your private areas such as your penis, vagina, rectum, buttocks, and breasts."

Instilling the concept of sexual self-sovereignty—one's ability to control their body and who could access it—in Washington, D.C.'s young Black children required that children possess accurate knowledge about sex. As Ferentz Lafargue has argued, "making sure to refer to [children's] body parts by their correct names" is a precondition to "treating them as sole proprietors of their bodies."[131] In CASAPP, the unembellished use of medically accurate terminology for sex organs provided the rudiments of sex education for a prepubescent Black audience. In a *Washington Post* article praising the CASAPP program as "among the nation's most effective," Nkenge Touré asserted that to properly arm children against sexual abuse "we have to go to the more specific things. We must give the children an idea of what you are talking about . . . you have to give a little more information than you might like."[132] Loretta Ross regarded the program as a "backdoor way of getting sex ed into the school system, because you can't teach a child safety around sexual assault if you don't teach them about sex."[133] Touré recalled that, although the reception for CASAPP was overwhelmingly positive, some resistance occasionally arose from parents who felt that feminist instructors covertly gave their children premature sex education.[134] The D.C. Rape Crisis Center preemptively dispelled parental discomfort by tactically labelling itself as a "child safety program" rather than a child sexual abuse prevention program. As Loretta Ross put it, "it was deeply euphemistic, it was disguised. Who can argue about keeping children safe? That's the way it was branded and framed. It insulated us from outright resistance, because it was not touted as an anti-rape or sex ed program. It was a child safety program."[135]

The churning moral panic over the safety of innocent children in the 1980s permitted Nkenge Touré and the D.C. Rape Crisis Center to refine the sexual vocabularies of Black children, equipping them to recognize assault when they encountered it. Instilling sexual self-sovereignty meant more than medically accurate terminology for body parts. Touré dedicated the first session of her presentation to familiarizing her students with the definitions of various sex crimes. Touré's curriculum prompted the program instructor to say the word, ask how many children had heard it before, and asked the children to define it themselves. Finally, the instructor would "share the proper term" as defined by Touré and her colleagues at the D.C. Rape Crisis Center. Touré defined rape for them as "when someone tries to do something to your body that you do not want them to do" and incest as "a family member trying to sexually assault or fondle you."[136] She illustrated these concepts through role-playing with the schoolchildren, approximating abusive situations and coaching them on how to respond.

The "Staying Safe" booklet continued the trend of recognizing children's sexual subjectivity. Following a brief foreword intended for parents, "Staying Safe" spoke directly to children. The child narrators, an African American girl named Andrea and a Hispanic boy named Miguel, engaged the young reader directly, alerting them that "now that the adults have read their part of the book, it's our turn. The rest of the booklet is for us."[137] The narrators defined

Figure 4. Illustration inside the "Staying Safe" booklet. Courtesy of the D.C. Rape Crisis Center.

relevant terms like "child abuse," "incest," and "child molester," repeated verbatim from the CASAPP curriculum. "Staying Safe" also reflected the program's commitment to medically accurate terms for sex organs. Miguel explained the importance of learning these definitions as a necessary step that children must take to become self-sufficient. "If we start taking the responsibility of going places alone or being home alone," Miguel explains, "we also have to be able to watch out for ourselves."[138] Andrea and Miguel went on to guide child readers through various scenarios of incest and child sexual abuse, from molestation by a babysitter to sexual assault by a mother's boyfriend to excessive hugging and kissing from an uncle. The scenarios described in "Staying Safe" replicated the roleplays Touré conducted in the classroom. After describing each scenario in exhaustive detail, Miguel and Andrea would stop the story, quiz the child reader on the appropriate response, and show the imperiled child taking the correct course of action.

Touré's transmission of sexual knowledge to children in the service of abuse prevention laid the foundation for their sexual self-sovereignty. To communicate the concept of sexual self-sovereignty, she leaned on the language of rights. Toward the end of each program, Touré called for the class to revisit the definition of words they had learned on the first day. For example, Touré interpreted the word "force" outside of physical coercion: "Even if the person does not have a weapon, it is still force; even if the person does not hit you, it is still force. If it is something that you do not want them to do to your body or you do not want to do to their body, it is force."[139] This capacious definition of force established the idea that any unwanted transgression across the boundaries of the body constituted a violent attack. Touré followed up with a sweeping pronunciation on the rights of children: "A right is something that you are entitled to, or something that you are supposed to have. You have a right to a decent free education; you have the right to shelter and clothing; and you have a right to be safe. You have the right to question what is done to your body. If what a person is doing to your body makes you feel scared, confused, or uncomfortable, you have the right to tell them to stop, even if they are an adult or a big person."[140] Touré's definition of children's rights contained traces of radical Black thought. She linked the rights of children to basic material needs—rights that she defended through the survival programs of the Black Panther Party and Save the People—and to the sexual self-sovereignty of Black children. "Staying Safe" reinforced the message of children's right to sexual self-sovereignty. The booklet concluded with a true-false quiz that affirmed that "children, as well as adults, have rights" and "you have the right to question anything that is done to your body."[141]

As she alerted Black children to their sexual self-sovereignty, Touré also authorized children to physically resist those who abused their authority over them. Touré's sanction of self-defense even translated into the diluted curriculum for preschoolers, kindergarteners, and first graders. "Your body belongs to you and no one has the right to touch it without your permission. If they try you can tell them to stop, you can scream, you can push them away."[142] The "Staying Safe" booklet modelled a variety of methods of resistance, including shouting at and striking their assailants, reminding readers that simply because their abuser is more powerful than them, "that doesn't mean that there is nothing that you can do or that you have to let what is happening continue."[143] The concluding quiz reiterated that "you have a right to tell that person to stop and leave you alone" and "you have the right to scream and yell to attract attention or walk or run away from that person and get help immediately."[144] Touré's prescription of self-defense for Black children challenged mainstream understandings of child sexual abuse and its prevention in the

1980s. First, it overturned assumptions about the helplessness of children that mobilized carceral state-building during the decade.[145] Second, it drew upon both Black feminism and Black Power, two movements that turned to arming their constituents as a preferable alternative to relying upon a racist and sexist criminal justice system. An unbroken line of Black feminist anti-rape activists, from the National Black Feminist Organization and the National Alliance of Black Feminists to Lynn Moncrief of Philadelphia WOAR, all embraced self-defense training as a key component of their caring labor that did not engage law enforcement as Black women's first line of defense. Within some Black Power circles, militaristic self-defense shored up a toxic strand of Black masculinity.[146] Touré's curriculum, in Black feminist fashion, unmoored self-defense from its masculinist associations by rendering it equally applicable to women and children.[147] Instructing children to physically resist authority figures who abused them was particularly liberatory for Black schoolchildren who increasingly experienced the classroom as a carceral space that surveilled and punished them for the most minor of offenses.[148]

The Child Assault Safety Awareness and Prevention Program piloted by Nkenge Touré engaged Black children with the practice of sexual self-sovereignty and self-defense when necessary. Though parents did not attend Touré's in-school presentations, the companion "Staying Safe" booklet interpolated them into the discourse of child sex abuse prevention in a manner that was neither punitive nor judgmental. While state involvement in child sexual abuse prevention assumed the inherent and unfixable dysfunction of the Black family, Touré's curriculum confirmed the competence of Black parents and basic wholesomeness of Black families. This avoided the pitfall of anti-violence advocacy described by Lynn Roberts in which an activist "removes the historical, familial and social contexts in which all our human interactions occur, freezes our most horrendous actions in time, stymies our opportunities for growth, and offers little hope that we can stop or prevent future harm."[149] The parental foreword of "Staying Safe," announced by the subheadings "To the Parents: This Part Is for You," called upon parents to reinforce the lessons imparted by the CASAPP. This section hailed the parent into the work of child abuse prevention and did not attempt to disguise the program's radical thrust. Touré hoped that the support of their parents would "aid children in the understanding that they too have resources and control over their bodies."[150] She assured the parent readers that "it is only through feeling a sense of their own power that children can become effective resisters." Touré's unusual description of children as "resisters," a term typically reserved for political combatants, aligned with the series of the commands to parents that concluded the forward of "Staying Safe": "Teach your children that they have control and autonomy over their bodies . . . Teach your children that they have the right to say NO . . . Blind obedience teaches children it is not okay to say no."[151]

* * *

In 1988, after a decade of instructing thousands of children in Washington, D.C. how to ward off assault, Nkenge Touré resigned from her post at the D.C. Rape Crisis Center. Like Lynn Moncrief, she cited emotional burnout as a major reason behind her departure.[152] A second significant reason for her resignation was Touré's growing impatience with the leadership of the D.C. Rape Crisis Center, who upheld a narrower definition of violence against women than she did. Touré attempted to expand the DCRCC's programming to address the multiple, intersecting violences experienced by poor women of color in the nation's capital. According to Touré, some of her white female colleagues used the Child Assault Safety Awareness and Prevention Program as a cudgel to deter her from more radical protests. She recalled how before her departure the Board of Directors repeatedly pressured her to "stay in your area" and limit her activism to "education for the children."[153] Though initially supportive of the CASAPP and its Black feminist politics, the DCRCC drifted toward the race-neutral perspectives and pushed for apolitical community education. In this way, the DCRCC illustrated the necessity of the diversion tactic for Black anti-rape organizers. As the 1980s approached, cash-strapped feminist rape crisis centers became too preoccupied with controlling rape through law enforcement partners to allow Black women's praxis of care to take place even subversively. The success of CASAPP in Washington, D.C. showed that other majority-Black institutions outside of the rape crisis center had potential to foster Black anti-rape organizers' care work.

As the 1980s pushed onward, the "Reagan Revolution" amplified the call for law and order that wormed its way into the feminist movement against sexual violence. The pairing of law-and-order rhetoric with welfare state retrenchment only deepened the vulnerability of Black victims. Under the Victims of Crime Act of 1984, policymakers mitigated the suffering of adult and child victims of sexual assault—and coaxed them to report and prosecute their assailants—by extending direct financial support from the state. With the other hand, Reaganites ruthlessly slashed social safety nets and so-called "entitlement" programs, shoving poor Black women and children into even greater precarity and exposing them to greater violence. Whereas Black women anti-rape organizers in Washington, D.C. enjoyed the benefits of a Black population majority and a local government sympathetic to Black Power, their counterparts in Chicago encountered far less accommodating political terrain. Witnessing the simultaneous expansion of the carceral state and decimation of the welfare state, the Black women who composed the Chicago Sexual Assault Services Network (CSASN) diverted their care work into the embattled social service landscape of the Windy City.

CHAPTER 5

Serving the Undeserving Victim

In the summer of 1979, Phyllis Pennese underwent training as a counselor for the Chicago-based Rape Victim Advocates (RVA).[1] Though she had no ties to any feminist or Black liberation groups, she was moved to activism out of concern for other Black women residing in the city's South and West Sides. Local newspapers offered persistent testimony to Black Chicago women's disproportionate vulnerability to sexual violence and the dearth of resources to cope with this vulnerability. According to one report from the *Chicago Tribune*, 10 percent of Chicago's reported rapes in 1979 occurred in the Robert Taylor Homes, a public housing project inhabited almost exclusively by poor Black women. A community group active there claimed that during the previous summer the housing project had averaged two rapes every three days.[2] Aurie Pennick, Ethel Payne's handpicked successor to lead the Coalition of Concerned Women in the War on Crime, complained to the *Chicago Tribune* that "as causes come and go, rape is starting to take a back seat to other issues" but "rape in the inner city was never properly addressed in the first place."[3] A year later, the *Chicago Defender* noted that "for women living on the poor side of town community based, crisis intervention, counseling, and referral services are practically nonexistent, and an energetic push to implement them is unforeseen."[4] Moreover, extant community organizations "lack the expertise needed to handle people in such delicate condition."[5]

One encounter with the Chicago police convinced Pennese that the issue of violence against Black women could not be satisfactorily addressed from within a system that aggressively criminalized Black bodies. Pennese accompanied an assaulted Black woman to the police station, where her assailant was held in custody. The police found her blood smeared on the man's clothing, positively identifying him as her attacker. However, when they discovered the victim had an outstanding warrant for prostitution, they arrested her. Pennese, outraged, protested the decision, asking "What about her victimization? That doesn't just wipe that away."[6] She received no answer. Instead, she learned that Black women, especially poor Black women who engaged in the illicit economy for survival, could not appear as deserving victims in the eyes of the state.[7] JoAnn Robinson of Chicago's Jackson Park Hospital Rape Victims Project echoed Pennese's observation that the police habitually assumed that welfare recipients supplemented their benefits with prostitution; therefore, their rape complaints were illegitimate. "Many Chicago policemen treat the rape of poor Black women as a joke," she concluded.[8] By 1982, Pennese departed RVA to join a new organization that was dedicated to ensuring that "the needs of Black [rape] victims are addressed within their own communities."[9]

The leadership of this group, the Chicago Sexual Assault Services Network (CSASN), came from vastly different political and socioeconomic backgrounds. Mary Scott Boria, who became CSASN's Executive Director in 1984, was a former member of the Chicago Chapter of the Black Panther Party who had recently earned her degree in social work.[10] Associate Director Sylvia Rush possessed only a high school diploma and had no formal political associations.[11] Phyllis Pennese, who succeeded Boria in 1988, would later become ordained through the Chicago Theological Seminary.[12] Beryl Fitzpatrick, like Boria, was educated in social work but also claimed membership in Brenda Eichelberger's National Alliance of Black Feminists and Angela Davis's National Alliance Against Racist and Political Repression.[13] Despite their different backgrounds, CSASN's members were united by two things: their concern with the dearth of services available to Black victims in Chicago and their commitment to providing these services outside the formal boundaries of the feminist movement against sexual violence.

Thus, the CSASN engaged the tool of diversion within the arsenal of practices cultivated by Black anti-rape organizers. They pried $35,000 from the Illinois Department of Health and Human Services to launch an intensive training program for representatives of community welfare agencies that were already established on the underserved South and West Sides. Such agencies included the Mile Square Health Center, the Bobby Wright Community Mental Health Center, and the Englewood Community Health Center. Upon completion, trained service professionals would offer cost-free comprehensive counseling to the rape victims they encountered.[14] Amid a national "die-off" of feminist rape crisis centers prompted by the decimation of federal funding streams under President Ronald Reagan, CSASN elected to carry their anti-rape activism into the besieged social welfare landscape of Chicago where they could better meet the needs of Black victims.[15] Whereas the Child Assault Safety Awareness and Prevention Program (CASAPP) piloted by Nkenge Tourè institutionalized self-defense training and culturally competent community education in the public school system of the District of Columbia, the CSASN institutionalized the emotional counseling element of Black anti-rape organizers' praxis of care in Chicago's social welfare agencies.

CSASN operated at the nexus of two interrelated political trends that dominated the 1980s: the slashing of social safety nets and the accelerated criminalization of Black life. The Victims of Crime Act (VOCA), signed into law by President Reagan in 1984, exemplified both trends.[16] VOCA was the "legislative centerpiece" of the victims' rights movement, which originated in the 1970s among crime victims who demanded that the criminal justice system redirect its ire toward the convicted instead of those harmed by the convicted.[17] VOCA established a national Crime Victims Fund comprised of fines levied against federal offenders and disbursed among the states to fund victim compensation programs and block grants for community organizations that provided services to victims of crime.[18] Feminist rape crisis centers relied upon VOCA grants as their sole source of federal funds during the 1980s, which tied them even more closely to carceral actors than the LEAA had.

The framers of the Victims of Crime Act geared its compensation scheme to only support *deserving victims* of crime. *Deserving victims* were morally upright, economically independent citizens who fell prey to criminals through no fault of their own and promptly reported the crime to the authorities. Provisions of the Victims of Crime Act of 1984 thus required "victim cooperation with the reasonable requests of law enforcement authorities" and threatened "diminishing compensation to the extent of the contributory misconduct of the victim."[19] For poor African American women, who frequently avoided reporting their rapes to the police precisely because of the perception that they invited assaults through their behavior, successfully filing for victim's compensation proved difficult. Meanwhile, the Reagan Administration worked diligently to eliminate public assistance that poor Black women relied on for survival.[20] This deprived poor Black rape victims of badly needed financial support from the state on two fronts. Poor Black women, whose innocence in crime and compliance with criminal justice could not be assumed, fell to the stigmatized status of *undeserving victims* who could not expect the financial support accorded to other, more prosperous citizens.

The Chicago Sexual Assault Services Network repudiated the framework of *deserving victims* codified by the Victims of Crime Act of 1984. Its

Black female leadership made therapeutic counseling accessible for poor Black women who had been deemed undeserving of support from the state by plugging services into the existing social service landscape that had also been ravaged by a conservative government. By caring for the minds, bodies, and souls of Black rape victims, CSASN proclaimed Black women worthy of the state's resources while contesting their susceptibility to its punishments. Through the tactic of diversion, the CSASN asserted that poor Black women and girls were entitled to counseling irrespective of their willingness to entrust themselves to the criminal justice system. In doing so, they elevated the healing of Black women and girls as an important mode of justice that did not automatically rest upon punishing offenders.

The Victims of Crime Act of 1984 and the Making of the "Deserving Victim"

Though intended to assist victims of all types of violent crimes, the Victims of Crime Act of 1984 centered rape victims in discourse and practice. This emphasis on sexual violence began with the Task Force on Victims of Crime convened by President Ronald Reagan in 1982.[21] The Task Force's Chairman opened the final report with the chilling statistic that in the United States, "every six minutes a woman is raped." The report went past dry statistics with an emotional composite portrait of the "human reality of victimization."[22] It featured a narrative of a middle-aged, presumably white woman sexually assaulted in her home and her ordeal as she attempted to wring justice from an indifferent court system and reconstruct her life in a fog of financial hardship and psychological distress. The final report concluded with sixty-eight recommendations, chief among them the creation of a national Crime Victims Fund and an Office of Crime Victims within the Department of Justice to administer these funds.[23] According to the Task Force, state compensation would salve the enormous mental anguish and physical injury endured by victims of crime and counteract their lost income from work absences. Well-compensated crime victims would have the stamina and security to press charges and testify against their assailants, increasing the chances of a guilty verdict and a substantial sentence for the assailant. The retributive logic of VOCA—taking resources from worthless criminals to give to blameless victims—reflected Reagan's compromise between anti-taxation small-government fiscal conservatism and perpetuating the federal "war on crime."

President Reagan signed the Victims of Crime Act into law on October 12, 1984, establishing a Crime Victims Fund that could collect up to $110 million annually. Criminal penalties collected from convicted federal defendants and bail bonds paid by defendants in federal criminal cases entirely comprised the fund with no contribution from general tax revenue.[24] By 1986, the Crime Victims Fund collected $85 million annually.[25] By 1990, a total of $500 million had been deposited into the Crime Victims Fund, a quarter of which was collected in 1989 alone.[26] The number of successful crime victim compensation claims for adult and child victims of sex offenses nearly tripled from 9,000 claims in 1986 to 25,000 claims in 1989. In the same period, claims paid on behalf of victims of sexual violence soared from $11 million to $29 million annually. While most of the Crime Victims Fund's annual revenue went toward compensating individual victims, VOCA also extended grants directly to rape crisis centers that served crime victims.[27] Compared to individual compensation claims, Victims of Crime Act grants extended to states grew sluggishly from $5.6 million in 1986 to $6.2 million in 1989.[28] Nevertheless, struggling rape crisis centers across the nation were grateful for renewed federal support. At the 1987 Congressional hearing to determine whether the Victims of Crime Act should be renewed past 1988, Susan Cameron of the Pennsylvania Coalition Against Rape celebrated VOCA as "a welcome and much needed addition to the resources available to those of us trying to provide services" that "represented a clear and continuing national commitment to the needs of victims."[29]

From the perspective of white anti-rape feminists like Susan Cameron, it was a resounding victory that the state actually counted rape survivors as victims of violent crime. Seventeenth-century British jurist Lord Matthew Hale's oft-quoted summation that rape was "an accusation easily to be made and hard to be proved and harder to be defended against by the party accused, tho never so innocent" informed the American legal system well into the twentieth century.[30] In his widely cited and studied *Treatise on the System of Evidence in Trials at Common Law* (1904), American legal scholar John Henry Wigmore affirmed Lord Hale's view that ordinary women routinely made false rape allegations as both a weapon of revenge against men who had wronged them and an outlet for their perverse sexual fantasies.[31] Attorneys and judges alike believed that women's rape accusations were suspect and exceptionally high standards of evidence were necessary to spare innocent men from false charges. When rape victims took the stand, they besieged them with prying and humiliating questions. Any inconsistencies in the woman's story or evidence of social behaviors that suggested a lack of chastity would be quickly deployed as proof that the sex in question was consensual. Juries were apparently swayed by the attacks on the credibility of rape victims, since conviction rates for rape remained notoriously low for much of the twentieth century.[32] Feminists spent much of the 1970s fighting for rape shield laws that rendered a woman's sexual history inadmissible as evidence. They feared that judges and juries bought into sexist rape myths and would refuse to see accusers as victims except under the rarest of circumstances: where the attack was egregiously violent and the woman was unquestionably chaste.[33] As early as 1972, feminist anti-rape groups like the New York Women Against Rape looked hopefully toward state-level victim compensation programs to achieve the same ends.[34] When VOCA arrived on the scene in 1984, the law appeared to them as favorable and even feminist legislation that checked the criminal justice system's bias favoring accused men.

VOCA may have fulfilled the feminist aim of encouraging the criminal justice system to believe and support victims of violent crime. But it also fulfilled a longstanding aim of the "war on crime": encouraging more victims to cooperate with law enforcement. The rhetoric surrounding VOCA preserved its forbearers' commitment to controlling rape through the machinations of law enforcement. Jane Nadley Burns, director of the Office for Victims of Crime, retraced the logic of the fifteen-year-old LEAA manual *Rape and Its Victims* while describing the importance of VOCA. She testified that "we need participation in the criminal justice system of victims as witnesses if we are going to end crimes. One of the things we know about sex offenders is that they are recidivists. If they are not stopped, they will continue to commit sex crimes."[35] Burns's testimony revealed that a desire to control crime through incarceration guided the Victims of Crime Act at least as much as compassion for the plight of crime victims.

Feminist rape crisis centers who received grants under VOCA discovered that the new law's emphasis on crime control exceeded that of the LEAA. Whereas the LEAA had strongly encouraged client anti-rape groups to refer victims to law enforcement for continued funding, VOCA required it as a precondition for funding. Under these circumstances, the subversion once practiced by Lynn Moncrief was impossible. Philadelphia Women Organized Against Rape successfully obtained VOCA grants to support their direct service provision between 1986 and 1989.[36] In-service training provided to their volunteers warned that "WOAR receives federal funds from the Victim of Crime Act (VOCA), which mandates us to more actively assist sexual assault victim / survivors with victim compensation by offering survivors information about victim's compensation as well as helping them with the claim forms."[37] To comply with this mandate, WOAR required its counselors to present all victims intercepted in the emergency room with a letter explaining their eligibility for crime victim's compensation, which invariably included a police report and full cooperation with the requests of law enforcement. The terms of VOCA support also compelled them to assist the victim in completing the claim form and filing it properly with the Philadelphia District Attorney's office and the Pennsylvania Commission on Crime and Delinquency. This assistance included reminder letters and phone calls to the residences of victims who dropped off during the application process.[38] To ensure future funding viability, organizations like WOAR were also required to submit performance reports to their state-level VOCA representatives detailing the demographics of the victims they served using these funds and, crucially, whether they elected to report their assault to the police.[39] In 1987, the Illinois Coalition Against Sexual Assault (ICASA) secured a VOCA grant worth nearly $500,000 to be distributed among its twenty-three-member rape crisis centers across the state. ICASA was governed by the same mandates as Philadelphia WOAR.[40] The examples of WOAR and ICASA show how VOCA secured the financial future of the feminist movement against sexual violence at the price of knitting the movement and the criminal justice system ever closer together.

By marking victims of violent crime as a special class of citizens entitled to compensation from the state, the Victims of Crime Act straddled punitive crime control policy and the retrenchment of the welfare state in the 1980s. During the 1970s, liberal and conservative policymakers lumped together welfare recipients and criminal offenders as an undesirable and unproductive class who ought to be expelled from the citizenry and stripped of their rights, including claims to public assistance.[41] By contrast, injured crime victims who were willing to pursue their cases in court and further the state's crime control agenda took their place as the exclusive recipients of financial support from the state. By supporting the Victims of Crime Act of 1984, the Reagan Administration departed from its habitual disdain for government "handouts" and social services. As the Republican Governor of California from 1967 to 1975, Reagan established his enduring political brand by launching an impassioned crusade against welfare "cheats" within the state. By the time he reached the White House in 1981, Reagan and his allies argued that Aid to Families with Dependent Children (AFDC) was more than a fiscally unsustainable burden on taxpayers. In their view, it actively eroded the family unit by disincentivizing wage labor and marriage, particularly among poor African Americans. The rising numbers of Black women heading households and collecting public assistance had vexed liberals and conservatives since the 1960s.[42] Reagan fed these anxieties by conjuring the image of the profligate Black "welfare queen" to discredit the entire welfare state. In 1981, the Omnibus Budget Reconciliation Act endorsed by President Reagan slashed AFDC's budget by 12 percent, or $1 billion. As a result, 400,000 AFDC recipients were purged from the welfare rolls and at least as many saw their benefits shrink.[43] Three years after sharply contracting AFDC, Reagan signed VOCA into law. While many poor families lost their cash payments from the state during the Reagan presidency, victims of crime became eligible for them. As legal scholar Marie Gottschalk has argued, "paradoxically, as social services began to shrink in the 1980s due to the tax revolt, the recession, and the Reagan revolution, services for crime victims, including rape victims, expanded."[44]

Though poor Black women were frequently victims of violent crimes, VOCA remained largely inaccessible to them. This was partly due to the lengthy and tedious application process for victim's compensation, which varied depending on the state but universally required survivors to promptly report their assaults to law enforcement officials who would relay applications to the state compensation board.[45] The criminal justice system was the only point of entry for crime victim's compensation, creating a serious obstacle for poor Black women who were reluctant to entrust themselves to the police. A second obstacle to compensation for poor Black women was the eligibility criteria of the Victims of Crime Act, which limited compensation to *deserving victims*, whose experiences fit easily into the narrow conceptual definitions of male violence upheld by state actors.[46] The Victims of Crime Act instructed state compensation boards to deny claimants whose "contributory misconduct" may have precipitated the crime.[47] In other words, state compensation boards required that the victim "must not have committed a criminal act or some substantially wrongful act that caused or contributed to the crime" for which they sought compensation.[48] This provision was ostensibly intended as a safeguard against fraud. Yet members of the *Feminist Alliance Against Rape* predicted that "taking into account provocation by the victim in determining restitution" would "raise serious issues for rape victims" who still labored under the assumption that rape victims "ask for it."[49] For Black women, historically entrenched stereotypes regarding their hypersexuality, irresponsibility, and criminality made authorities even more inclined to conclude that they invited assault through their immoral behavior. As Phyllis Pennese and JoAnn

Robinson knew, poor Black women who incurred sexual violence while engaging in prostitution or partaking in illegal drugs were not recognized as the innocent, injured victims of crime that VOCA was designed to serve. The criminalization of both groups peaked in the 1980s, as the War on Drugs escalated and urban planners around the country sought to expel sex workers from sectors of their cities that were slated for economic redevelopment.[50] In this respect, VOCA manifested what scholar Kali Gross has termed "the exclusionary politics of protection" in which institutionalized racism prevents Black women from claiming protection under the law while disproportionately subjecting them to legal punishment.[51]

Federal officials knew that Black women, particularly Black rape survivors, were chronically underserved by VOCA. In the National Evaluation of State Victims of Crime Act Assistance and Compensation Programs, commissioned by the Department of Justice in 2002, researchers within the Urban Institute concluded that Black women comprised only 14 percent of victim compensation claimants for sexual assault while white women made up 76 percent of claimants.[52] They admitted that this ratio was "not in line with typical victim statistics," namely the National Crime Victimization Survey, which consistently identified Black women in lower socioeconomic classes as the group most victimized by rape.[53] They suggested that the "eligibility criteria" for successfully filing for victim's compensation might explain the severe underrepresentation of Black women among claimants.[54] Reagan had pushed huge numbers of poor Black women out from under AFDC, but the alternative social welfare program he and his allies devised for white middle- and upper-class victims of violent crime did not welcome them.

The Victims of Crime Act fused two bipartisan political trends in the 1980s: the racially selective retrenchment of the welfare state and the invigoration of punitive crime control efforts. VOCA empowered *deserving victims*, whose race and class status made them compelling witnesses for the state, through cash payments. From the vantage point of the criminal justice system, financially supporting *deserving victims* would ease the successful prosecution of rapists, which would in turn lead to far fewer rapes being committed in the first place. *Undeserving victims*, whose Blackness and poverty lessened their chances of sustaining a rape conviction, were of little use to state officials committed to punitivity as a deterrent to violent crime. The stipulations built into the Victims of Crime Act excluded *undeserving victims*, specifically those who engaged in criminal activity or could incur greater harm by appealing to the police for protection.[55] Unsurprisingly, poor Black women seldom filed for compensation under VOCA.[56] Through the de facto exclusion of poor women of color, the Victims of Crime Act implicitly constructed the *deserving victim* as a white, middle-class woman whose violation merited state compensation because she was morally irreproachable and economically viable. By contrast, Black women and girls on the South and West Sides of Chicago were *undeserving victims* entitled to no public assistance, let alone victim's compensation.

The Women of Color Caucus of the National Coalition Against Sexual Assault (NCASA)

The passage of VOCA in 1984 inaugurated a new chapter in the state's efforts to control the crime of rape under the less costly modality of "victim assistance." The nation-wide feminist movement against sexual violence, weakened by the suspension of other state funding streams in the early 1980s, worked diligently to ensure their movement would not lose the federal government's attention again. In August 1978, the National Coalition Against Sexual Assault (NCASA) formed as the first national network for anti-rape activists and advocates, as well as professional service providers who worked with rape victims. NCASA's comprehensive mission was "to end sexual violence and rape in our society, to unite all centers, to establish a national communications network, to serve as a lobbying unit, [and] to investigate funding sources for the continuation of programs and rape crisis centers."[57] NCASA was born during the annual meeting of the National Organization for Victim Assistance, when over fifty attendees representing anti-rape groups determined that they needed a network that specialized in service provision for rape victims.[58] By 1989, nearly half of the nation's rape crisis centers were represented in NCASA's membership.[59]

In March 1983, Mary Ann Largen, director of governmental policy for NCASA, testified in support of VOCA. She acknowledged that "crime victim compensation is not a panacea for all victims of crime" since "only victims who cooperate with criminal justice agencies may benefit."[60] Still, Largen threw NCASA's support behind VOCA, believing the act would secure the financial future of the rape crisis center movement. After the enactment of the Victims of Crime Act, NCASA devoted its Legislative Committee to ensuring the renewal of the law. During a 1987 Congressional hearing, NCASA's Susan Mooney reiterated Largen's argument on the centrality of VOCA funds for rape crisis centers.[61] Appealing to the concept of the *deserving victim*, Mooney reminded Congress that the renewal of VOCA was an obligatory measure for controlling crime and ensuring public safety. She argued that in recent years "the American public has made it increasingly clear that they expect our government to assist in the provision of services for victims of crime."[62] The inevitable closure of rape crisis centers and victim service organizations deprived of VOCA funds would hinder the state's crime control project and "result in a tremendous step backwards in the effort to encourage victims to report crimes." Even as the larger victims' rights movement came to question the efficacy of incarceration in achieving restitution for victims, NCASA remained committed to VOCA as an economic lifeline for the feminist movement against sexual violence.[63] Their pro-reporting and pro-arrest stance meshed with the get-tough approach of the state.[64]

While NCASA's leaders spent much of the 1980s defending VOCA, its non-white members clamored for better representation within the organization. The Women of Color Caucus formed during NCASA's first annual conference in Lake Geneva, Wisconsin, in 1979. Headed by Deirdre Wright of the D.C. Rape Crisis Center, the Women of Color Caucus connected non-white women from across the nation who were engaged in anti-rape activity.[65] In effect, NCASA's Women of Color caucus was to the national feminist movement against sexual violence what the Third World Women's Caucus was to Philadelphia WOAR. Between 1979 and 1988, NCASA approved numerous anti-racist resolutions proposed by the Women of Color Caucus. At the 1980 Conference, to combat "an obvious unawareness of the issues which were important to women of color," NCASA designated the annual keynote speech to be given by a woman of color.[66] In 1984, NCASA pledged that the first day of its annual conferences would be reserved for the Women of Color Institute. The Women of Color Institute would provide space for non-white members of NCASA to "network with each other apart from the total body" and strategize ways to "expand [NCASA's] services to women of color and to act in a manner that will ensure the participation of women of color." The work of anti-racism and racial inclusivity did not fall solely on the shoulders of non-white women. At the 1987 conference, Fern Ferguson, the new head of the Women of Color Caucus, directed NCASA's white women to form an anti-racism group that would be "accountable to the Women of Color Caucus."

NCASA's annual Women of Color Institute, directed by its Women of Color Caucus, provided a permanent space for Black women anti-rape organizers, many of whom were the sole women of color working within their respective institutions, to forge connections with other Black women on a national level. The Women of Color Institute (and, by extension, the Women of Color Caucus) of NCASA secured a foothold for Black women in the nationwide anti-rape movement while pushing service providers to look beyond the implicitly white *deserving victim* upheld by the Victims of Crime Act. Many of their proposals moved against the state's crime control interests. NCASA heeded the Women of Color Caucus and acknowledged the claim made during the NCPCR's "Special Populations" Conferences that racism and sexism within the criminal justice system made reporting rapes to law enforcement an undesirable option for poor non-white women. They resolved to "undertake concerted efforts in our communities and at the state and national levels to secure a variety of alternative actions" that did not hinge on law enforcement cooperation, such as women's self-defense groups and word-of-mouth warnings about known offenders within communities.[67] When NCASA held its annual conference in Philadelphia in 1987, many of Philadelphia WOAR's Black members volunteered to organize the Women of Color Institute. Meloney J. Sallie, the chair of WOAR's own Women of Color Caucus (formerly the Third World Caucus), published a short essay preemptively justifying the racially exclusive Women of Color Institute. Sallie pointed to the potential of anti-rape advocacy to fuel the state's crime control agenda as an example. Although she felt "very strongly that any man who rapes any woman should be held accountable," she also realized that "men of color are drastically overrepresented in prison."[68] Sallie argued that the Women of Color Institute afforded Black anti-rape organizers like herself a place to theorize careful modes of anti-rape advocacy that were responsive to those inhabiting marginal intersections. She explicated the inseparability of interpersonal and state violence within non-white communities, which underscored the importance of Black women's care work as a non-punitive form of prevention: "If you train one woman not to become a victim of sexual assault, you have prevented one woman from becoming a victim. If you train one man not to be a perpetrator, you have prevented approximately fifteen women from being victims. And if that man is a man of color, you have kept one man of color out of prison. This dilemma, and others like it, are why I feel it is necessary to have a Women of Color Network and any other tools women of color need to organize themselves and get the cultural support which is needed to do this work effectively."[69] The reactions of NCASA's white membership to the annual conferences demonstrate that the Women of Color Caucus made some headway with injecting Black women's perspectives into the predominantly white anti-rape movement. *Aegis* contributor Gail Sullivan amplified the racist potential of an overreliance on law enforcement. "Laws are made by those in power to protect their own interests," Sullivan surmised. "We need to understand that under such a system, when men are punished for their behavior, it is not because the system is protecting women but because to do so supports and reflects an aspect of the system, such as racism and the isolation of Third World communities."[70]

The Black Chicago women who founded CSASN were members of NCASA and regular attendees of the Women of Color Institute. Phyllis Pennese chaired NCASA's Women of Color Caucus in the late 1980s while also participating in the organization's lesbian coalition.[71] Mary Scott Boria also attended NCASA's national conference annually until the coalition's demise in the mid-1990s. Both Pennese and Boria averred that the Women of Color Institute of NCASA provided badly needed space for them to cultivate their anti-rape advocacy as Black women on a national scale. While the Women of Color Caucus enjoyed some influence within NCASA's agenda, this does not mean that the annual conferences were devoid of racial tension. Mary Scott Boria recalled the "public struggles at conferences" over issues of non-white women's representation in NCASA leadership and organizational agenda, not unlike the contentious "Special Populations" Conferences organized by the NCPCR. Boria reported feelings of frustration each year after the Women of Color Institute adjourned and the white NCASA attendees arrived. According to Boria, after two days of uninterrupted sisterhood and solidarity among women of color, "suddenly the whole conference opened up and it was like 'Oh my god, we're being invaded by these white women.'"[72]

The Women of Color Caucus of NCASA fostered a Black women's network within the feminist movement against sexual violence that looked beyond the limiting framework of the *deserving victim*. Though their white colleagues within NCASA respected their interventions, they did not or could not consistently implement them. Despite Black women persistently pressing their white colleagues to incorporate the perspectives of Black victims, NCASA remained committed to the Victims of Crime Act as an economic lifeline for the movement.[73] Consequently, they upheld the framework of the *deserving victim* as defined by the federal government. To reach the thousands of Black women and girls excluded by this framework, the Chicago Sexual Assault Services Network would need to work outside the feminist rape crisis centers funded by VOCA and represented by NCASA. As Nkenge Tourè did in Washington, D.C., CSASN diverted counseling for victims into existing public institutions that Black communities already frequented.

Fighting the "Disgrace of Black Chicago" with Diversion

In Chicago, a cluster of anti-rape organizations that opened during the 1970s continued to offer an uneven assortment of services into the 1980s.[74] But these groups, such as Rape Victim Advocates (RVA), Women in Crisis Can Act (WICCA), the Women's Services division of the Loop YWCA, and the Citizen's Committee for Victim Assistance (CCVA), were geographically and culturally removed from Black Chicago. Although more than 1,600 Black and Hispanic women reported rapes to the Chicago police in 1981, only half of the 452 rape victims counseled at the Loop YWCA that year were women of color.[75] Both the National Alliance of Black Feminists and the Coalition of Concerned Women in the War on Crime disintegrated that decade, leaving Black rape victims in the lurch. Exacerbating the situation was the pronounced die-off of feminist rape crisis centers across the country. Between 1978 and 1981, the nation lost nearly half of its rape crisis centers due to lack of funds as the LEAA shuttered and local administrations declined to pick up the tab.[76] Chicago was no exception.[77] When the LEAA-funded Citizen's Committee for Victim Assistance folded in 1981, director Marty Goddard lamented the "totally disgraceful . . . lack of services on the South and West Sides of Chicago, where a majority of our Black victims reside."[78] Despite valiant efforts, the crisis had only deepened, leading the *Defender* to declare rape "the disgrace of Black Chicago."[79]

To address the dire state of rape services in Chicago, Black and white anti-rape organizers pooled their combined thirty-five years of experience and founded the Chicago Sexual Assault Services Network (CSASN) in 1982. CSASN's mission statement upheld the provision of no-cost counseling services for survivors of sexual assault independent of the criminal justice system. From its inception, CSASN targeted "Black and Hispanic neighborhoods where there is currently a dearth of services for sexual assault victims."[80] CSASN would combat the "sketchy, scattered, underfunded and inadequate" services in Chicago from a central coordinating office that would train personnel within existing neighborhood centers in the underserved South and West Sides to offer on-site counseling for rape victims.[81] CSASN would expand its reach each year, eventually encompassing the Near and Far West Sides, Near South, Midsouth, and Southwest Sides, as well as the Northwest and North Lakefront areas. Appealing to the fiscal conservatism that dominated the 1980s, CSASN marketed itself to the Illinois Department of Human Services as "a cost-effective model for citywide neighborhood-based services for sexual assault victims." Their successful pitch secured a multi-year Community Development Block Grant that allocated $35,000 annually to cover the costs of conducting training, maintaining a central office, and employing two full-time staff members.[82]

Mary Scott Boria and Sylvia Rush served as the first executive director and associate director respectively.[83] They established a salient Black presence within CSASN with the help of other African American women who served CSASN as volunteers. The core group included Saundra Bishop, Phyllis Pennese (who would eventually take the position of director after Boria's departure in 1988), and Beryl Fitzpatrick, among others. CSASN was also ensconced within the lively social service world of metropolitan Chicago, seamlessly connecting the network to already practicing Black women community workers. CSASN was also firmly tethered to the electoral politics of Black Chicago. Mary Scott Boria and Saundra Bishop campaigned aggressively for Harold Washington, who became the city's first Black mayor in February 1983.[84]

Through previous experiences organizing Chicago's Black community, CSASN members knew firsthand that poor Black women were disproportionately impacted by rape and had few options for care after an assault. They also knew that the criminal justice system was indisposed to provide justice, let alone care, to poor Black women. Mary Scott Boria was a self-described "Afro-and-black-leather-jacket Black radical" recruited to the Chicago Chapter of the Black Panther Party while studying at Malcolm X College (formerly Crane Junior College).[85] Boria chafed under the "damn sexist organization" and departed a few months after the assassination of Fred Hampton in late 1969. But she never forgot the Panthers' lessons on the Chicago police force's horrendous brutality toward its Black denizens. During her tenure as a Cook County Hospital social worker and a city planner in Chicago's Department of Human Services, Boria tempered her radical disposition. She arrived at CSASN with a more pragmatic—but ultimately pessimistic—attitude toward law enforcement officials. Boria knew that "Chicago's system of criminal justice was not to be trusted."[86] At the same time, she acknowledged that "we certainly aren't going to get rid of it."[87]

Beryl Fitzpatrick's experiences as a political activist and professional social worker convinced her that Chicago's law enforcement officials offered little meaningful recourse for raped Black women. Like Phyllis Pennese, Beryl had undergone training with Rape Victim Advocates. She did so at the urging of the National Alliance of Black Feminists.[88] In addition to NABF,

Fitzpatrick was an active member of the Chicago Alliance Against Racist and Political Repression, a radical organization that grew out of the struggle to acquit Angela Davis from specious conspiracy charges in 1970. Trained as a social worker, Fitzpatrick worked in a variety of community health organizations in Chicago. Once, while employed by a daytime homeless shelter, Fitzpatrick received a distressed Black woman seeking relief from the mobile healthcare unit stationed at the shelter that day. Requesting to speak with Fitzpatrick in private, the woman disrobed and revealed a putrefied breast injury she had suffered from a homeless man who had raped her several days prior.[89] Unwilling to turn to the police for assistance due to her own criminal record and unable to afford proper medical attention, the woman was forced to let the wound fester until she discovered the mobile health unit. Poverty, Blackness, and criminalized status barred the women Pennese and Fitzpatrick counseled from the class of *deserving victims* who became the exclusive beneficiaries of state support in the 1980s.

The Black women who comprised CSASN's founding membership were well-versed in the racist, sexist, and classist logic that determined victimhood for Chicago law enforcement. The Victims of Crime Act of 1984 would consecrate the narrow criteria for victimhood for those seeking individual compensation as well as feminist rape crisis centers who survived on VOCA grants. But CSASN never sought nor received funding from VOCA. Unlike the much larger Illinois Coalition Against Sexual Assault with whom they occasionally partnered, CSASN did not interface directly with victims of sexual assault and therefore did not qualify for VOCA grants.[90] Irrespective of their lack of standing with VOCA, CSASN did not develop a robust relationship with Chicago's criminal justice system. Instead of convincing the city's intractable criminal justice system to recognize poor Black women as *deserving victims,* they committed themselves to establishing counseling services for poor Black women in Chicago who had been sexually assaulted. CSASN remade anti-rape advocacy in Chicago around the needs of *undeserving victims*: women whose race branded them as lascivious and therefore complicit in all violence they incurred, whose enduring poverty marked them as shiftless abusers of state resources, whose histories of crime cast them beyond the pale of citizenship. From their perspective, what *undeserving victims* needed above all was care in the form of accessible therapeutic counseling. Although CSASN supported victims who chose to pursue assailants in court, they believed that actual justice for poor Black survivors must proceed from no-cost, community-based care. This kind of care provision served the dual purposes of declaring Black women deserving of state resources amid welfare state retrenchment while sidestepping a criminal justice system that had embedded itself within the feminist movement against sexual violence.

Mary Scott Boria confirmed that for CSASN, "the aim was to get these services to non-white women in these communities who did not have access to the very basic care after being assaulted."[91] As noted by the *Defender* and the *Tribune*, Black women's access to counseling services was mitigated by both geographical and cultural factors. The location of the remaining rape crisis centers in Downtown Chicago made them practically inaccessible to Black women in the South and West Sides who could seldom afford bus or train fare. In addition to geographical constraints, Boria noted a strong tradition of dissemblance that forbade Black women from publicly exposing their interior selves lest they provide ammunition for anti-Black theories of inferiority.[92] Placing highly trained counselors within existing neighborhood centers that impoverished Black women already utilized would ameliorate both issues. Though CSASN provided its trademark forty-hour training module to professionals employed in hospitals, community mental health centers, and women's centers throughout the city, Boria recalled that most trainees were Black women social service professionals based in South and West Side community agencies. The Bobby E. Wright Mental Health Center and the Englewood Community Mental Health Center, located on the West and South Sides respectively, frequently dispatched their personnel for CSASN training. As a result of training, African American social service professionals "would be better prepared in their local agencies to provide services to women who were sexually assaulted, who maybe showed up at their center for something else."[93]

Integrating rape counseling services into the roster of services offered by community agencies in the South and West Sides, as opposed to localizing services exclusively within a single rape crisis center or hitching them to police operations, enabled CSASN to develop a more "successful working relationship with Chicago's Black community" than other feminist anti-rape groups.[94] Phyllis Pennese recalled that during her time at Rape Victim Advocates, "we were being trained to advocate for white women" and consequently "the issues that were different for women of color weren't really being addressed."[95] Geography also stunted RVA's attempts to embrace Black Chicago.[96] During its heyday, RVA reached the eight or nine hospitals that dotted the North Side and Downtown Chicago, only belatedly extending to St. Bernard's Hospital in Englewood in 1986. By contrast, CSASN was rooted to the predominantly Black West Side through its central office in Mt. Sinai Hospital from the start. Unlike the rape victim service ventures that had appeared in Chicago in the previous decade, CSASN was expressly devoted to meeting the needs of indigent Black rape victims and equipping Black social service providers to meet these needs. CSASN channeled the provision of counseling to poor Black women through community agency workers who were typically middle-class and college-educated, leaving the class dynamic of social service provision intact. Nevertheless, CSASN was committed to serving Black Chicagoan women practically to a fault. According to Pennese, their attention to poor non-white rape victims and the community agencies that served them hindered their ability to raise money, compared to predominantly white groups like Rape Victim Advocates.[97]

Care for the minds, bodies, and souls of Black women formed the bedrock of CSASN's anti-rape advocacy. Its members drew upon personal experience when they spoke of the importance of therapeutic counseling services for indigent Black victims. Assistant Director Sylvia Rush first garnered Mary Scott Boria's notice when in 1985 she singlehandedly organized a march in Downtown Chicago in support of rape victims in the wake of the high-profile Gary Dotson–Cathleen Webb case.[98] After accusing Dotson of sexual assault, Webb later recanted her testimony. Rush, a rape survivor herself, desperately "wanted people to know that maybe [Webb] lied, but the majority of victims are telling the truth."[99] Rush declined assistance from well-heeled Black organizations like Reverend Jesse Jackson's Operation PUSH when they told her she "would have to do things the way they wanted to." Instead, she forged ahead on her own, impressing Boria with her grassroots ethic. Rush was attracted to CSASN because, as a survivor of rape, she intimately understood the importance of accessible high-quality counseling. Before CSASN's existence, Rush ventured out of the South Side once a week to attend counseling sessions at the Loop YWCA. Rush understood restoration of her mind, body, and soul as a means of "getting control back" from her rapist. This understanding of "getting control back" through wellness stood in contrast to Philadelphia WOAR's "empowerment model," which sought the same end through police reporting. It also reclaimed the concept of "control" that law enforcement agencies had been striving to make synonymous with heavy-handed police response since the mid-1970s. Rush's definition of control was more aligned with that of the First National Conference on Third World Women and Violence, which saw anti-rape activism as "giving [Black women] some control over their lives and assistance in times of crisis."[100] Orchestrating CSASN's training program promoted Rush's own healing process, underscoring the reciprocity of care and control in Black anti-rape organizing. By embedding affordable counseling services into community agencies on the South and West sides of the city, Rush asserted, "I helped more people than [my rapist] hurt."[101]

Beryl Fitzpatrick similarly viewed care as a vital aspect of anti-rape advocacy for Black women. Once, a group of concerned Black women called Fitzpatrick and her Rape Victim Advocate colleagues to the notoriously decrepit and dangerous Henry Horner public housing development on the West Side. A resident, a young Black single mother, had been raped and, as Fitzpatrick recalled, "she was practically losing her mind."[102] Before RVA's arrival on the scene, a group of neighbors managed the victim's most basic material and emotional needs. The women of Henry Horner took turns "bathing her, combing her hair, keeping her warm, supporting her, [and] taking care of her children."[103] Fitzpatrick described the care these women performed for their devastated neighbor as the essence of effective counseling for Black rape victims. In Fitzpatrick's view, "they actually helped that woman not go to the other side, lose her mind, and not come back." Fortunately, RVA was able to connect the woman to long-term counseling, but Fitzpatrick made clear that the counselor simply "continued the work of these Black women and the nurturing that they had done so she could be whole again."[104] The state's preference for supporting *deserving victims* in the 1980s left women like the Henry Horner resident to lean on their communities for care and support. It was the task of CSASN to formalize networks of community care upon which poor Black women had always relied, integrating them into existing institutions to render them truly accessible. Reaching Chicago's large population of poor Black rape survivors, deemed undeserving by the political order of the day, demanded that CSASN prioritize community-based care and counseling in their advocacy. The criminal justice system, and the conduit to it provided by the Victims of Crime Act, would be irrelevant to their advocacy.

Serving the Undeserving Victim

In August 1984, the Chicago Sexual Assault Services Network allocated its first Community Development Block Grant from the Department of Human Services toward hiring Mary Scott Boria as Executive Director. With Boria at

A rape survivor, Sylvia Rush (l.) reviews data with her former supervisor Mary Scott-Boria at the Chicago Sexual Assault Services Network headquarters. After becoming assistant to the director of the network earlier this year, Ms. Rush says she has come to realize that many women are raped by men they know. Ms. Scott-Boria, now with the YWCA, puts the figure at about 60 percent.

Figure 5. Sylvia Rush (*left*) converses with Mary Scott Boria (*right*). Renee D. Turner, "Rape: the Myths and Realities," *Ebony*, October 1988, 110. Courtesy of the National Museum on African American History and Culture.

the helm, CSASN devised its signature training regimen.[105] CSASN's training spanned forty hours but was subdivided into eight five-hour sessions. To avoid monopolizing the time and resources of the community agency personnel they trained, CSASN held one day of training per week. Each session was led by a different CSASN member who specialized in the subject area. Mary Scott Boria herself conducted the first session, which introduced trainees to definitions of sexual assault and deconstructed the cultural myths that blamed women (especially women of color) for being raped. The second session imparted intervention strategies for community workers, such as "crisis management" and "empathic listening and response." This session also provided guidelines for continuing the counseling relationship after the initial crisis period had passed.[106] The third session covered the procedures and infrastructure established to process rape accusations within the medical and criminal justice systems as well as the difficulties rape survivors faced within these systems. The fourth and fifth sessions were designated for "special issues," an umbrella term encompassing the problems of rape survivors who were not *deserving victims*. These sessions discussed "heterosexism, racism, and sexism" and "Black, Mexican, and Puerto Rican cultural issues" in the provision of services to rape survivors.[107] Incest, domestic violence, child sex abuse, and drug addiction also fell under "special issues." The final three sessions consisted of workshops in which trainees practiced their newly acquired counseling skills, punctuated by a final evaluation.

CSASN's members directed six training sessions per calendar year, often in the Loop YWCA on Wabash Avenue, since their Mt. Sinai Hospital office could not accommodate large training groups. CSASN initially approached forty community agencies, hospitals, and health centers based in the South and West Sides and asked them to release their personnel for intensive training as rape counselors. Of these forty organizations, twenty-five attended CSASN's inaugural training session on October 15, 1984. Institutions that served the West Side, such as the Mile Square Health Center, Bobby E. Wright Community Mental Health Center, Mount Sinai Hospital, and Cook County Hospital, sent representatives to the first CSASN training session. South Side institutions such as the Englewood Health Center, the Hospital of Englewood, and Chicago Osteopathic Medical Center were also represented.[108] The Illinois Department of Human Services and Department of Children and Family Services sent their Chicago-based caseworkers. Even North Side institutions that served comparatively few non-white women like the Edgewater-Uptown Community Mental Health Center and the Loop YWCA saw the benefit of CSASN training in making their services more relevant to racial minorities.

Attending organizations responded enthusiastically to CSASN's mission. Kennise Herring of the Edgewater-Uptown Community Mental Health Center noted that "there are few mental health services geared to the needs of rape victims in this ethnically diverse city—and existing services for rape victims may not take into account the minority victim's special needs."[109] She knew that "minorities tend to rely upon family members or respected members of their communities in times of trouble." But women who had been sexually assaulted "often cannot rely upon the people they would otherwise turn to in times of trouble" if those communities remain mired in sexist rape myths.[110] Herring believed that no-cost community-based care was the key to reaching survivors of color and was elated by the emergence of CSASN. She urged the personnel of the Edgewater-Uptown Community Mental Health Center to undergo training. Edgewater-Uptown Community Mental Health Center even offered to pay the training fees for professionals unaffiliated with the center who provided social services, mental health services, or spiritual guidance to communities of color.

On the South and West Sides of Chicago, interest in rape counselor training remained high among community agencies into 1985. Mary Scott Boria replicated CSASN's success during the second training session, which ran from January 23 to March 20, 1985. The session attracted twenty-two participants from thirteen community agencies, including the Hospital of Englewood, Southwestern Women Working Together, and Chicago's Department of Mental Health.[111] Among those twenty-two participants, Boria recorded eleven African Americans. With the second training session underway, Boria could confidently report that CSASN was effectively reaching its targeted cohort of Black community workers and measurably augmenting the counseling services available to non-white women on the South and West Sides of the city. In 1985, CSASN's apparent success emboldened Boria and her colleagues to request an even larger Community Development Block Grant from the Department of Human Services, one that would allow CSASN to better serve the city's public housing by placing part-time community advocates within the Chicago Housing Authority. Steep budget cuts precluded CSASN from diverting their care work into the new venue of public housing. Still, CSASN was well-regarded by Black community workers and organizers and remained a fixture in Chicago's social service landscape. Cook County State's Attorney Richard M. Daley recognized Mary Scott Boria alongside twenty-five other community organizers for "improving conditions for women in society," lauding CSASN for "developing support services for rape victims, particularly in Black and Hispanic neighborhoods."[112]

The fact that CSASN diverted Black women's care work on behalf of victims into the existing social service system prompted some criticism.[113] Some veterans of the feminist movement against sexual violence argued that "the emphasis on services conflicts with a strategy of organizing a movement to end violence against women" because it relegated anti-rape organizations to palliative rather than revolutionary forces.[114] Like generations of Black women care workers before them, the women of CSASN did not view service provision and political engagement as mutually exclusive.[115] As Mary Scott Boria asserted, CSASN's social service orientation was not a shortcoming but a strength that enabled them to reach broad swaths of poor Black survivors of sexual assault.[116] CSASN "started with the assumption that most of the community service agencies already were seeing rape victims" and designed their advocacy to support these agencies rather than supplant them. With feminist rape crisis centers geographically isolated from Black victims and biased toward police reporting by their law enforcement-adjacent funders, it made sense to divert Black-focused anti-rape advocacy in the embattled but expansive social service networks of the city. As Sylvia Rush neatly surmised, CSASN's philosophy was that "there's people out here suffering . . . This is what's needed. Let's just do it."[117] In this way, CSASN's diversion of anti-rape activism into Chicago's social service sector mirrored the D.C. Rape Crisis Center's child sexual abuse prevention education in public schools. These spaces were already populated by Black victims and more amenable to Black-centered advocacy than a feminist movement against sexual violence that was beholden to an ever-tighter carceral funding base from the state.

CSASN's particular brand of anti-rape advocacy embodied the ethic of community care upheld by African American women professionals and volunteers throughout the twentieth century that seldom separated the provision of services from reckoning with injustice and inequality.[118] The Black women who formed the network infused their caring labor with a vocal political critique of the systemic racism and cultural misogyny that fostered violence against Black women.[119] Moreover, attending to the physical, mental, and emotional health of poor Black women within their own communities was an inherently radical political act amidst the ruthless welfare state retrenchment of the 1980s. During the first years of the Reagan Administration, many Black women in Chicago experienced the simultaneous violences of sexual assault and slashed welfare benefits. Physical violation within their own communities compounded their struggle to scrape resources from an ever-shrinking welfare state. By expanding the services offered by the decimated social welfare institutions of Chicago to include rape counseling, CSASN addressed the most pressing bodily needs of poor Black women who found themselves newly demonized and dispossessed under Reagan's neoconservative order. Attending to the needs of those victims labelled undeserving of state support by the Omnibus Budget Reconciliation Act of 1981 and the Victims of Crime Act of 1984 imbued CSASN's care work with a radical thrust.

Both Phyllis Pennese and Beryl Fitzpatrick believed the counseling services they created through CSASN were radical ventures because they targeted poor Black women. In turn, the work itself actively sustained and encouraged their own political development. Pennese found that her time with CSASN reinforced her budding womanism.[120] Coordinating community-based counseling confirmed for her that the sexual violence Black women incurred was inseparable from their experience of racial and class oppression. "We didn't have the luxury of not looking at the parallels and intersections of our feminism and the other issues in our communities," she explained.[121] Pennese realized that community-based counseling was a necessary addendum to a thoroughly racist criminal justice system that routinely dismissed Black women's complaints of violence and a profit-driven healthcare system that ignored poor women's traumas. Beryl Fitzpatrick agreed that CSASN's care work on behalf of poor Black rape victims necessitated a radical political understanding of patriarchy, systemic racism, and class oppression. According to Fitzpatrick, CSASN encouraged her to marry her Black feminist background in the National Alliance of Black Feminists and her social work training from Roosevelt University.[122] She always strived "to be the activist and be the political thinker and bring that into social work." She instructed the social service professionals that she trained to counsel rape victims through CSASN to "look at the total woman who comes into the health center," acknowledge the interlocking oppressions that forced her to seek the assistance of community health centers, and respond appropriately.

Not all members of CSASN agreed that the network was as radical as it could or should have been. Mary Scott Boria admitted that CSASN's financial dependence on the Illinois Department of Human Services, though not as constrictive as carceral funders like the LEAA and VOCA, "limits your ability to be as radical as maybe you wanted to be."[123] According to the terms of their Community Development Block Grant, CSASN was forbidden from engaging in any institutional advocacy or direct-action protest. These tactics had been mainstays of the feminist movement against sexual violence since the early 1970s. This indicates one shortcoming of the tactic of diversion overall: non-carceral funding sources outside of the feminist movement against sexual violence were relatively more pliant, but not totally open-ended. Still, Boria did not see the stipulations as completely compromising CSASN's ability to perform radical care work. In 1988, Mary Scott Boria resigned from the directorship of the Chicago Sexual Assault Services Network. She left to take the position of Director of Women's Services at the

Loop YWCA, where she could expect higher pay and a more generous funding stream for instituting services for rape victims.[124] Sylvia Rush departed from CSASN shortly after Mary Scott Boria's resignation, citing disillusionment with the network's direction. Rush felt that CSASN's client relationship to the Department of Human Services entailed "a bunch of bullshit" that detracted from the network's mission.[125] Marching through the streets of Downtown Chicago felt more efficacious than currying political favor with state's attorney Richard M. Daley and quibbling over the wording of grant applications. Rush felt that CSASN could not honestly consider themselves radical because "there was just more effort going into bureaucracy" than serving victims. In 1988, Phyllis Pennese and Beryl Fitzpatrick replaced Mary Scott Boria and Sylvia Rush as executive director and assistant director, respectively.

Between 1988 and 1990, CSASN showcased its politics by taking to a national platform with a uniformly Black readership to debunk rape myths that flourished within the Black community. CSASN members were featured twice in *Ebony* magazine: Sylvia Rush appeared alongside Mary Scott Boria in the October 1988 issue and Phyllis Pennese sat for an interview two years later in December 1990. Their commentary underscored their understanding of rape in the Black community as a political act that must be answered by service provision and social change simultaneously. In substance, their comments directly echoed the commentary issued by organized Black feminists in *Essence* fifteen years prior. Sylvia Rush utilized *Ebony*'s platform to tout the emotional benefits of the community-based rape counseling CSASN established in Chicago's poor Black neighborhoods. "Rape is on the rise and Black women disproportionately are its target," she explained, but "the family support network in place for other crises is missing when there is a rape."[126] Rush emphasized that talking to trained counselors provided badly needed catharsis and clarity for Black women survivors. In the same breath, she debunked the rape myths that persisted within the Black community that prevented a complete understanding of the issue. Revitalizing the Black feminist indictment of intraracial Black-on-Black rape, Rush reminded readers that "many women are raped by men they know" and "the idea that all rapists are strangers is but one myth that permeates our thinking about rape."[127]

In 1990, Phyllis Pennese affirmed Sylvia Rush's earlier statement that the Black community was "still very much rooted in the myths around sexual assault."[128] She spoke specifically on the prevalence of date rape in the

Black community, lamenting how "our community still buys into the notion that 'She went with him or she had on a tight leather miniskirt, so she must have wanted it' . . . We have to recognize that no one incites sexual assault because rape is not about sex. It's about degradation, humiliation, violence, and control."[129] Like the original Black feminists of the early 1970s, Pennese confronted the Black community about the reality of intraracial rape. She insisted that only a sweeping cultural change would dislodge stubborn rape myths. "A man takes what he has grown up with as cues," she explained.[130] "When all the while she is saying no, he's been told that means yes."

Letters to the editor of *Ebony* in response to the coverage of CSASN reveal that the male and female readership internalized the network's political message. Donald Bankston of San Jose, California, commended the October 1988 article entitled "Rape: Myths and Realities" for addressing a "long overdue" topic.[131] Bankston was "very sad to hear that a lot of our sisters are being raped by sick brothers" and recognized Black men's responsibility for affecting positive change. "There should be something we all can do to stop this," he reasoned. Vivian Billups of San Bernardino, California, applauded the January 1991 article and its "efforts to educate your readers about a subject that is often disregarded or denied."[132] She affirmed Donald Bankston's point that "Men and women must realize that victimization of women is not another 'female problem.'"

In the early 1990s, financial support for the Chicago Sexual Assault Services Network waned considerably. The Community Development Block Grants offered by the Illinois Department of Human Services shrank each year, forcing CSASN to appeal to local charities and foundations to patch together revenue. Indeed, CSASN may have been a victim of its own success. After nearly a decade, most of Chicago's operational community health centers, hospitals, and social welfare agencies had already submitted their personnel for CSASN training. As demand for training declined, CSASN's inability to fundraise stunted the network's growth. By November 1992, Pennese had "virtually given up" attempting to secure funds to expand CSASN's resources, such as a twenty-four-hour rape hotline at CSASN's Mount Sinai central office.[133] Personal burnout among the leadership compounded CSASN's financial hardship and the network dissolved into the larger Illinois Coalition Against Sexual Assault. The network conducted their last signature training program in 1993.

* * *

In the 1980s, the Victims of Crime Act resumed the state's interest in supporting feminist anti-rape activity following the shutdown of the Law Enforcement Assistance Administration and the National Center for the Prevention and Control of Rape. The structure of this support, though markedly different from the large block grants offered by the LEAA and the NCPCR, still advanced the merger of the war on rape and the federal "war on crime." Heavily focused on individual victim compensation for victims of violent crime, VOCA offered smaller, inflexible grants to feminist rape crisis centers for the sole purpose of facilitating individual claims. Under this modality of funding, cash-strapped feminist rape crisis centers saw their priorities further reduced to victim assistance. Through its qualification criteria, VOCA privileged a class of implicitly white middle class *deserving victims* as the exclusive beneficiaries of financial support from the state. The fledgling National Coalition Against Sexual Violence (NCASA) lobbied aggressively for the passage and renewal of VOCA each year, fusing the feminist rape crisis centers it represented to the same exclusionary framework.

At the same time, NCASA's Women of Color Caucus and Institute continued to foster mistrust in criminal justice approaches to anti-rape advocacy and direct the movement's attention toward the *undeserving victims* whose cases were not immediately useful to the state's crime control agenda. The Black women leaders of the Chicago Sexual Assault Services Network, many of whom were active members of NCASA's Women of Color Caucus, implemented this approach locally. Through CSASN, Black women anti-rape organizers provided community-based care for indigent Black women survivors on the South and West Sides of Chicago. This care helped to offset the welfare state dispossession faced by many Black women in Chicago during the 1980s and early 1990s.

At its founding in 1983, the Atlanta-based National Black Women's Health Project (NBWHP) practiced the same diversion tactic as CSASN. The NBWHP was comprised of Black women who were concerned about the gender violence other Black women faced, but they had no concrete connections to the feminist movement against sexual violence. Their novel framing of male violence as an issue of Black women's health that was systemic in origin led them to address the issue through their signature "self-help" sessions within Black community spaces. The funding they secured from private foundations accommodated the diversion tactic. It also suited an increasingly neoliberal government's preference that private charities foot the bill for solving problems of social inequality. The Violence Against Women Act (VAWA) of 1994 would revive the older practice of heavy federal investment in feminist anti-rape activity. Couched within the Violent Crime Control and Law Enforcement Act, VAWA foregrounded carceral responses to sexual violence by tethering operational grants for rape crisis centers to enormous surges in prison construction and police hiring. The NBWHP responded to these developments by trading diversion for open resistance, battling the punitive legislation before them.

CHAPTER 6

Self-Healers Resist

In 1981, Byllye Avery was a board member of the National Women's Health Network. A Florida-based reproductive healthcare worker by trade, Avery was struggling to research a report about Black women's health issues. She was shocked to discover the paucity of reliable data about Black women's health, finding only superficial statistics about Black women's susceptibility to psychological disorders.[1] Two years later, she and a handful of Black women colleagues convened the First National Conference on Black Women's Health Issues. Over two thousand African American women descended on Spelman College, seeking both information and a space to voice their anxieties about their vulnerability to premature death.[2] The sessions offered during the 1983 conference encompassed the typical medical concerns faced by African American women, such as hypertension, diabetes, and breast cancer. The program also featured two panels on gender violence. The first discussed Black women's experiences within rape crisis centers and battered women's shelters; the second imparted intervention strategies for child sexual abuse and incest.[3] While these offerings appeared to deviate from the conference theme, Avery later asserted that any comprehensive examination of Black women's health issues required a discussion of violence. "What causes all this sickness?" she asked. "Like cardiovascular disease—it's the number one killer [of Black women]. What causes all that heart pain?"[4] As Avery understood it, Black women's physical maladies stemmed from the male violence that kept them in a lifelong state of emotional distress.[5] "When sisters take their shoes off and start talking about what's happening, the first thing we cry about is violence," she explained. "The number one issue for most of our sisters is violence—battering, sexual abuse. Same thing for their daughters, whether they are twelve or four."[6]

The enormous success of the 1983 conference led Avery to incorporate the National Black Women's Health Project (NBWHP) as an autonomous organization headquartered in Atlanta, Georgia, in 1984. By the time Byllye Avery was awarded a "Genius Grant" from the MacArthur Foundation in 1989, the National Black Women's Health Project spanned over 150 chapters in 22 states.[7] The "self-help" method developed by the original conference attendees in 1983 became a mainstay of the movement. Rooted in a tradition of care-oriented community uplift pioneered by Black women in the late nineteenth century, the "self-help" practiced by the project saw groups of Black women gathering to address the intractable community problems that white institutions elected to ignore.[8] The NBWHP's iteration of "self-help" featured cathartic discussions of the traumatic source of their poor health. But it was designed to guide participants toward understanding their poor health as the product of systemic forces—namely institutionalized racism, unchecked sexism, and grinding poverty. The "self-help" method proved a deft tool for "breaking the conspiracy of silence" that continued to shroud intraracial sexual violence despite the protests of Black feminists.[9] Panels addressing rape, battering, and sexual abuse appeared every year in the NBWHP's annual conference program.[10] Local chapters folded gender violence into their organizational agendas well into the late 1990s.[11] By doing so, the NBWHP expanded twentieth century Black health activism to explicitly tackle gender-based violence and "introduced violence as a public health issue."[12]

This novel combination of Black feminism and Black health activism was sorely needed at the tail end of the century. By approaching gender violence as a Black women's health issue, the project avoided the state's preferred framing of gender violence as a crime issue to be solved by apprehending and punishing offenders. Through the LEAA, the NCPCR, the NCCAN, and VOCA, the federal government had spent two decades honing its crime control response to rape. The availability of federal funds for the feminist movement against sexual violence ebbed with the decline of the administrative state model of the "war on crime" and rise of individualistic fiscal conservatism in the 1980s. Irrespective of the repackaging, these funds pressured feminist anti-rape activists and organizations to treat police reporting and prosecution as the lynchpin of their advocacy. Funds flowed freely once again with the Violence Against Women Act (VAWA) of 1994, the single largest federal investment in the feminist movement against sexual violence. As a component of the $30 billion Violent Crime Control and Law Enforcement Act of 1994, VAWA allocated $1.6 billion over six years toward maintaining services for rape and domestic violence survivors.[13] However, the vast majority of VAWA funds were earmarked for projects that defined "services" as promoting the prosecution of gender violence.[14] In its first year, VAWA slated $300 million in funding for "boosting law enforcement and creating more secure public environments."[15] VAWA funding itself was dwarfed by the Violent Crime Control and Law Enforcement Act's $10 billion federal investment in prison construction and police officer hiring.[16] With the benefit of hindsight, scholar Victoria Law points to VAWA as the zenith of carceral feminism, which "sees increased policing, prosecution, and imprisonment as the primary solution to violence against women" and ignores the systemic roots of gender violence.[17]

Avery, her associates, and her successors framed violence against women as a Black women's health issue that derived from intersecting forms of systemic inequality and was treatable in the short and long term through self-help. Their cognizance of the systemic racism and welfare state retrenchment that exacerbated violence against Black women compelled them to reject the carceral logic that had become commonplace throughout much of the feminist movement against sexual violence by the 1990s. Employing the diversion tactic first honed by Black anti-rape organizers in the early 1980s, they housed their anti-rape activity in an entirely separate movement. In the same way that the D.C. Rape Crisis Center and the Chicago Sexual Assault Services Network made use of state and municipal human services grants to sidestep crime control agencies, the National Black Women's Health Project sustained itself through private charitable funding streams that did not readily dictate cooperation with the criminal justice system. The project distinguished itself from DCRCC and CSASN by engaging another tactic that had all but disappeared from the mainstream feminist movement against sexual violence: open resistance to carceral legislation. While their contemporaries in the feminist movement against sexual violence cheered VAWA, the project publicly denounced it as an inadequate solution for poor Black women.

Self-Help and Anti-Violence

Three years prior to the First National Conference on Black Women's Health Issues, Loretta Ross facilitated the First National Conference on Third World Women and Violence in her role as executive director of the Washington, D.C. Rape Crisis Center. She carried the Black feminist analysis of rape she had developed in Washington, D.C. to Atlanta for the First National Conference on Black Women's Health Issues. Ross resigned from her post at the D.C.

Rape Crisis Center in 1982, citing conflicts with white feminist colleagues who had grown increasingly resistant to Ross's capacious definition of violence against women that included state violence.[18] After a brief stint as a coordinator for the National Organization for Women, Ross identified the Black women's health movement as a venue where a Black anti-rape organizers' care work could still flourish. For Ross, violence against women was a literal matter of life or death for Black women when "being raped and beaten and murdered by the men in our lives, not strangers, kills us more than cancer, childbirth, hypertension, car accidents, and heart attacks combined."[19] Even if the assaults did not kill them directly, living in constant fear of these assaults bred stress-induced illness that ultimately would.[20] At Byllye Avery's urging, Ross accepted the position of NBWHP Project Director in 1989.[21]

Lillie Allen introduced the "self-help" method of interpersonal counseling during a workshop at the First National Conference on Black Women's Health Issues, inventing the vehicle through which the National Black Women's Health Project would launch its anti-violence organizing. After three hundred conferencegoers packed a Spelman College classroom designed to hold fifty, Allen repeated the wildly popular workshop each day of the conference to ensure that all who wished to attend it could.[22] In "self-help," a group of participants divulged to one another traumatic occurrences that, when undisclosed, kept them from living healthful, self-actualized lives. Describing self-help as the "backbone of the project," Avery noted that stories of gender violence frequently surfaced during these sessions. "They talk about being beaten. They talk about being passed around sexually as little girls. They talk about all of that, and how it feeds into a negative self-image, and how we carry that with us."[23] Loretta Ross attributed the popularity of "self-help" to its ability to transcend the strictly clinical concerns that preoccupied other health organizations and demonstrate the inseparability of physical, mental, and emotional health problems in Black women's lives. "We always knew about the Black women's health issues," Ross recalled, "the obesity and diabetes, the lupus, the sickle-cell disease . . . but those soul issues, nobody was talking about [them]." Sexual abuse and domestic violence fell squarely into the category of "soul issues."[24] Avery recalled that this attention to the nexus of psychological wellbeing and intractable violence separated the Black women's health movement from the white-led women's health movements, which often focused on reproductive health issues.[25] She praised self-help as "a wonderful way to learn about our health issues, to learn about how much violence . . . we were living with—be it domestic violence, be it sexual violence."[26]

The practice of "self-help" within the National Black Women's Health Project made it a suitable candidate for diverting Black women's anti-rape advocacy in the 1980s. "Self-help" resembled the practice of consciousness-raising popularized by the earliest feminist anti-rape collectives in the late 1960s.[27] But the same infiltration of law enforcement rape control tactics that compelled Black anti-rape organizers to divert their advocacy in the first place had rendered such practices virtually extinct within feminist rape crisis centers. "Self-help" also stood in contrast to the individualistic bent of "victim assistance" that characterized many state-funded feminist rape crisis centers in the late 1980s. By design, "self-help" used its group context to deconstruct power relations structured by race, sex, and class. Allen distinguished "self-help" from professional modes of therapy by focusing on peer-to-peer counseling among a group of Black laywomen. This leveled the power disparity inherent in most counseling relationships, where credentialed middle-class white women unilaterally advised unfortunate Black women whose problems they did not share. More importantly, self-help simply but powerfully exposed to Black women the systemic roots of violence in their lives, galvanizing them to work for structural change. By practicing self-help "in the presence of other Black women," Avery explained, "we understand that we have an institution of sexism that's going on in our lives that tends to oppress us, and that the only way we can get out from under it is to learn how to unhook."[28] The practice of self-help triggered a necessary shift from focusing on the maladies afflicting Black women to the systems that inflicted them.[29] This transition was often easier said than done. Loretta Ross commented that participants in "self-help" sessions would occasionally "get stuck in how bad they felt" and fail to progress toward a political understanding of their pain.[30] Still, Ross agreed that self-help was "the glue that held the Project together [and] spurred people's interest."[31]

By the time that the National Black Women's Health Project formally coalesced in 1984, self-help had, in the words of Loretta Ross, "caught on like wildfire."[32] With the support of the national headquarters in Atlanta, local chapters from Los Angeles to Philadelphia had adopted the practice. For the next decade, rape, domestic violence, and sexual abuse occupied a crucial place in the agendas of the national leadership and local grassroots. At both levels, Black women spoke freely about the gender violence in their lives and connected that violence to interlocking systemic oppressions. The concept of "self-help" was not entirely novel for many African Americans. From the late nineteenth through the twentieth centuries, Black club women and national sororities used the phrase "self-help" to describe their practice of constructing alternative social welfare institutions, from kindergartens to settlement homes to health clinics, to ameliorate the social problems endemic to Black America that were caused by white discrimination.[33] Two key differences separated the self-help practiced by Black club women and members of the National Black Women's Health Project. First, the group-counseling tactic of the NBWHP eliminated the unequal class relations that frequently characterized the racial uplift projects of Black club women. Second, the NBWHP did not adhere to the respectability politics that forbade Black women from speaking openly about intimate matters. The influence of organized Black feminism of the 1970s underpinned their direct confrontation with intracommunity rape and abuse in the 1980s and 1990s.[34] The self-help method piloted by the NBWHP even sparked discussion of and mobilization against gender violence beyond the borders of the United States. At the behest of the W. K. Kellogg Foundation, Byllye Avery and her colleagues traveled to South Africa at the height of apartheid. They taught the self-help method to Black South African women they met in Johannesburg, who used it to broach the issues of domestic violence, sexual abuse, and HIV / AIDs, in that order.[35]

In keeping with Black feminist interventions, Byllye Avery directly linked Black women's vulnerability to gender violence to the broader sexual politics of Black America. She pointed out that high rates of unemployment and incarceration among Black men "often lead to permissible forms of sexual and child abuse and domestic violence" within Black communities.[36] As the 1985 "Fact Sheet on Black Women's Health" elaborated, chronic Black male unemployment and mass incarceration resulted from the systemic racism inherent in hiring patterns and policing practices during the 1980s.[37] This systemic racism was exacerbated under a capitalist neoliberal order that left the systemic obstacles isolating Black men from gainful employment intact and correlated men's self-worth to their economic viability.[38] Avery did not lay the blame for Black women's vulnerability to violence solely upon systemic racism and poverty. She took Black men to task for channeling their rage over inescapable systemic racism into abuse.[39] In a 1989 article for the feminist magazine *Sojourner*, she railed against the moral hypocrisy whereby Black girls are lectured to abstain from sex when self-help revealed that "most of these girls did not get pregnant by teenage boys; most of them got pregnant by their mother's boyfriends or their brothers or their daddies."[40] Avery called upon Black women and men to open a dialogue that directly interrogated Black men's sexual privilege: "We need to talk to our brothers. We need to tell them the incest makes us crazy . . . We need men to stop giving consent, by their silence, to rape, to sexual abuse, to violence. You need to talk to your boyfriends, your husbands, your sons, whatever males you have around you—talk to them about talking to other men."[41] These appeals to community dialogue were a frequent refrain of Black anti-rape organizers working to avoid partnerships with the criminal justice system, from the National Black Feminist Organization to Lynn Moncrief of Philadelphia WOAR to the dissenters from the NCPCR's "Special Populations" Conferences. Avery shared their understanding that incarceration did little to shield Black women from male violence and exacerbated the systemic inequalities that exposed them to violence in the first place. Reflecting on her stewardship of self-help groups, Avery recalled how the NBWHP "watched the lives of women whose men were in prison and how the men controlled the women's lives from prison."[42]

Local chapters of the National Black Women's Health Project coupled the practice of the self-help method with a searing indictment of the social dynamics that exposed Black women to gender violence. McDaniel Glenn Homes, a public housing project in the southwestern corner of Atlanta almost exclusively inhabited by Black women, formed its own self-help group in 1987.[43] Marie Rasheed, president of the McDaniel Glenn Tenants Association, stated that the self-help group afforded McDaniel Glenn's Black female tenants "the time and the space we need [for] making ourselves well in every respect—the mental, and the physical and the emotional."[44] The group immediately identified interpersonal violence as a community problem that was devastating their health. Cheryl Boykins, a staff project director for the National Black Women's Health Project, took notice of the McDaniel Glenn tenants. In 1988, she hired Marie Rasheed and her neighbors Mary Sanders and Annie Williams to jumpstart self-help group formation in Atlanta's other public housing projects through the Center for Black Women's Wellness.[45]

Funded through a grant by the W. K. Kellogg Foundation, the center served Black women and their families in Atlanta's public housing communities as "a one-stop opportunity to access health screening and assessment, continuing education and job training, career development, social services information and referral, [and] cultural and recreational activities."[46] The grant was consistent with the W. K. Kellogg Foundation's half-century-long record of promoting community health and welfare through grassroots participation. Being funded by a private foundation proved a boon for the Center for Black Women's Wellness and the National Black Women's Health Project generally. By the mid-1980s, many veteran anti-violence feminists had witnessed the corrosive effect that dependence upon state funding had on the movement's politics and agenda. Grants issued by state agencies to provide services almost always came with strings attached, most commonly a preference for professional social workers to provide victim services and the criminal justice system as the primary solution to the problems of marginalized people.[47] Although a private funding base allowed the NBWHP to avoid the crime control ethos that complicated advocacy within rape crisis centers, it also bound them to the "non-profit industrial complex" described by activist Suzanne Pharr. Under the "non-profit industrial complex," the efficiency-obsessed neoliberal state had abandoned the provision of social services (aside from policing and incarceration) and allowed these essential tasks to fall to nonprofits. Their reliance on foundation grants prevented them from becoming too radical in their words and actions lest they jeopardize their funding.[48] Funding through private philanthropy never guaranteed total freedom of prerogative. The example of the Ford Foundation and its efforts to dampen the Black Power drift of the civil rights movement by favoring liberal-integrationist leaning projects like CORE remains instructive.[49] However, this was not the experience of the Project. The W. K. Kellogg Foundation did not prevent them from assessing their histories of physical and emotional trauma politically and organizing against the structural causes of that trauma. It allowed them to successfully divert Black-centered anti-rape advocacy into Black community institutions.

With private Kellogg funds, the Center for Black Women's Wellness was able to hire McDaniel Glenn tenants and operate as a launchpad for anti-violence organization for Black women public housing tenants who participated in self-help groups. In early 1991, Marie Rasheed and her colleagues hosted a workshop on "Stopping Violence Through Self-Help Group Development" at the Center for Black Women's Wellness.[50] The workshop demonstrated in microcosm how the self-help method led to concrete action against domestic violence and sexual violence. It began as a typical self-help session, allowing the Black women in attendance to share their experiences with violence. Marian Grier shared that she had been trapped in a physically abusive marriage for nearly twenty years. She underscored the necessity of disclosing interpersonal violence in the self-help setting for her own mental health, concluding that "we do violence to ourselves if we do not see our own worth and dignity."[51] Quickly, other participants in the workshop such as D'borah James declared that "talking [is] not enough to remedy these problems." She rallied fellow workshop attendees to "community cohesiveness," combatting domestic violence by opening and maintaining dialogues between McDaniel Glenn tenants to resolve conflicts. The creation of the Center for Black Women's Wellness by the National Black Women's Health Project headquarters and the sustaining of that center by grassroots participants illustrate how the self-help method fostered decisive group action to end violence against Black women.

The tenants of the McDaniel Glenn public housing project equated the gender violence they experienced to the violent street crimes that garnered public attention in the 1980s. Occasionally, these women invoked the language of personal responsibility when they addressed rape and battering within their community. One anti-violence workshop attendee asked aloud, "If we don't take charge [of crime in our community], who will?"[52] Though reminiscent of the rhetoric of Ethel Payne's Coalition of Concerned Women in the War on Crime, the McDaniel Glenn tenants' appeals to internal community dialogues attended to the systemic roots of interpersonal violence and did not engage law enforcement entities. They effectively reversed the formulation of CCWWC. Ethel Payne and her followers flattened gender violence into a problem of crime control. The National Black Women's Health Project and its members took up gender violence—already configured as a problem of crime control by the mid-1980s—and reframed it as an issue of gender inequality. Put another way, groups like the CCWWC fixated on the "fast violence" afflicting Black women and girls and structured activism to address the spectacular instance of violation. By contrast, the NBWHP predicated their activism on what scholar Rob Nixon has termed "slow violence," or the gradual, cumulative harm that besets marginalized people living in toxic environments over the course of their lives and seldom garners much activist attention. In dedicating themselves to Black women's health issues, the NBWHP calibrated their anti-rape activism to the context of "slow violence." This led them to markedly different solutions than their feminist and non-feminist peers.[53]

The NBWHP's practice of self-help within the Center for Black Women's Wellness in Atlanta paralleled CSASN's focus on institutionalizing cost-free counseling within existing social welfare and community health agencies that served Black women. Both groups treated physical and mental wellness as Black victims' most pressing needs and turned to venues that were not rape crisis centers to ensure those needs were met. In both cases, the decision to divert Black-led anti-violence advocacy to alternative venues was a response to feminist rape crisis centers that were more concerned with controlling rape than caring for victims. The key difference was that CSASN's choice of alternative venues—community and social welfare agencies in Chicago—were still beholden to perpetually endangered state funding sources. NBWHP's alternative venue—the Black women's health movement—enjoyed funding from private foundations. While not free of political construction, these foundations did not invest in activist groups explicitly for crime control purposes.

Feminist rape crisis centers in Atlanta, like their counterparts in Chicago, had struggled to meaningfully integrate Black women within their advocacy and organizational structures in the past. In the fall of 1973, a group of concerned feminists founded the Metropolitan Atlanta Rape Crisis Council (MARCC). The following summer, these feminists established a rape crisis center at Atlanta's Grady Memorial Hospital where volunteers would offer counseling to the rape victims being treated there. Portia LaSonde, the founder of MARCC, was originally hired by Grady Memorial Hospital using funds from the Department of Family Planning to administer the project and train volunteers. Shortly thereafter, Grady Memorial Hospital "reassigned" LaSonde, assumed control of the rape crisis project, and recruited a new crop of white volunteers, none of whom had been active in MARCC.[54] The switch stemmed from the desire of Grady Memorial Hospital's administrative hierarchy to "professionalize" the Grady Rape Crisis Center. MARCC's membership saw this as a blatant "whitewashing of the Grady Rape Crisis Center" by hospital officials. By dismissing LaSonde, "a black woman [who] probably has more experience counseling rape victims than anyone in Atlanta," Grady Memorial Hospital was alienating Black volunteers and depriving Black rape victims of effective services. As one white volunteer named Krista wondered, "How can we pretend to meet the needs of Atlanta rape victims without having black counselors; over 50 percent of the rape victims who come to Grady are black?"[55] In addition to its uniformly white staff, the Grady Rape Crisis Center was an uninviting space for Atlanta's Black rape victims due to its lockstep adherence to police procedure. Georgia state law mandated that hospitals file a police report for every rape victim that they treated. This meant that Black rape victims who sought care at the Grady Rape Crisis Center would automatically find themselves at the center of a police investigation regardless of their wishes.[56] Whereas the Grady Rape Crisis Center, a formal node of the feminist movement against sexual violence, was practically devoid of Black staff and fused to law enforcement, the Center for Black Women's Wellness provided an alternative venue for anti-violence action where poor Black women could care for other poor Black women and themselves.

The Policy Turn of the National Black Women's Health Project

After winning a MacArthur Fellowship in 1989, Byllye Avery decided that she needed to relinquish some control over the growing National Black Women's Health Project. Years of simmering tension between Avery and Lillie Allen over the significance of the "self-help" method further convinced her to step back. She resigned as executive director but remained closely involved with the NBWHP, adopting the title "founding president." Interim Director Julia Scott initiated layoffs (including Loretta Ross) to rein in spending, drastically altering the composition and character of the NBWHP. In the summer of 1991, Cynthia Newbille took over as executive director at the Atlanta headquarters and Julia Scott assumed control of the Public Policy and Education Program (PPEP) in the Project's Washington, D.C. office.[57] As the focus of the National Black Women's Health Project migrated toward public policy in the 1990s, its leadership and grassroots continued to frame violence against Black women primarily as a health issue that manifested as both physical injury and mental anguish.

Raised in a public housing project, Newbille was an avid supporter of the Center for Black Women's Wellness. According to the October 1991 edition of the *Vital Signs* newsletter, "Cynthia believes that the poor must realize that their situation is borne [sic] of the socio-political and economic realities of American society and not inferior character."[58] This conviction about the political nature of Black women's health problems led her to set an anti-violence agenda for the NBWHP that pushed beyond grassroots self-help and community organizing and toward policy input. The National Black Women's Health Project would relocate its headquarters from Atlanta to the District of Columbia in 1996.[59] Some lamented this development as a stultifying sell-out, whereby the Project abandoned grassroots micromobilization for the comforts of institutionalization.[60] Others saw policymaking as another weapon in the group's arsenal, alongside self-help, to care for Black victims by attacking the systemic origins of their vulnerability to violence.[61]

Despite mixed feelings about this change in direction, Newbille retained Avery's original emphasis on gender violence as a dire threat to Black women's health. Speaking at an August 1991 rally hosted by the National Organization for Women in Atlanta, Newbille recited grim statistics: three to four million women were beaten by their partners every day and domestic violence resulted in more injuries to women annually than rape, car accidents, and muggings combined.[62] She confirmed that the project was still categorizing rape and battering as health issues, declaring that "domestic violence is one of the major health threats to women in this country." Newbille also made clear that this violence was rooted in sexism, racism, and poverty. According to Newbille, gender violence happened because "society teaches men to control their women, to dominate and to be in charge" and "for African American women, this situation is further exacerbated due to institutional racism, rendering them powerless to have appropriate redress through the criminal justice system."[63] Newbille encouraged all Black women living with violence to "seek assistance from women's organizations, such as the National Black Women's Health Project" and instructed the remainder of her audience to "begin a dialogue" with women who were being abused and "support them in pursuing alternatives."[64] She also called for specific steps that challenged the racism, sexism, and poverty that enabled gender violence. She insisted that "men must begin to seek assistance in learning new models of conflict resolution and interpersonal relationships." Newbille also addressed poverty by calling for an expansion of Head Start funding, a social service that would extend high-quality childcare and nutritional assistance to poor women, better equipping them to flee the clutches of an abuser.

The 1992 annual meeting of the National Black Women's Health Project held in Los Angeles affirmed that the health threat posed by gender violence remained a target of the movement. Panels and workshops titled "Loving Without Violence" and "Violence Against Women and the Ongoing Challenge to Racism" peppered the conference program. Anita Hill, fresh off her testimony before Congress accusing then–Supreme Court nominee Clarence Thomas of sexual harassment, delivered the keynote address. Avery personally invited Hill, since "we know the issue that Black women want to hear and talk about is that of sexual harassment and abuse they have received in their lives."[65] She credited Hill with jumpstarting the self-help process for Black women victims across the nation, noting that "since the hearings, I have been astonished at the number of women who have broken the 'conspiracy of silence' and talked about their victimization." In her speech, Hill affirmed "speaking truth to power" as a pathway to healing from the trauma of sexual violence, an obvious parallel to the grassroots practice of self-help.[66]

The centerpiece of the 1992 meeting was an issue panel dedicated to "Black Women's Health: The Impact of Violence / The Challenges of Healing," featuring Black feminist luminaries Kimberlé Crenshaw and Angela Y. Davis. As they spoke, Crenshaw and Davis noticeably distanced the project's health-issue approach to violence against Black women from the crime-issue framing that flourished in the mainstream anti-violence-against-women movement. Crenshaw saw the project as perfectly illustrating her signature theory of intersectionality by attending to the collision of multiple simultaneous vectors of oppression, or, in her words, "bring[ing] together that double vision of Black and woman."[67] She praised the National Black Women's Health Project for providing a space "to speak to these issues and to heal ourselves . . . so that we can look squarely at the problem of violence without the fear of misrepresentation, reprisal, or exclusion." This space stood in contrast to the feminist movement against gender violence because it was created and controlled by Black women who acknowledged that gender violence flowed from sexism and racism simultaneously. Crenshaw remarked upon the double valence of the NBWHP's foundational self-help practice. It not only promoted individual healing from past traumas, but also served as a conduit for organizing the community to address sexual violence. To build a future where Black women are spared gender violence and the practice of self-help is obsolete, "it's important that we engage in a process within our community to examine where this misogyny comes from."[68] Black feminist anti-rape organizers had consistently prescribed this practice of care as a community-sustaining alternative to criminalization since the 1970s.

While Kimberlé Crenshaw heralded the capacity of self-help to inspire community organizing against sexual violence, Angela Davis issued a stern warning against framing gender violence narrowly in terms of crime. She argued that Black women could not rely on the criminal justice system to shield them from violence, since the state was so often a perpetrator of violence toward them. This was essentially the same argument Davis had made in criticism of the feminist movement against sexual violence at Sonoma State College in 1977. But she marshalled contemporary evidence to support her point. Davis reminded her audience that barely two months prior, the city that hosted their annual meeting had exploded into a devastating week-long rebellion ignited by unchecked police brutality toward South Central

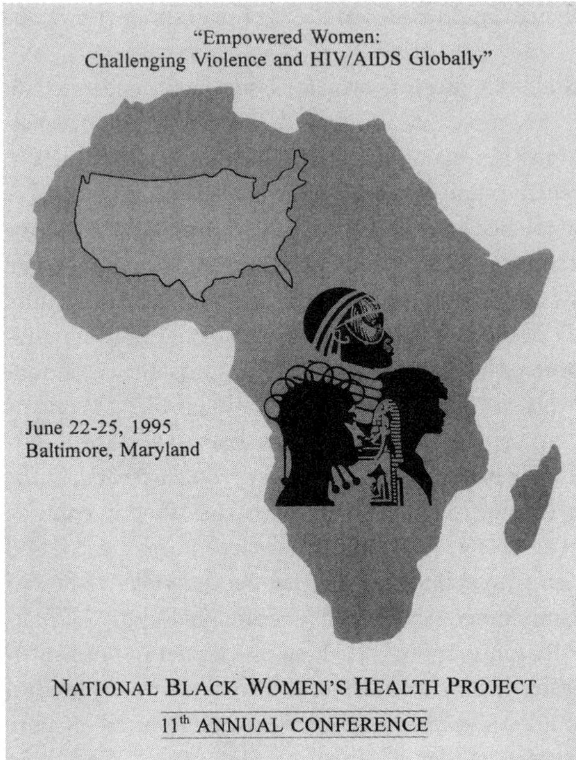

Figure 6. Program of the 11th Annual Meeting of the National Black Women's Health Project in Baltimore, Maryland (June 22–25, 1995): "Empowered Women: Challenging Violence and HIV / AIDS Globally." Courtesy of Smith College Special Collections.

residents. Though Rodney King was a Black man, Black women undoubtedly shared his experience of ruthless police aggression.[69] Davis implored conferencegoers to "look at the ways in which what is normally constructed as domestic violence takes place within the context of the state as well . . . What about the police who commit sexual violence, molest, harass, assault, rape the women that they arrest? . . . I would like us to think about the connection between those realms and the fact that you cannot separate the one from the other."[70] Through her comments, Davis demonstrated that entrusting law enforcement to end violence against Black women was incompatible with the philosophy of the National Black Women's Health Project. The NBWHP framed rape and battering as problems of physical and mental health and prescribed self-help counseling because it promoted the healing of survivors, exposed the systemic roots of gender violence, and empowered survivors to collectively challenge these systems. The criminal justice system, by contrast, did nothing to ease Black women's pain and perpetuated the systemic inequality that put them in harm's way. Davis's speech proved highly prescient as the NBWHP waded into the waters of public policy and the temptation to align their organization with the carceral state was stronger than ever.

The Violence Against Women Act of 1994

The National Black Women's Health Project's gravitation toward public policy in the early 1990s mirrored the state's renewed interest in generously subsidizing feminist anti-rape activity. In 1990, then-senator Joseph Biden of Delaware introduced the Violence Against Women Act as the first major piece of federal legislation that specifically targeted rape and domestic violence. VAWA languished in the Senate for four years until it was passed as Title IV of the Violent Crime Control and Law Enforcement Act thanks to the relentless lobbying of the National Coalition Against Sexual Assault.[71] The Violent Crime Control and Law Enforcement Act of 1994, commonly referred to as the "Clinton Crime Bill," was designed to dispel the Democratic Party's reputation as weak on the issue of crime and coax moderate voters back into the Democratic fold. In addition to funding enormous surges in prison construction and police hiring, the Clinton Crime Bill instituted a "three-strikes-and-you're-out" law mandating life imprisonment for recidivist federal offenders; sanctioned the death penalty for dozens of new offenses; established increased sentences and new mandatory minimums for a wide array of crimes; and created a national sex offender registry.[72] By the time Clinton vacated the White House in 2001, the American prison population had doubled and national spending on incarceration had ballooned to \$351 billion from \$10 billion in 1990.[73] The inclusion of the Violence Against Women Act within the Violent Crime Control and Law Enforcement Act was key for securing the support of liberal politicians who were skeptical of mass incarceration as a social policy.[74] This included twenty-six of the thirty-eight members of the Congressional Black Caucus, who voted for the Clinton Crime Bill despite their misgivings over law and order in part because of their approval of the Violence Against Women Act.[75]

VAWA contained several commendable provisions worthy of feminist praise. The act financially maintained shelters, hotlines, counseling, and educational prevention programs that were originally launched by the feminist anti-violence movement during the 1970s. VAWA also provided an avenue for undocumented women to apply for legal resident status in order to escape their abusers, extended federal protections and services to Native American women who were assaulted on tribal lands, and automatically required convicted abusers to pay restitution to their victims.[76] In 1994, many feminist organizations celebrated VAWA as a permanent state commitment to addressing gender violence. NOW Legal Defense Fund applauded the provisions of VAWA that categorized rape and battering as discriminatory "crime[s] motivated by gender," opening the door for survivors to sue their assailants under federal civil rights law.[77] This provision was struck down by the Supreme Court in 2000, but the remainder of VAWA stands pending congressional reauthorization every five years. Feminist organizations have invariably rallied for each reauthorization and pushed for expansions of the law's provisions.[78] Feminist historian Maria Bevacqua describes VAWA as "perhaps the most significant accomplishment of the anti-rape movement."[79]

But the crime control mentality that inspired the larger Violent Crime Control and Law Enforcement Act stained the Violence Against Women Act. Every element of VAWA emphasized policing, prosecution, and punishment as the ideal remedies to rape and battering. VAWA established the Office on Violence Against Women within the Department of Justice, described by INCITE! as "the federal arm of the prison-industrial complex," to channel funds to service providers.[80] This action ensured that collaboration with law enforcement would be an important criterion for feminist anti-rape groups hoping to receive federal funds. INCITE! noted that after 1994, "many antiviolence organizations are now located within police departments."[81] "Community coordination," VAWA's predominant funding model, was premised on strengthening ties between service providers and law enforcement entities. The Office on Violence Against Women evaluated the success of anti-violence organizations funded under the "community coordination" model explicitly in terms of increased rates of prosecution and conviction.[82] VAWA also monetarily incentivized police and prosecutors to take on gender violence as a serious crime and supplied new tools for punishing offenders, including increased sentences for repeat offenders and mandatory arrest policies when responding to domestic violence complaints.[83]

Scholars and activists have retrospectively criticized the legislation for ignoring the dynamics of patriarchy, racism, and poverty that enable gender violence, and especially for its uncritical partnership with the criminal justice system that endangered women of color.[84] Like the Victims of Crime Act of 1984, the automatic restitution awarded to survivors required successful prosecution of their assailants and therefore sustained engagement with the criminal justice system.[85] Mandatory arrest policies posed an even greater threat to Black victims. INCITE! member Ana Clarissa Rojas Durazzo confirms that responding police officers steeped in racist stereotypes about Black women's immorality and incorrigibility frequently arrested them alongside or in lieu of their abusers "if she so much as scratched her abuser in self-defense."[86] Scholar Nancy Whittier concludes that a diverse coalition of activists brought forth the Violence Against Women Act, but their arguments ultimately did not "fit into the gendered crime frame that facilitated conservative support for VAWA," resulting in a law containing "mixed . . . carceral, non-carceral, and intersectional elements."[87]

Operating at a remove from the feminist movement against sexual violence, the National Black Women's Health Project was well-positioned to critique and ultimately reject the Violence Against Women Act as it emerged. Byllye Avery, Cynthia Newbille, and all of their associates approached violence against women as a health issue that derived from structural inequality and demanded grassroots solutions that interrogated said structural inequality. VAWA apprehended rape and battering primarily in carceral terms: as violent crimes to be solved through punishment. Phrased as a medical analogy, the National Black Women's Health Project maintained that VAWA hastily treated the symptoms of rape and battering without curing the underlying diseases that caused them: the sexism that encouraged men of all races to abuse women of all races, the racism that precluded legal protection for Black survivors, and the classism that denied poor women the means to escape abusive situations. As they formulated the project's stance on VAWA, they remained committed to a systemic understanding of violence against Black women. Consequently, they rejected an invigorated criminal justice system as an appropriate or proportionate response to rape and battering.

The National Black Women's Health Project's earliest engagement with the Violence Against Women Act began in 1991, when the Women's International League for Peace and Freedom dispatched a letter to Byllye Avery seeking her support for the proposed legislation. The letter exposed the carceral grounding of VAWA, assuring Avery that "if made into law, this act would provide a great deal of services for women all across the country . . . It would also provide safer streets for women through an expansion of police and security forces."[88] WILPF acknowledged that "many African American women do not report their assaults due to poor relations with the police," suggesting that lower rates of reporting may result in Black communities being "robbed of the opportunity to receive monies that will increase their safety," since allocations would be determined by official crime rates recorded by the Federal Bureau of Investigation.[89] It is unclear how Byllye Avery and her associates responded to the WILPF, if at all. But from that letter, there was no mistaking the intentions of the proposed Violence Against Women Act to control rape without caring for its most marginalized victims.

On August 21, 1994, the Representatives of the 103rd Congress approved the Violent Crime Control and Law Enforcement Act that contained the Violence Against Women Act by an impressive margin (235 to 195). Four days later, the Senate followed suit and approved the measure (61 to 38). In keeping with its newfound interest in public policy, the National Black Women's Health Project meticulously reported on every piece of relevant legislation passed by Congress to its membership. Each issue of *Hill Briefs* summarized the content of the bills and stated the NBWHP's official position. For the Violent Crime Control and Law Enforcement Act of 1994, Julia Scott and her team determined that "a no vote was in support of the NBWHP position."[90] The stated rationale for their opposition was the death penalty provisions embedded in the larger bill.[91] In June 1995, the National Black Women's Health Project enumerated their complaints with the Violence Against Women Act on its own terms.[92] Before launching into their critique, they recognized the gravity of the issue. The NBWHP reminded readers that poor Black women have borne the brunt of the "wave of violence." They agreed that "adequate local, state, and federal resources must be allocated to improve conditions and reduce crime in public housing projects and inner-cities." They were pleased to see that the original language of the Violence Against Women Act authorized $10 million to nonprofit organizations for the improvement of domestic violence intervention and prevention programs. However, it would not be enough to redeem VAWA in their sight.

Foremost among their complaints was that the monies funneled by VAWA to police departments and victim assistance groups would not fix dilapidated public housing, lack of job opportunity, and meager social welfare programs. The NBWHP's own statistics confirmed that low-income women were three times more likely to suffer abuse than higher income women.[93] They listed four conditions that would be necessary to protect women: education for employers on the obstacles abused women face, the creation of job training programs, the expansion of affordable daycare, and an increased minimum wage. VAWA would satisfy none of these conditions. These shortcomings were especially glaring considering President Bill Clinton's looming threat to "end welfare as we know it."[94] This threat would come to fruition the following year as the Personal Responsibility Work Opportunity Reconciliation Act (PRWORA). The act abolished Aid to Families with Dependent Children (AFDC), the public assistance program commonly referred to as "welfare." Conservatives and liberals had decried AFDC for decades for supposedly encouraging dependency and single parenthood, particularly among African American women.[95] In its place, PRWORA substituted Temporary Aid for Needy Families (TANF), which limited recipients to two consecutive years of benefits and a lifetime total of five. Like the Chicago Sexual Assault Services Network before them, the NBWHP was acutely aware of Black women's reliance on public assistance. Both recognized that conducting anti-rape advocacy in tandem with social welfare provisions allowed them to access previously unreachable Black women victims. They also recognized that the elimination of public assistance—whether by tethering it exclusively to cooperation with law enforcement or ending it completely—rendered Black women even more vulnerable to gender-based violence. NBWHP projected that "the potential benefits of VAWA could easily be undermined by Congressional initiatives such as the proposed cuts to AFDC, Food Stamps, Medicaid, and public housing."[96] Such cuts would "seriously impact the lives of poor unemployed women who rely on AFDC, Food Stamps, and public housing to provide the safety net that might enable them to flee violent domestic situations."[97] The NBWHP clearly articulated their understanding of gender violence as a health issue rooted in economic inequality in their opposition to VAWA. They urged that the federal funds allotted to VAWA be "redirected to ensure the availability of shelters and public housing and to strengthen the safety net." As Black anti-rape organizers had done for decades, the NBWHP took the state to task for reneging on its obligation to care for Black women.

The project also took issue with VAWA's framing of rape and abuse solely in terms of violent crime since the criminal justice system was so saturated with racism and sexism as to be useless, if not actively harmful, to Black women survivors. The NBWHP elaborated that "the racism and prejudice inherent in our society and in our institutions explains why Black women may be at the most risk for violence."[98] Yet VAWA tasked those same institutions with defending and assisting survivors. For Black survivors, this created a contradiction whereby "they must turn to a system that has traditionally mistreated Black women" and "has traditionally disregarded the seriousness of violence against women." In the view of the National Black Women's Health Project, the Violence Against Women Act failed Black survivors on two fronts. By addressing gender violence solely in terms of controlling crime, it ignored the broader economic conditions that condemned them to cyclical abuse and punted poor Black women to a criminal justice apparatus they understandably did not trust. The NBWHP knew VAWA was settled law, and they entertained no delusions of rolling it back. Still, they warned that "without mechanisms to eliminate serious gaps in access to health care and legal advocacy services that separate poor women, particularly women of color, from more affluent white women, VAWA fails to address the full scope of the problem."[99]

* * *

Six years after resigning the NBWHP's executive director role, Byllye Avery returned to preface the NBWHP's annual meeting program. Her message to conference participants retraced the first decade of the National Black Women's Health Project, describing gender violence as a raison d'être. "About 12 years ago brave sisters in the Project took the risk to talk about the high amounts of violence they were experiencing in their lives," Avery recalled. "Many were surprised to learn that their experiences were repeated many times in the lives of other women."[100] Avery continued that upon uncovering the extent of gender violence in their lives, "we moved past feeling ashamed and blaming ourselves to open sharing and action." Even with the Violence Against Women Act enshrined in law, Avery still believed in the potential of self-help to ignite community organizing against gender violence and expected the members of the movement she built to feel the same way.

Three years later, the California branch of the National Black Women's Health Project held its second annual Evening of Awareness on "Domestic Violence in the African American Community," during which attendees publicly divulged their experiences of abuse. For one attendee, who went by Adessina, the event dredged up repressed memories of the battering that took place in her childhood home. Linking her experiences with gender violence to her present physical afflictions, she welcomed the workshop as an opportunity "to feel my anger and rage and wrench it from the places in my body where it is manifesting in fibroid tumors."[101] Adessina fully recapitulated the self-help process, demanding that community action immediately follow the workshop. "I will no longer be afraid to write about or voice those thoughts of fear; of 'airing our dirty laundry in public.' I will be silenced no more! This is a problem that needs to be addressed within the Black community . . . We must stand united together to expose this ugly monster of patriarchal domination."[102]

The National Black Women's Health Project carried Black feminists' understanding of interlocking systemic oppression, mistrust of law enforcement, and commitment to care work into the 1990s. From the group's inception, they framed violence against Black women as a health issue to be addressed through self-help counseling and subsequent community action. Even as the NBWHP forayed into the world of public policy in the 1990s, the organization consistently linked rape and battering to the forces of sexism, racism, and poverty. Their unique framing accommodated the intersectional analysis that the mainstream feminist movement against violence had mostly marginalized. Thus, the National Black Women's Health Project was equipped to roundly reject the otherwise popular Violence Against Women Act in real-time. As they bridged the 1980s and 1990s, they swapped the tactic of diversion for resistance to promote Black women's care work as the partnership between the feminist "war on rape" and the federal "war on crime" reached its apex.

The critique of the Violence Against Women Act by the National Black Women's Health Project was refined in the new millennium by INCITE! Women of Color Against Violence. Upon the passage of VAWA, Black women operating within the feminist movement against sexual violence warned their white colleagues with a renewed urgency that "the now-naturalized response to gender violence is to 'call the cops,' a tactic that doesn't work too well for communities already under attack by the racism of law enforcement, immigration laws and enforcement, and the prison industrial complex."[103] Frustrated Black anti-violence organizers responded in the same manner that Margaret Sloan and Brenda Eichelberger had responded to the intransigence of male-led Black liberation groups and white-dominated feminist groups in the early 1970s. In 2000, they founded a racially separate organization, INCITE! Women of Color Against Violence, where they could better parse the overlapping terrain of interpersonal and state violence.[104]

EPILOGUE

The Making of "Me Too"

Despite the protests emanating from groups like the National Black Women's Health Project, the passage of the Violence Against Women Act (VAWA) of 1994 completed the decades-long merger of the federal "war on crime" and the feminist "war on rape." VAWA radically altered the funding landscape for feminist rape crisis centers by reestablishing a direct and reliable cash flow from the federal government. The fretting over funds that attended the anti-rape movement from its birth largely subsided, though not without political and ideological costs. The funds made available under VAWA flowed from the Office on Violence Against Women, a branch of the Department of Justice, closely knitting together feminist anti-violence activity and law enforcement operations.[1] Like the Law Enforcement Assistance Administration (LEAA) of the 1970s, the Office on Violence Against Women maintained that high rates of gender violence in the United States derived from underreporting by victims and lack of consequences for offenders. Recipients of VAWA funds were firmly pressured, if not outright required, to recommend police reporting to victims as the surest path to safety, healing, and justice. Congress reauthorized the act in 2000, 2005, 2013, and 2022, despite partisan bickering over government spending and extending protections to Native American, undocumented, and queer victims of gender violence.[2]

The ascension and survival of VAWA indicated that the Black feminist praxis of care lost substantial ground within the mainstream feminist movement against sexual violence. For decades, Black women in Philadelphia, Chicago, the Bay Area, Washington, D.C., and Atlanta warned that the police-centric approach to rape control would only inflict greater violence and precarity upon assaulted Black women and girls. Some attempted to subvert the agencies of the federal "war on crime," steering state funds away from police reporting and toward community education programs, self-defense training, and other projects that sustained Black life. Subversion had limited utility following the decline of block grants and the rise of individualistic "victim assistance." Frustration with this development, along with the defensiveness of their white colleagues within feminist rape crisis centers, drove some to divert their anti-rape activism to the fields of public education, social welfare, and public health. There, solutions that attacked the roots of sexual violence and transferred badly needed resources to victims could proceed without the persistent oversight of law enforcement. But these alternative venues were also vulnerable to the vicissitudes of state funding. In any case, they would be obviated by VAWA and the federal government's reinstatement of an enduring carceral apparatus for rape control.

By the new millennium, many Black anti-rape organizers found their diverse arsenal of tactics exhausted. Some women of color attending a board meeting of the National Coalition Against Sexual Violence grumbled that the organization, which once fostered Black feminist critique through its Women of Color Caucus, now seemed uninterested in addressing their concerns.[3] Years of expensive lobbying campaigns had taken their toll and the board of directors would vote to fold after failing to obtain funds.[4] Much like the Black women who attended the National Center for the Prevention and Control of Rape's "Special Populations" conference series in 1977, the disenchanted NCASA members resolved then and there to convene an independent organization where women of color could combat the multiple violences that affected them. This new group would be known as INCITE! Women of Color Against Violence.

INCITE! Women of Color Against Violence officially emerged in 2000 when over a thousand women of color activists gathered in Santa Cruz, California, for a conference titled "The Color of Violence." Like the First National Conference on Third World Women and Violence held in Washington, D.C. twenty years prior, "The Color of Violence" united Black, Latina, Asian, and Native American women in the common cause of developing an anti-violence movement that was more caring and less carceral. Loretta Ross, who attended the earlier meeting, would later assert that "the 1980 conference was a precursor to INCITE!,"[5] and Beth Richie, an INCITE! cofounder, noted that "Black women's visionary leadership helped to shape ["The Color of Violence"], and Black women's work featured prominently in the workshops."[6] The conference keynote was delivered by Angela Davis, who had persistently cautioned the feminist movement against sexual violence not to collaborate with carceral actors since the 1970s.

"The Color of Violence" conference signaled that a Black feminist perspective on gender-based violence had evolved from a skepticism of state actors during the 1970s toward treating state violence as inseparable from the rape and battering that women of color suffered within their homes and communities.[7] INCITE! cofounder Ana Clarissa Rojas Durazzo pointed to the Violence Against Women Act as a major obstacle to this brand of activism. She declared that "VAWA . . . merged in policy the interests of the state—to criminalize society, populate the cheap labor force of the PIC [prison-industrial complex], manage the nation's shifting racial demographics (specifically, the declining white population) by quarantining more people of color in prison, and deflect attention from its role in the production and reproduction of domestic violence—with the interests of the anti-violence movement."[8] Organizations beholden to VAWA funds perpetuated "the ideology of the criminalization of violence against women" that actively harmed victims who were not middle-class white women. In this way, INCITE! repudiated the simplistic "everywoman analysis" described by Beth Richie.[9] Instead, they embodied what legal scholar Aya Gruber has termed a "neofeminism" that substituted a "forward-looking distributional approach" to justice in lieu of the dominant retributive model.[10] Such an approach not only rejected state control of rape as violent and counterproductive. It also called upon the state to provide the caring labor Black women had been performing interstitially for over a century.

In 2001, INCITE! partnered with Critical Resistance, the organization founded by Angela Davis and Ruth Wilson Gilmore in 1997 to push for the abolition of the prison system. The two groups jointly released a "Statement on Gender Violence and the Prison Industrial Complex" that reconciled the priorities of the anti-violence and anti-carceral movements.[11] The statement reprised the comments made by Loretta Ross and Nkenge Touré in their reports on the proceedings of the First National Conference on Third World Women and Violence in 1980. INCITE! and Critical Resistance took issue with the fact that "the mainstream anti-violence movement has increasingly relied on the criminal justice system as its front-line approach towards ending violence against women."[12] They noted that higher rates of prosecution and incarceration for rapists in recent decades did not correspond to a decrease in the rate of sexual assault. In fact, the criminalization approach to stopping gender violence had made women less safe by driving marginalized groups of women—such as women of color, sex workers, lesbians, trans women, immigrant women, and disabled women—into the clutches of hostile law enforcement entities. INCITE! and Critical Resistance blamed the influx of state funding for installing an "individualistic approach towards ending violence such that the only way people think they can intervene in stopping violence is to call the police." The anti-violence movement's embrace of carceral tactics, however well-intentioned, had "fueled the proliferation of prisons which now lock up more people per capita in the U.S. than any other country."

By constructing their advocacy around a presumed white middle-class victim, the feminist movement against sexual violence contributed to the crisis of mass incarceration. Conversely, those seeking to dismantle the prison-industrial complex had "conceptualized men of color as the primary victims of state violence" and ignored the women of color who were also victimized by the same forces. Moreover, their narrow focus on eliminating prisons and related punitive institutions that confined, maimed, and killed people of color at alarming rates "generally failed to provide a sufficient mechanism for safety and accountability for survivors of sexual and domestic violence."[13] The alternatives prison abolitionists had imagined to incarceration, such as community policing, failed to realize that communities in their present state were frequently sources of harm and danger for women and girls of color. INCITE! and Critical Resistance, recognizing their respective movements' shortcomings, called for a capacious analysis that refused incarceration as a solution to gender violence while also confronting the systems that allowed gender violence to fester in communities of color. The "Statement on Gender Violence and the Prison Industrial Complex" enumerated the ways that each movement could achieve this. The feminist movement against sexual violence could "critically assess the impact of state funding, . . . develop alternative fundraising strategies," and "oppose legislative change that promotes prison expansion, criminalization of poor communities and communities of color and thus state violence against women of color, even if these changes also incorporate measures to support victims of interpersonal violence." For its part, the prison abolition movement could "center stories of state violence committed against women of color" and "challenge men of color . . . to take particular responsibility to address and organize gender violence in their communities as a primary strategy for addressing violence and colonialism." Both anti-violence movements should "link struggles for personal transformation and healing with struggles for social justice."

By the end of the decade, INCITE! chapters had been founded in eleven states and dozens of organizations across the country counted themselves as allies.[14] During this time, INCITE! published several anthologies based on their conferences.[15] One of these anthologies, *The Revolution Will Not Be*

Funded (based on the conference of the same name held in Santa Barbara, California, in 2004), stated that state funding and the prison-industrial complex were not INCITE!'s only opponents. A booming "non-profit industrial complex" had also cropped up in the two decades since President Ronald Reagan decimated social welfare spending while abetting carceral expansion. During this conference, attendees discussed how anti-violence organizers who hoped to avoid state funding and its emphasis on criminalization found themselves bogged down in an endless cycle of applying to private foundations for meager grants to keep themselves afloat. Frequently, these private foundations kept them focused on short-term "deliverables," such as reaching a quota of women who received counseling services, and discouraged political agitation.[16] The National Black Women's Health Project lived through this precise predicament. INCITE! was not calling on anti-rape organizers to spurn their grant proposals, abandon counseling, and take to the streets. Rather, they were pushing organizers to, in the words of historian Lisa Levenstein, "think about how to preserve their integrity while navigating a fundamentally flawed system."[17] Black anti-rape organizers were quite adept at such maneuvering. While providing care for victims in spaces premised on controlling rape, they never lost sight of changing systemic inequality.

One Black anti-rape organizer, Tarana Burke of Harlem, New York, successfully navigated the "non-profit industrial complex," securing private funding to facilitate Black-centered service provision. She launched Just Be Inc. in 2007 to assist assaulted Black girls who lived in places "where rape crisis centers and sexual assault workers weren't going."[18] She had been inspired to organize to stop violence from her experiences as a youth worker, specifically one heartbreaking encounter in which an overwhelmed Burke failed to counsel and comfort a Black girl who disclosed that her stepfather was routinely assaulting her.[19] Burke, a survivor of sexual abuse, was determined to never allow such a scenario to unfold again.[20] Just Be Inc. "focused on the health, well-being, and wholeness of young women of color" by providing them with a safe space to disclose their abuse, a supportive network of sympathetic Black women and girls, and social services to regain some control over their lives.[21] The criminal justice system was conspicuously absent from Burke's formulation of "empowerment through empathy."[22] Within Just Be Inc., she originated the slogan "Me Too" as "a catchphrase to be used from survivor to survivor to let folks know that they were not alone and that a movement for radical healing was possible." With its emphasis on emotional healing, community building, resource redistribution, and irrelevance to law enforcement, Burke's original "Me Too" movement exemplified Black women's tradition of caring labor for victims.

By late 2017, the phrase "me too" had migrated far from its humble origins. Actress Alyssa Milano unintentionally co-opted Burke's slogan as a Twitter hashtag (#MeToo) that was meant to demonstrate the enormous number of women in the United States that had been victims of gender violence. This online gesture tipped off a seismic national reckoning about the pervasiveness of gender violence in American society. This iteration of #MeToo garnered sufficient public outrage to fell powerful serial abusers who had long evaded social and legal consequences, including USA Gymnastics team doctor Larry Nassar, producer Harvey Weinstein, comedian Bill Cosby, and music mogul R. Kelly. Many other high-profile offenders were not purged from public life. Christine Blasey Ford's courageous testimony against Supreme Court nominee Brett Kavanaugh in October 2018 for an attempted rape mirrored Anita Hill's testimony during the confirmation hearings of Justice Clarence Thomas in 1991. Relentless Republican railroading delivered both women's assailants a seat on the highest court in the land. President Donald Trump faced scores of sexual assault allegations, one of which resulted in a multimillion-dollar judgment in favor of author E. Jean Carroll but no criminal charges.[23] Meanwhile, a growing chorus of conservatives (and even some self-proclaimed feminists) droned that the #MeToo movement had devolved into a hysterical witch hunt that ruined men and infantilized women by collapsing the distinctions separating unpleasant dates, inappropriate workplace leering, and serial rape.[24] But even its detractors could not deny that #MeToo represented a cultural watershed in the history of sexual violence in the United States. The cracks in the patriarchally sanctioned rape culture cut by Susan Brownmiller and Susan Griffin had widened into chasms. For the first time, a person who flagrantly disregarded the sexual autonomy of women would receive more grief than sympathy from the American public.

Tarana Burke reported feeling "panicked" after #MeToo went viral.[25] Though Burke saluted those who publicly shared their violation, she also "felt a sense of dread, because something that was part of my life's work was going to be co-opted and taken from me and used for a purpose that I hadn't originally intended." Upon learning that she had inadvertently copied the ongoing work of a woman of color, Alyssa Milano moved quickly to make amends. But #MeToo had already taken on a life of its own. An image of the #MeToo movement rendered in American public consciousness of affluent white women cheerleading the criminal justice system as it sent rapists to prison. With its focus on salacious stories of obscenely rich and corrupt men finally punished for their heinous crimes, #MeToo acquired a vengeful flavor and dispensed with the tedious analysis of whether incarceration was an effective deterrent to rape. Legal scholar Aya Gruber has argued that although the movement encompasses a diverse array of responses to sexual violence, "much of #MeToo is punitive and carceral" and "the #MeToo era reinvigorated the declining feminist inclination to fight sexism through strict law enforcement."[26]

Burke publicly expressed her frustration with the #MeToo movement's increasingly carceral bent. In an interview with *The Nation* in November 2017, she explained how the media's fixation on the downfall of individual perpetrators "defeats the purpose" of the original "Me Too" movement, which was intended to return resources and visibility to the most marginalized victims.[27] "The conversation is largely about Harvey Weinstein or other individual bogeyman," she fumed. "No matter how much I keep talking about power and privilege, they keep bringing it back to individuals . . . I'm talking [about] black and brown girls, queer folks." A year later, Burke's view had only hardened. She told *New York Magazine* that she felt #MeToo had "lost its way" by indulging in the theatrics of the rich and famous vindictively accusing and angrily deflecting and needed to return to its roots. "We have to shift the narrative that it's a gender war, that it's anti-male, that it's men against women, that it's only for a certain type of person—that it's for white, cisgender, heterosexual, famous women. That has to shift."[28] Burke was not simply concerned that spotlighting the transgressions of perpetrators was forcing assaulted Black women and girls back into the shadows. She also feared that the online mutation of #MeToo was uncritically championing the criminal justice system as a heroic entity that offered safety and comfort to survivors. Burke knew—as Angela Davis, Brenda Eichelberger, Lynn Moncrief, Nkenge Touré, Mary Scott Boria, and Byllye Avery knew—that cooperating extensively with law enforcement offered none of these things to the Black women and girls she served. Burke said she was "appalled" to discover that many rape crisis centers were hitched to local police stations.[29] "That's a big hurdle for [Black women], because we don't trust the police." Beyond the logistical difficulties, Burke questioned whether carceral approaches to gender violence actually helped survivors to heal or contributed to ending gender violence at all. Reiterating INCITE!'s critique of the criminalization of gender violence, Burke announced that to re-center women of color within the #MeToo movement, "We have to start talking about nontraditional methods of pursuing justice . . . I'm talking restorative justice and transformative justice. Because the other part of this is that many perpetrators are themselves survivors of sexual violence, particularly child sex abuse . . . We've got to get a clearer understanding of what justice is and what people need to feel whole. And if we're ever going to heal in our community, we have to heal the perpetrators and heal the survivors, or else it's just a continuous cycle."[30] In late 2018, Burke attempted to wrest #MeToo from unproductive Hollywood gossip by relaunching metoomvmt.org with new materials and resources for organizers and allies. The revised "Me Too" website declared that "'me too' isn't a trend . . . We have the reach and moral authority to change public discourse around sexual assault, accountability, and restorative justice."[31] Burke and her colleagues explicitly recognized the carceral state as a source of violence for women of color by curating an alarming set of statistics. They publicized the fact that 86 percent of women incarcerated in the United States were survivors of sexual violence, that Black women who were incarcerated were more likely to experience sexual assault by prison staff than their white peers, and that police officers committed sexual assault at significantly higher rates than the general population.[32] An attached glossary defined the concept of restorative justice as a "theory of justice" that "seeks to address the needs of those who have been harmed, while encouraging those who have caused harmed to take responsibility."[33] Burke's retooling of "Me Too" rebuffed the carceral state and committed to restorative justice as a superior method of healing Black girls and their communities, building upon the diverse arsenal of practices forged by Black anti-rape organizers three decades prior.

Serendipitously, the Twitter-born iteration of the #MeToo movement reached a fever pitch during the same months that over a dozen Black women who had spent part of their lives fighting to end rape sat for interviews for this book. Though my prepared questions focused on their rich activist lives and their memories of the daily struggles within rape crisis centers, our conversations inevitably drifted toward explosive contemporary developments that involved sexual violence. Some took these tangents as opportunities to reflect upon the impact of their anti-rape activities. Though most were aware of Tarana Burke's origination of the slogan and Alyssa Milano's inadvertent co-optation of it, they universally praised the #MeToo movement. Beryl Fitzpatrick, an alumna of the National Alliance of Black Feminists (NABF) who later joined the Chicago Sexual Assault Services Network (CSASN), spoke approvingly of #MeToo in February 2019. She was glad to contribute her memories to a study of Black women's anti-rape activity in light of the fact that "we now have two rapists on the Supreme Court."[34] Though #MeToo failed to prevent the confirmation of Justice Brett Kavanaugh, she had faith that more women speaking out would convince more Americans that "violence against women is real" and alert them "to what Black women have endured in particular." Loretta Ross, formerly of the D.C. Rape Crisis Center and the National Black Women's Health Project, saw the same forces that originally drove her and other Black women to anti-rape advocacy at work within #MeToo. In the 1970s, Ross and her colleagues "were survivors who had never gotten counseling. There was no counseling to be had at the time. So that might have had something to do with why we channeled our rage into activism."[35] In her view, #MeToo helped "survivors become activists" by coaxing them to publicly acknowledge their violations and connecting them to the activist structures feminists had laid over the course of four decades.

Others were less sanguine in their outlook on #MeToo. Samia Cherry, formerly of Philadelphia Women Organized Against Rape (WOAR), felt that #MeToo was far from the most important social movement ignited by social media. Personally, she was more invested in Black Lives Matter, since "there's been so much abuse of power. Not just in the city of Philadelphia but around the nation . . . my opinion about police and police abuse of power has not changed [since my time as a Black Panther]."[36] Sylvia Rush, who left CSASN after becoming discouraged by the seemingly endless politicking and bureaucracy, noted with dismay in January 2019 that the damning Lifetime series *Surviving R. Kelly*, which went into production at the peak of #MeToo, had yet to result in real legal or social consequences for R. Kelly.[37] Phyllis Pennese, also of CSASN, strongly endorsed #MeToo but her endorsement was tinged with regret. The very necessity of a widescale movement to confront the nation's permissiveness toward sexual misconduct in the 2010s suggested that she had fallen short in her own organizing in the 1980s. "It saddens me that we're still dealing with some of these issues . . . There are times where I step back and I look and shake my head in grief that all these years later, there hasn't been enough change and progress around this area."[38]

Others saw the social and cultural conditions that #MeToo aimed to correct as a consequence of their failure to forestall the merging of the feminist "war on rape" and the federal "war on crime." Ross maintained that she left anti-rape work permanently in the late 1980s because the increasing professionalization of advocacy that attended the state funding of rape crisis centers had ushered in a weaker "bad apples" analysis of rapists. "That's when it moved from looking at the structural to the individual," she argued. "The radical feminist in me screams, 'It's not that individuals are not committing these crimes, but they are supported by rape culture. They are allowed to get away with it by a rape culture.'"[39] According to Ross, organizers' emphasis on locking up deviant perpetrators detracted attention from the systems that fostered sexual violence. For every one rapist that was placed behind bars, ten more cropped up to take his place. "That's how we got Brett Kavanaugh," she declared.

Mary Scott Boria was even more self-critical. She spoke of the irony whereby contemporary restorative justice activists in Chicago cut their political teeth in the anti-violence movement. "A lot of folks who were involved in victim services, victim rights, domestic violence, sexual assault are now all restorative justice . . . and so a lot of those folks are really sort of seeing that the work that we did around criminal justice reform really handed over to the criminal justice system our work. And it didn't change the outcome for victims at all."[40] Boria detected the incongruence between #MeToo's cathartic portrayal of prosecutors throwing the book at unrepentant offenders and the disappointing reality facing women of color who engage the criminal justice system. They were unlikely to see their abusers suffer the fates of Harvey Weinstein, Larry Nassar, Bill Cosby, and R. Kelly and far more likely to find themselves swept up in punitive law enforcement. Retrospectively, Boria wished she had pressed her white colleagues within the feminist movement against sexual violence on avoiding carceral collaborations and entanglements. "I think had we had a more open and honest dialogue about the role that criminal justice plays in our communities, and thought through that, had we been able to really fight through that together, we might have come to some of that point. But we tiptoed around it because our movement was so fragile."[41]

Scott's concern over the movement's fragility was not baseless. The National Coalition Against Sexual Assault (NCASA) has been dissolved for a quarter century and supplanted by the Rape, Abuse & Incest National Network (RAINN). RAINN unites over a thousand local sexual assault organizations through operating a National Sexual Assault Hotline and spearheads "programs to prevent sexual violence, help survivors, and ensure that perpetrators are brought to justice."[42] While Philadelphia WOAR, the D.C. Rape Crisis Center, and INCITE! still stand, the NABF and the CSASN shuttered long ago. The National Black Women's Health Project lives on in the Black Women's Health Imperative, but gender violence has been marginalized in its agenda. Aside from the Victims of Crime Act of 1984 and the Violence Against Women Act of 1994, all the federal interventions designed to control the crime of rape have vanished into the sea of defunct state agencies. The pace of change has only accelerated in recent years, with #MeToo implanting an anti-rape disposition in public consciousness and catapulting Tarana Burke to the status of national celebrity. But the Black feminist praxis of care is nothing if not durable. It survived the merging of the feminist "war on rape" and the federal "war on crime," preserved in a diverse arsenal of practices. Amid the growing political currency of prison abolitionism and restorative justice since 2020, Black women's caring labor for Black victims may no longer need to stand athwart an increasingly carceral state.

NOTES

Introduction

1. "Women: Rape, 1975–1978," Papers of Angela Y. Davis, 1937–2017 (inclusive), 1968–2006 (bulk), MC 940, 194.14, box 194, Schlesinger Library, Radcliffe Institute, Harvard University, Cambridge, MA.

2. Danielle L. McGuire, *At the Dark End of the Street: Black Women, Rape, and Resistance; A New History of the Civil Rights Movement from Rosa Parks to the Rise of Black Power*, 1st ed (New York: Knopf, 2010), 275; Christina Greene, *Free Joan Little: The Politics of Race, Sexual Violence, and Imprisonment* (Chapel Hill: University of North Carolina Press, 2022), 1–4.

3. Angela Y. Davis, "Forum: Joanne Little; The Dialectics of Rape," *Ms.* 3, no. 12 (June 1975): 74–77.

4. "Women: Rape, 1975–1978," Papers of Angela Y. Davis, 1937–2017 (inclusive), 1968–2006 (bulk), MC 940, 194.14, box 194, Schlesinger Library, Radcliffe Institute.

5. Crystal Feimster, *Southern Horrors: Women and the Politics of Rape and Lynching* (Cambridge, MA: Harvard University Press, 2009); Estelle B. Freedman, *Redefining Rape: Sexual Violence in the Era of Suffrage and Segregation* (Cambridge, MA: Harvard University Press, 2013).

6. "Women: Rape, 1975–1978," Papers of Angela Y. Davis, 1937–2017 (inclusive), 1968–2006 (bulk), MC 940, 194.14, box 194, Schlesinger Library, Radcliffe Institute.

7. Emily Thuma, *All Our Trials: Prisons, Policing, and the Feminist Fight to End Violence* (Urbana: University of Illinois Press, 2019), 5–6; Greene, *Free Joan Little*, 225.

8. Sally Quin, "The Rape Crisis Center: An Alternative to the Police," *Washington Post*, June 15, 1975, E17; Catherine O. Jacquet, "Fighting Back, Claiming Power: Feminist Rhetoric and Resistance to Rape in the 1970s," *Radical History Review* 126 (2016): 71–83.

9. Thuma, *All Our Trials*, 123–124.

10. "Third World Women and Rape: Report from the First National Conference on Third World Women and Violence, August 1980," Loretta Ross Papers, SSC-MS-00504, box 5, folder 2, Smith College Special Collections, Smith College, Northampton, MA.

11. "Third World Women and Rape: Report from the First National Conference on Third World Women and Violence, August 1980."

12. "Third World Women and Violence by Loretta J. Ross, August 1980," Loretta Ross Papers, SSC-MS-00504, box 5, folder 3, Sophia Smith Collection, Smith College.

13. My conceptualization of Black women's ethic and practice of care is indebted to pathbreaking historians like Jacqueline Jones and Stephanie Shaw. See Jacqueline Jones, *Labor of Love, Labor of Sorrow: Black Women, Work, and Family from Slavery to the Present*, revised 2nd edition (New York: Basic Books, 2010); Stephanie Shaw, *What a Woman Ought to Be and to*

Do: Black Professional Women Workers During the Jim Crow Era (Chicago: University of Chicago Press, 1996).

14. Sarah Haley points out "the stark contrast between the complete mode of austerity that is policing and incarceration and the commitment to resources and the creation of infrastructure and holistic—material, psychic, and emotional—care that is abolitionist queer and trans feminism." See Sarah Haley, Andrea J. Ritchie, Emily L. Thuma, "'Criminalization Is the Antithesis of Care': Contextualizing the *Dobbs* Decision with Black Queer Abolitionist Feminism," *GLQ* 30, no. 1 (January 2024): 61–74.

15. Darlene Clark Hine, "Rape and the Inner Lives of Black Women in the Middle West: Preliminary Thoughts on the Culture of Dissemblance," *Signs* 14, no. 4 (summer 1989): 912–20; Sharon Block, *Rape and Sexual Power in Early America* (Chapel Hill: University of North Carolina Press, 2006); Hannah Rosen, *Terror in the Heart of Freedom: Citizenship, Sexual Violence, and the Meaning of Race in the Postemancipation South* (Chapel Hill: University of North Carolina Press, 2008); McGuire, *At the Dark End of the Street*; Feimster, *Southern Horrors*; Freedman, *Redefining Rape*; Sarah Haley, *No Mercy Here: Gender, Punishment, and the Making of Jim Crow Modernity* (Chapel Hill: University of North Carolina Press, 2016); Catherine O. Jacquet, *The Injustices of Rape: How Activists Responded to Sexual Violence, 1950–1980* (Chapel Hill: University of North Carolina Press, 2019); Greene, *Free Joan Little*; Emily A. Owens, *Consent in the Presence of Force: Sexual Violence and Black Women's Survival in Antebellum New Orleans* (Chapel Hill: University of North Carolina Press, 2023).

16. Patricia Hill Collins, *Black Sexual Politics: African Americans, Gender, and the New Racism* (New York: Routledge, 2004), 75.

17. Dawn Rae Flood, *Rape in Chicago: Race, Myth, and the Courts* (Urbana: University of Illinois Press, 2012), 76.

18. Deborah Gray White, *Too Heavy a Load: Black Women in Defense of Themselves, 1894–1994* (New York: W. W. Norton, 1999), 15.

19. Kimberly Springer, *Living for the Revolution: Black Feminist Organizations, 1968–1980* (Durham, NC: Duke University Press, 2005), 1–2.

20. Aya Gruber, *The Feminist War on Crime: The Unexpected Role of Women's Liberation in Mass Incarceration* (Oakland: University of California Press, 2020), 84–89.

21. Andrea J. Ritchie, *Invisible No More: Police Violence Against Black Women and Women of Color* (Boston: Beacon Press, 2017), 118–20.

22. Beth E. Richie, *Arrested Justice: Black Women, Violence, and America's Prison Nation* (New York: New York University Press, 2012), 36–37.

23. Jones, *Labor of Love, Labor of Sorrow*; Shaw, *What a Woman Ought to Be and Do*.

24. Annelise Orleck, *Storming Caesar's Palace: How Black Mothers Fought Their Own War on Poverty* (Boston: Beacon Press, 2005), 3, 215; Cheryl Hicks, *Talk with You Like a Woman: African American Women, Justice, and Reform in New York, 1890–1935* (Chapel Hill: University of North Carolina Press, 2010), 108; Alondra Nelson, *Body and Soul: The Black Panther Party and the Fight Against Medical Discrimination* (Minneapolis: University of Minnesota Press, 2011), 10, 27.

25. Treva B. Lindsey, *America, Goddam: Violence, Black Women, and the Struggle for Justice* (Oakland: University of California Press, 2022), 119.

26. Freedman, *Redefining Rape*, 1–3.

27. Maria Bevacqua, *Rape on the Public Agenda: Feminism and the Politics of Sexual Assault* (Boston: Northeastern University Press, 2000), 50.

28. Jacquet, "Fighting Back, Claiming Power," 73.

29. Jacquet, *The Injustices of Rape*, 81.

30. Jacquet, *The Injustices of Rape*, 88.

31. Bevacqua, *Rape on the Public Agenda*, 102.

32. Bevacqua, *Rape on the Public Agenda*, 79.

33. Elizabeth Kai Hinton, *From the War on Poverty to the War on Crime: The Making of Mass Incarceration in America* (Cambridge, MA: Harvard University Press, 2016), 27.

34. Marie Gottschalk, *The Prison and the Gallows: The Politics of Mass Incarceration in America* (Cambridge: Cambridge University Press, 2006), 124–126.

35. Thuma, *All Our Trials*, 7.

36. While these agencies did not directly subsidize feminist rape crisis centers, they did fund research and community coordination projects in conjunction with anti-rape organizers. Many feminist rape crisis centers, such as Philadelphia Women Organized Against Rape (WOAR), the Washington D.C. Rape Crisis Center (DCRCC), and the Chicago Sexual Assault Services Network (CSASN), carved out niches in state and municipal budgets as well, though these sources were far less generous and dependable than their federal counterparts and kept feminist rape crisis centers in the orbit of local police and prosecutors.

37. Jacquet, *The Injustices of Rape*, 160–161.

38. Flood, *Rape in Chicago*, 81.

39. Bevacqua, *Rape on the Public Agenda*, 204.

40. Bevacqua, *Rape on the Public Agenda*, 96.

41. Thuma, *All Our Trials*, 6.

42. Gottschalk, *The Prison and the Gallows*, 159; Julilly Kohler-Hausmann, *Getting Tough: Welfare and Imprisonment in 1970s America*, Politics and Society in Modern America (Princeton, NJ: Princeton University Press, 2017), 2; Gruber, *The Feminist War on Crime*, 63.

43. Nancy A. Matthews, *Confronting Rape: The Feminist Anti-Rape Movement and the State* (New York: Routledge, 1994), 119.

44. Gottschalk, *The Prison and the Gallows*; Michelle Alexander, *The New Jim Crow* (New York: The New Press, 2012); Naomi Murakawa, *The First Civil Right: How Liberals Built Prison America* (Oxford: Oxford University Press, 2014); Hinton, *From the War on Poverty to the War on Crime*; James Forman, *Locking Up Our Own: Crime and Punishment in Black America* (New York: Farrar, Straus and Giroux, 2017).

45. Alexander, *The New Jim Crow*, 178.

46. Anne Gray Fischer, *The Streets Belong to Us: Sex, Race, and Police Power from Segregation to Gentrification* (Chapel Hill: University of North Carolina Press, 2022), 3.

47. Paul Renfro, *Stranger Danger: Family Values, Childhood, and the American Carceral State* (Oxford: Oxford University Press, 2020), 13.

48. Gruber, *The Feminist War on Crime*, 171.

49. Erica Meiners, *For the Children? Protecting Innocence in a Carceral State* (Minneapolis: University of Minnesota Press, 2016), 157.

50. Thuma, *All Our Trials*, 7.

51. Matthews, *Confronting Rape*; Gottschalk, *The Prison and the Gallows*; Kristin Bumiller, *In an Abusive State: How Neoliberalism Appropriated the Feminist Movement Against Sexual Violence* (Durham, NC: Duke University Press, 2008); Richie, *Arrested Justice*; Meiners, *For the Children?*; Thuma, *All Our Trials*; Gruber, *The Feminist War on Crime.*

52. Gottschalk, *The Prison and the Gallows*, 115.

53. Matthews, *Confronting Rape*, 61–64.

54. Bumiller, *In an Abusive State*, xiii.

55. Haley, Ritchie, and Thuma, "'Criminalization is the Antithesis of Care,'" 61; Randi Gill-Sadler and Erica R. Edwards, "Taking Over, Living-In: Black Feminist Geometry and the Radical Politics of Repair," *Radical History Review*, no. 148 (January 2024): 107–129.

56. Carrie N. Baker and Maria Bevacqua, "Challenging Narratives of the Anti-Rape Movement's Decline," *Violence Against Women* 24, no. 3 (March 2018): 350–376.

57. Lindsey, *America, Goddam*, 25.

58. Thuma, *All Our Trials*; Anne Gray Fischer, *The Streets Belong to Us*; Lindsey, *America, Goddam*.

59. For more on the rise of neoliberal governance since the 1970s, see Lily Geismer, *Don't Blame Us: Suburban Liberals and the Transformation of the Democratic Party* (Princeton, NJ: Princeton University Press, 2014); Brent Cebul, *Illusions of Progress: Business, Poverty, and Liberalism in the American Century* (Philadelphia: University of Pennsylvania Press, 2023).

60. Matthews, *Confronting Rape*, 111.

61. "Budget Growth 1972–1986," Women Organized Against Rape Records, box 1, folder 29, Special Collections Research Center, Temple University Archives, Philadelphia.

62. Nkenge Touré, "Special Populations Conference: Black Focus," *Feminist Alliance Against Rape Newsletter* (May/June 1977): 8.

63. Gottschalk, *The Prison and the Gallows*, 125–126.

64. Nkenge Touré, interview with the author, October 16, 2018.

65. "Proposal for CSASN," HERS records, box 1, folder 7, Special Collections and University Archives, University of Illinois at Chicago.

66. United States Congress, *Legislation to Help Crime Victims: Hearings Before the Subcommittee on Criminal Justice of the Committee on the Judiciary, House of Representatives, Ninety-eighth Congress, Second Session, on H.R. 2661, H.R. 2978, H.R. 3498, and H.R. 5124 . . . February 2, 7, March 15, 22, April 2, and August 2, 1984* (Washington, D.C.: US Government Printing Office, 1984), 4.

67. Gottschalk, *The Prison and the Gallows*, 151–152.

68. Byllye Avery, "Black Women's Health: A Conspiracy of Silence," *Sojourner*, January 1989, 15–16; "Hill Briefs Vol. 1 No. 6 June 1995," Black Women's Health Imperative Records, SSC-MS-00487, box 2, folder 37, Smith College Special Collections.

69. See Matthews, *Confronting Rape*, 104–120; Bevacqua, *Rape on the Public Agenda*, 37–38; Wini Breines, *The Trouble Between Us: An Uneasy History of White and Black Women in the Feminist Movement* (Oxford: Oxford University Press, 2006), 157–171; Jacquet, *The Injustices of Rape*, 133–159; Greene, *Free Joan Little*, 173–182.

70. Bevacqua, *Rape on the Public Agenda*, 78.

71. Richie, *Arrested Justice*, 90.

72. Thuma, *All Our Trials*; Greene, *Free Joan Little*.

73. Collins, *Black Sexual Politics*; Freedman, *Redefining Rape*; Jacquet, *Injustices of Rape*.

74. Ruth Wilson Gilmore, *Golden Gulag: Prisons, Surplus, Crisis, and Opposition in Globalizing California* (Oakland: University of California Press, 2007), 178.

75. Kimberle Crenshaw, "Mapping the Margins: Intersectionality, Identity Politics, and Violence Against Women of Color," *Stanford Law Review*, no. 6 (1991): 1246.

76. Elizabeth Bernstein, "The Sexual Politics of the 'New Abolitionism,'" *Differences* 18, no. 3 (2007): 128–151.

77. Nancy Hewitt, ed., *No Permanent Waves: Recasting Histories of Feminism* (New Brunswick, NJ: Rutgers University Press, 2010).

78. Mary Scott Boria, interview with the author, June 13, 2018; Sylvia Rush, interview with the author, January 23, 2019; Loretta Ross, interview with the author, September 27, 2018; Nkenge Touré, interview with the author, October 16, 2018.

79. Springer, *Living for the Revolution*, 78. For non-feminist usage of the term "Third World" by Black activist women, see Ashley Farmer, *Remaking Black Power: How Black Women Transformed an Era* (Chapel Hill: University of North Carolina Press, 2017), 159.

80. Richie, *Arrested Justice*, 102–103.

Chapter 1

1. Springer, *Living for the Revolution*, 27–28.

2. Springer, *Living for the Revolution*, 53–59.

3. "Charlie Cherokee Says," *Chicago Defender*, November 12, 1974, 17.

4. "Rape Crisis Line on Southside," *Chicago Defender*, November 2, 1974, 2.

5. Collins, *Black Sexual Politics*, 65–66.

6. Dawn Rae Flood adduces evidence of African American women in mid-century Chicago successfully bringing intraracial rape charges against African American men. She also notes that these women found virtually no support among civil rights leaders or within the Black press, as victims of interracial rape regularly did. See Flood, *Rape in Chicago*, 75–77.

7. "Black Feminism—A New Directive: Consciousness Raising Guidelines for Black Men and Women," National Black Feminist Organization Collection, folder 1, Special Collections and University Archives, University of Illinois at Chicago.

8. Louis Martin, "The Big Parade: Summit Meet Needed for Crime War," *Chicago Defender*, October 19, 1974, 3.

9. Greene, *Free Joan Little*, 220.

10. Richie, *Arrested Justice*, 133; Thuma, *All Our Trials*, 127–128; Gruber, *The Feminist War on Crime*, 87; Lindsey, *America, Goddam*, 119; Greene, *Free Joan Little*, 228.

11. Most Black anti-rape organizers did not belong to chapters of the NBFO, NABF, or CRC. They evinced Kimberly Springer's observation that the true measure of Black feminism's success is not the size or longevity of its organizations but the enduring influence of its ideas. See Springer, *Living for the Revolution*, 168.

12. Robyn Spencer, *The Revolution Has Come: Black Power, Gender, and the Black Panther Party* (Durham, NC: Duke University Press, 2016), 88–89.

13. Breines, *The Trouble Between Us*, 55–56.

14. Spencer, *The Revolution Has Come*, 46–48; Farmer, *Remaking Black Power*, 76.

15. bell hooks, *Ain't I a Woman: Black Women and Feminism* (New York: Routledge, 2015), 105.

16. Eldridge Cleaver, *Soul on Ice* (New York: Dell Publishing Company, 1968), 14.

17. Spencer, *The Revolution Has Come*, 44.

18. Ashley Farmer asserts that Black Power movements attracted Black women in the 1960s who were outraged by sexual assault and other "gender-specific forms of discrimination" that the civil rights movement largely failed to address. They initially saw the promise of Black community empowerment to address this issue. See Farmer, *Remaking Black Power*, 54.

19. Farmer, *Remaking Black Power*, 76, 122.

20. Jacquet, *The Injustices of Rape*, 67–69.

21. Breines, *The Trouble Between Us*, 66–67; Spencer, *The Revolution Has Come*, 188–189.

22. Wadiyah Nelson, interview with the author, May 10, 2018.

23. Wadiyah Nelson, interview with the author, May 10, 2018.

24. Collins, *Black Sexual Politics*, 225, 243–245.

25. Collins, *Black Sexual Politics*, 227–228.

26. Richie, *Arrested Justice*, 47.

27. hooks, *Ain't I a Woman*, 115–117.

28. White, *Too Heavy a Load*, 220; Flood, *Rape in Chicago*, 141.

29. Unlike its peer Black feminist organizations, the Third World Women's Alliance (originally created by radical Black activist Fran Beal as the Black Women's Liberation Committee of SNCC) dedicated little direct attention to rape and sexual abuse in its statements and activities. This should by no means suggest that the TWWA was apathetic on the question of sexual violence. Historian Ashley Farmer locates TWWA's anti-rape politics in their rejection of the "promise of protection" framework cribbed by some Black Power groups from the Nation of Islam and embrace of self-defense for the revolutionary Black woman. See Farmer, *Remaking Black Power*, 187.

30. Springer, *Living for the Revolution*, 33–34.

31. Springer, *Living for the Revolution*, 51.

32. Breines, *The Trouble Between Us*, 120–121.

33. Margaret Sloan, "Woman; Margaret Sloan on Black Sisterhood," interview by Sandra Elkin, WNED New York, American Archive of Public Broadcasting, August 4, 1974, http://americanarchive.org/catalog/cpbaacip-81-47rn8v5q.

34. New York Radical Feminists, *Rape: The First Sourcebook for Women*, ed. Noreen Connell and Cassandra Wilson (New York: Plume Books, 1974), 246.

35. New York Radical Feminists, *Rape: The First Sourcebook for Women*, 246.

36. "NYWAR Meeting Minutes January 10, 1974," New York Women Against Rape Records, 1971–1984, MC 353, folder 5, Schlesinger Library, Radcliffe Institute, Harvard University.

37. "NYWAR Meeting Minutes May 30, 1974," New York Women Against Rape Records, 1971–1984, MC 353, folder 5, Schlesinger Library, Radcliffe Institute, Harvard University.

38. Jacquet, *The Injustices of Rape*, 94.

39. Sloan, "Woman; Margaret Sloan on Black Sisterhood."

40. "Women's Anti-Rape Coalition Meeting Minutes, September 16, 1975," Yolanda Bako Papers, 1970–1995, MC 943, folder 5, Schlesinger Library, Radcliffe Institute, Harvard University.

41. Letter from Hortense Barber, May 27, 1975, Yolanda Bako Papers, 1970–1995, MC 943, folder 5, Schlesinger Library, Radcliffe Institute, Harvard University. Emphasis in original.

42. "Women's Anti-Rape Coalition's 3rd Annual New York City Rape Conference, Friday August 22, 1975," Yolanda Bako Papers, 1970–1995, MC 943, folder 5, Schlesinger Library, Radcliffe Institute, Harvard University.

43. Flood, *Rape in Chicago*, 142.

44. Springer, *Living for the Revolution*, 53.

45. "Minutes of the Sixth Meeting of the National Organization of Black Feminists Provision Chicago Chapter (July 24, 1974)," National Black Feminist Organization Collection, folder 2, Special Collections and University Archives, University of Illinois at Chicago.

46. Brenda Eichelberger to Jo Benet, August 30, 1974), National Black Feminist Organization Collection, folder 8, Special Collections and University Archives, University of Illinois at

Chicago; Brenda Eichelberger to Fran P. Hosken, September 1, 1974, National Black Feminist Organization Collection, folder 3, Special Collections and University Archives, University of Illinois at Chicago.

47. Brenda Eichelberger to Herman Roberts, September 25, 1974, National Black Feminist Organization Collection, folder 3, Special Collections and University Archives, University of Illinois at Chicago.

48. Eichelberger to Roberts, September 25, 1974.

49. "Newsletter November 1974," National Black Feminist Organization Collection, folder 12, Special Collections and University Archives, University of Illinois at Chicago; "Newsletter January 1975," National Black Feminist Organization Collection, folder 13, Special Collections and University Archives, University of Illinois at Chicago.

50. Kathryn Christensen, "Black Women Battle Double Prejudice," *Chicago Daily News*, January 4, 1975, 19.

51. Springer, *Living for the Revolution*, 54–55.

52. "Black Women's Bill of Rights, 1976," National Alliance of Black Feminists Collection, folder 1, Special Collections and University Archives, University of Illinois at Chicago.

53. Forman, *Locking Up Our Own*, 76.

54. Brenda Eichelberger, "Voices on Black Feminism," *Quest: A Feminist Quarterly* 3, no 4 (spring 1977): 21.

55. Marcia Ann Gillespie, "Getting Down," *Essence*, June 1976, 35.

56. Bernette Golden, "The Ugly Crime of Rape," *Essence*, June 1976, 36.

57. Golden, "The Ugly Crime of Rape," 72.

58. Golden, "The Ugly Crime of Rape," 73.

59. Robert Staples, "The Myth of Black Macho: A Response to Angry Black Feminists," *The Black Scholar* (March / April 1979): 24.

60. Staples, "The Myth of Black Macho," 24.

61. Reprinted as Audre Lorde, "Sexism: An American Disease in Blackface," in *Sister Outsider: Essays and Speeches by Audre Lorde* (New York: Crossings Press, 1984), 60–65.

62. Lorde, "Sexism: An American Disease in Blackface," 60, 64.

63. Lorde, "Sexism: An American Disease in Blackface," 63.

64. Barbara Smith, "An Open Letter on Black Feminism," *Plexus*, October 1979, 16.

65. Alice Claire, "Ask Alice," *Chicago Defender*, November 2, 1974, 14.

66. Michael Sneed, "Rapes Increasing but More Women Reporting Them," *Chicago Tribune*, January 3, 1974, N4.

67. Flood, *Rape in Chicago*, 142; "Rape Group Meets Thursday," *Chicago Defender*, April 9, 1974, 16.

68. "Women Launch Fight on Crime," *Chicago Defender*, February 25, 1974, 3.

69. James McGrath Morris, *Eye on the Struggle: Ethel Payne, the First Lady of the Black Press* (New York: Amistad Press, 2015).

70. Forman, *Locking up Our Own*, 50.

71. "Women Meet to Map Strategy for War on Crime," *Chicago Defender*, March 2, 1974, 13.

72. "Rochford Pledges Action," *Chicago Defender*, March 11, 1974, 1; "Rochford and Coalition of Concerned Women," *Chicago Defender*, March 18, 1974, 15.

73. Leah Wright Rigueur, *The Loneliness of the Black Republican: Pragmatic Politics and the Pursuit of Power* (Princeton, NJ: Princeton University Press, 2015), 87.

74. Jennifer Mayer, "A Review of the War on Crime," *Chicago Defender*, September 7, 1974, 24.

75. "On Southside: Organize Rape Crisis Line," *Chicago Defender*, February 6, 1975, 4.

76. Historian Leah Wright Rigueur notes that even for Black Republicans, the "law-and-order" rhetoric that emerged from Richard Nixon's 1968 presidential campaign was an "alienating concept" because it implied violent state repression while overlooking injustice. Rigueur, *The Loneliness of the Black Republican*, 126–127.

77. Flood, *Rape in Chicago*, 110.

78. Mayer, "A Review of the War on Crime," 24.

79. "Call to Action in War on Crime," *Chicago Defender*, November 9, 1974, 1.

80. Paul Delaney, "Blacks, in Shift, Organize to Combat Rise in Crime," *New York Times*, November 13, 1974, 22.

81. Delaney, "Blacks, in Shift, Organize to Combat Rise in Crime," 22. Emphasis added.

82. White, *Too Heavy a Load*, 70–71; Freedman, *Redefining Rape*, 118.

83. Bernard Headley, "'Black on Black' Crime: The Myth and the Reality," *Crime and Social Justice* no. 20 (1983): 50.

84. Headley, "'Black on Black' Crime," 51.

85. Pearl Reed, "Calling the Kettle the Right Color," *Chicago Defender*, December 12, 1974, 8.

86. Lawrence Muhammad, "Our Man, a Law and Order Convert," *Chicago Defender*, October 29, 1977, 8.

87. Lawrence Muhammad, "Black-on-Black Crime Still Highest," *Chicago Defender*, July 21, 1979, 1.

88. Forman, *Locking Up Our Own*, 146.

89. Rigueur, *The Loneliness of the Black Republican*, 277.

90. Ethel Payne, "War on Crime: Can It Be Won?," *Chicago Defender*, November 30, 1974, 8.

91. Payne, "War on Crime: Can It Be Won?," 8.

92. Greene, *Free Joan Little*, 220.

93. Hinton, *From the War on Poverty to the War on Crime*, 134–136.

94. "What to Do in Case of Rape," *Chicago Defender*, March 8, 1975, 13.

95. "Women Crime Fighters Celebrate First Year," *Chicago Defender*, February 25, 1975, 2; "War on Crime . . ." *Chicago Defender*, March 1, 1975, 16.

96. "League of Black Women Director Resigns," *Chicago Defender*, March 29, 1975, 11.

97. Roxane Brown, "Rape, a Black Problem," *Chicago Defender*, April 22, 1978, 9.

98. Edith Herman, "A 'Forgotten' Story of Pain in the Inner City," *Chicago Tribune*, July 15, 1979, M3.

99. The *Defender* specified a handful of other small but significant differences. The NABF survived on private donations and membership dues. These politically flexible but unpredictable revenue streams would contribute to the disbanding of several Black feminist organizations. Springer, *Living for the Revolution*, 84–85. The coalition enjoyed stable funding from the Illinois Law Enforcement Commission, the state-level representative of the Law Enforcement Assistance Administration (LEAA). As the historian Christina Greene has noted, the LEAA was "the federal agency that helped to spur the disproportionate incarceration of Black and brown men and women" amid the "war on crime." Greene, *Free Joan Little*, 178.

100. Jacqueline Moore, "3 Women's Groups Common Goal: Aid Black Women," *Chicago Defender*, June 26, 1976, 12.

101. Keeanga-Yamahtta Taylor et al., ed., *How We Get Free: Black Feminism and the Combahee River Collective* (Chicago: Haymarket Books, 2017), 66–67.

102. Richie, *Arrested Justice*, 145–146.

103. Lindsey, *America, Goddam*, 19–23.

104. Greene, *Free Joan Little*, 228.

105. New York Radical Feminists, *Rape: The First Sourcebook for Women*, 242.

106. Jacquet, *The Injustices of Rape*, 81–82.

107. New York Radical Feminists and rape conference, 1970–1981 [4 folders], Papers of Susan Brownmiller, 1935–2000, MC 523, T-326, 30.14–31.2, box 30, box 31, Schlesinger Library, Radcliffe Institute.

108. New York Radical Feminists, *Rape: The First Sourcebook for Women*, 246.

109. New York Radical Feminists, *Rape: The First Sourcebook for Women*, 246.

110. "Rape Coalition," 1973–1979, Papers of Yolanda Bako, 1970–1995, MC 943, Vt-105, 1.5, box 1, Schlesinger Library, Radcliffe Institute.

111. "Rape Coalition."

112. Janette C. Tolbert, "Rape!," *Encore American & Worldwide News*, February 17, 1975, 21.

113. Sloan, "Woman; Margaret Sloan on Black Sisterhood."

114. "The Empty Cell," Pauline Bart Papers, box 2, folder 1, David M. Rubenstein Rare Book & Manuscript Library, Duke University.

115. "The Empty Cell."

116. Robin McDuff, Deanne Pernell, and Karen Saunders, "Feminists Critique the Anti-Rape Movement," *Feminist Alliance Against Rape Newsletter* (January / February 1977): 2–5.

117. Scholar Beth Richie has noted that "as the broader political discussion about crime, violence and justice [became] more conservative, a number of women in positions of power within the anti-violence movement made a series of strategic decisions, moving to work inside the system rather than against it. Subsequently, Black women and other women of color . . . [found] themselves in conflict with other leaders in the anti-violence movement." Richie, *Arrested Justice*, 47.

118. Gruber, *The Feminist War on Crime*, 63.

119. "Third World Women and Rape: Report from the First National Conference on Third World Women and Violence, August 1980," Loretta Ross Papers, SSC-MS-00504, box 5, folder 2, Smith College Special Collections.

120. Beryl Fitzpatrick, interview with the author, February 1, 2019.

121. Loretta Ross, interview with the author, September 27, 2018; Wadiyah Nelson, interview with the author, May 10, 2018.

122. Greene, *Free Joan Little*, 189.

123. Anne M. Valk, *Radical Sisters: Second-Wave Feminism and Black Liberation in Washington, D.C.* (Urbana: University of Illinois Press, 2008), 158.

124. Deb Friedman, Jackie Macmillan, and Patrice & Nkenge Touré, "Judgment on Justice," *Feminist Alliance Against Rape Newsletter* (September/October 1977), 2–5.

125. Loretta Ross, interview by Joyce Follet, transcript of video recording, November 3, 2004, Voices of Feminism Oral History Project, Sophia Smith Collection, Smith College, 122.

126. Audre Lorde and bell hooks had yet to compose their most famous Black feminist tracts, but according to Ross the group was "doing a lot of black feminist stuff" even in the absence of a "theoretical basis" handed down by writers. Loretta Ross, interview by Joyce Follet, 87.

127. William Fuller, "Prisoners Against Rape," *Feminist Alliance Against Rape Newsletter* (September / October 1974): 5.

128. Fuller, "Prisoners Against Rape," 6.

129. Valk, *Radical Sisters*, 163.

130. Sally Quin, "The Rape Crisis Center: An Alternative to the Police," *Washington Post*, June 15, 1975, E17.

131. Shatema Threadcraft, *Intimate Justice: The Black Female Body and the Body Politic* (New York: Oxford University Press, 2016), 64.

132. Quin, "The Rape Crisis Center."

133. Ross recalled that their white colleagues within the DCRCC ultimately stood by their decision to exclude white conferencegoers. The lawsuit was advanced by an unaffiliated white policewoman who "had no consciousness." Loretta Ross, interview by Joyce Follet, 128.

134. Nkenge Touré, interview with the author, October 16, 2018.

135. "Third World Women and Rape: Report from the First National Conference on Third World Women and Violence, August 1980."

136. "Working With Minority Men Committing Violence Against Women: Report from the First National Conference on Third World Women and Violence, August 1980," Loretta Ross Papers, SSC.MS.00504, box 5, folder 12, Smith College Special Collections.

137. "Working With Minority Men Committing Violence Against Women: Report from the First National Conference on Third World Women and Violence, August 1980."

138. "Third World Women and Rape: Report from the First National Conference on Third World Women and Violence, August 1980."

139. "Third World Women and Rape: Report from the First National Conference on Third World Women and Violence, August 1980."

140. "Black Feminism—A New Directive: Consciousness Raising Guidelines for Black Men and Women," National Black Feminist Organization Collection, folder 1, Special Collections and University Archives, University of Illinois at Chicago.

141. Threadcraft, *Intimate Justice*, 68.

Chapter 2

1. *HOTLINE*, October 1979, Women Organized Against Rape Records, box 29, folder 7, Special Collections Research Center (SCRC), Temple University Archives.

2. *HOTLINE*, May 1978, Women Organized Against Rape Records, box 29, folder 5, SCRC, Temple University Archives.

3. "Minutes of the Program Planning Committee, June 14, 1978," Women Organized Against Rape Records, box 4, folder 33, SCRC, Temple University Archives.

4. Timothy J. Lombardo, *Blue-Collar Conservatism: Frank Rizzo's Philadelphia and Populist Politics* (Philadelphia: University of Pennsylvania Press, 2018), 2.

5. Lisa Levenstein, *A Movement Without Marches: African American Women and the Politics of Poverty in Postwar Philadelphia* (Chapel Hill: University of North Carolina Press, 2009), 180. Levenstein adds that the African American women who patronized Philadelphia General Hospital forced the healthcare institution to take the problem of sexual violence seriously decades before white feminists captured the issue. See Levenstein, *A Movement Without Marches*, 155.

6. "WOAR After PGH Meeting, July 29, 1976," Women Organized Against Rape Records, box 4, folder 20, Special Collections Research Center, Temple University Archives.

7. "Ten Years After Rape Crisis Centers," *off our backs* (August–September 1984): 17–23.

8. As police commissioner, Frank Rizzo oversaw a notoriously contentious relationship between the Philadelphia Police Department and the Black community that included the raiding of Black Panther Party offices in 1970. For more on Frank Rizzo's career as a "law and order" figure, see Lombardo, *Blue-Collar Conservatism*.

9. "Budget Growth 1972–1986," Women Organized Against Rape Records, box 1, folder 31, SCRC, Temple University Archives.

10. Hinton, *From the War on Poverty to the War on Crime*, 2.

11. Hinton, *From the War on Poverty to the War on Crime*, 253.

12. Lisa Brodyaga et al., *Rape and Its Victims: A Report for Citizens, Health Facilities, and Criminal Justice Agencies* (Washington, D.C.: Law Enforcement Assistance Administration, U.S. Department of Justice, 1975), xii.

13. Greene, *Free Joan Little*, 304.

14. Bevacqua, *Rape on the Public Agenda*, 82.

15. Matthews, *Confronting Rape*, 58–59; Gottschalk, *The Prison and the Gallows*, 125; INCITE! Women of Color Against Violence, ed., *The Revolution Will Not Be Funded: Beyond the Non-Profit Industrial Complex* (Boston: South End Press, 2007); Thuma, *All Our Trials*, 5–6; Greene, *Free Joan Little*, 228–229.

16. "Overview of Third World Women and Violence, First National Conference on Third World Women and Violence, August 1980," Nkenge Touré Papers, SSC-MS-00563, box 4, folder 14, Smith College Special Collections.

17. "HOTLINE December 1976: Staff Profiles," Women Organized Against Rape Records, box 29, folder 3, SCRC, Temple University Archives.

18. "Memorandum: June 21, 1979," Women Organized Against Rape Records, box 4, folder 44, SCRC, Temple University Archives.

19. "Third World Caucus Objectives, Adopted June 9, 1978," Women Organized Against Rape Records, box 4, Folder 44, SCRC, Temple University Archives.

20. Hinton, *From the War on Poverty to the War on Crime*, 143.

21. INCITE!, *The Revolution Will Not Be Funded*, 119.

22. Brodyaga et al., *Rape and Its Victims*, 14.

23. Brodyaga et al., *Rape and Its Victims*, 30.

24. Hinton, *From the War on Poverty to the War on Crime*, 183.

25. Brodyaga et al., *Rape and Its Victims*, 33.

26. Jacquet, "Fighting Back, Claiming Power," 73.

27. Flood, *Rape in Chicago*, 11.

28. Richie, *Arrested Justice*, 37.

29. Bumiller, *In an Abusive State*, 6–7.

30. Gottschalk, *The Prison and the Gallows*, 126.

31. Jacquet, "Fighting Back, Claiming Power," 71.

32. Brodyaga et al., *Rape and Its Victims*, 131.

33. "Public Confidence in Criminal Justice System Must Be Restored: Dogin," *LEAA Newsletter* 8, no. 1 (January 1979): 1.

34. Brodyaga et al., *Rape and Its Victims*, 131.

35. Brodyaga et al., *Rape and Its Victims*, 69.

36. Brodyaga et al., *Rape and Its Victims*, 333.

37. "Review of *Rape and Its Victims*," Pauline Bart Papers, box 20, David M. Rubenstein Rare Book & Manuscript Library, Duke University, Durham, NC.

38. "Review of *Rape and Its Victims*."

39. Barbara Allen, "WAR: Women Against Rape," *Feminist Alliance Against Rape Newsletter* (May / June 1974): 1–3.

40. Mary Ann Largen, "LEAA Rape Funding Review," *Feminist Alliance Against Rape Newsletter* (September / October 1974): 10.

41. Judy Smith, "Alabama Conference Report," *Feminist Alliance Against Rape Newsletter* (January / February 1975): 12–13.

42. Jacquet, "Fighting Back, Claiming Power," 80.

43. Gerald Bryant, *A Community Response to Rape : Polk County Rape / Sexual Assault Care Center, Des Moines, Iowa* (Washington, D.C.: Law Enforcement Assistance Administration, 1977), i.

44. Deborah Carrow, *Rape: Guidelines to a Community Response* (Washington, D.C.: Law Enforcement Assistance Administration, 1980), 4.

45. Bevacqua, *Rape on the Public Agenda*, 83.

46. "Baton Rouge: Louisiana," *Feminist Alliance Against Rape Newsletter* (September / October 1976): 11–12.

47. Carrow, *Rape: Guidelines to a Community Response*, 5.

48. United States Congress, *Research into Violent Behavior: Overview and Sexual Assaults; Hearings Before the Subcommittee on Domestic and International Scientific Planning, Analysis, and Cooperation of the Committee on Science and Technology, U.S. House of Representatives, Ninety-fifth Congress, Second Session, January 10, 11, 12, 1978* (Washington, D.C.: US Government Printing Office, 1978), 402.

49. Deborah Carrow, *Rape: Guidelines to a Community Response*, 198.

50. Gail Sullivan, "A Funny Thing Happened on Our Way to Revolution," *Aegis* (spring 1982): 15–17.

51. Stuart Taylor Jr., "Rape Crisis Centers Reduced," *New York Times*, August 31, 1981, B4.

52. Janet Howard, "Battered and Rape: The Physical / Sexual Abuse of Women," in *Fight Back!: Feminist Resistance to Male Violence*, ed. Frèdèrique Delacoste and Felice Newman (Minneapolis: Cleis Press, 1981), 82.

53. "Crisis Center Project 1978–1979," Women Organized Against Rape Records, box 21, folder 36, SCRC, Temple University Archives; "Statewide Outreach Project 1977–1978," Women Organized Against Rape Records, box 19, folder 7, SCRC, Temple University Archives; "LEAA Juvenile Advocacy, 1980," Women Organized Against Rape Records, box 19, folder 13, SCRC, Temple University Archives.

54. *HOTLINE*, November 1979, Women Organized Against Rape Records, box 29, folder 7, SCRC, Temple University Archives.

55. "Letter to Frank Rizzo, January 15, 1974," Women Organized Against Rape Records, box 5, folder 9, SCRC, Temple University Archives.

56. Matthew Countryman, *Up South: Civil Rights and Black Power in Philadelphia* (Chapel Hill: University of North Carolina Press, 2006), 316.

57. Lombardo, *Blue Collar Conservatism*, 145–147.

58. Lombardo, *Blue Collar Conservatism*, 145–147.

59. "Introspective Look at Our Volunteers, 1977," Women Organized Against Rape Records, box 34, folder 32, SCRC, Temple University Archives.

60. Glenavie Norton, interview with the author, April 12, 2019.

61. Letty Thall, interview with the author, April 10, 2019.

62. Letty Thall, interview with the author, April 10, 2019.

63. "Application for Subgrant March 14, 1975," Women Organized Against Rape Records, box 18, folder 17, SCRC, Temple University Archives.

64. "Application for Subgrant 1975," Women Organized Against Rape Records, box 18, folder 39, SCRC, Temple University Archives.

65. Richie, *Arrested Justice*, 83.

66. Wadiyah Nelson, interview with the author, May 10, 2018.

67. "GJC / LEAA Grant Application for Crisis Center Project 1975," Women Organized Against Rape Records, box 18, folder 27, SCRC, Temple University Archives.

68. "GJC / LEAA Grant Application for Crisis Center Project 1975."

69. *HOTLINE*, September 1976, Women Organized Against Rape Records, box 29, folder 3, SCRC, Temple University Archives.

70. "GJC Crisis Center Project Third Year 1977–1978," Women Organized Against Rape Records, box 18, folder 23, SCRC, Temple University Archives.

71. "GJC Crisis Center Project Continuation Application 1978–1979," Women Organized Against Rape Records, box 18, folder 36, SCRC, Temple University Archives.

72. "Application for Continuation of Statewide Outreach Project," Women Organized Against Rape Records, box 19, folder 7, SCRC, Temple University Archives.

73. "Statewide Outreach Project Quarterly Report January 1977-March 1977," Women Organized Against Rape Records, box 19, folder 4, SCRC, Temple University Archives.

74. "Board of Directors Meeting, May 19, 1977," Women Organized Against Rape Records, box 1, folder 3, SCRC, Temple University Archives.

75. *HOTLINE*, September 1977, Women Organized Against Rape Records, box 29, folder 4, SCRC, Temple University Archives.

76. Berit Lakey, interview with the author, April 29, 2019.

77. "Update: Fighting Rape," Women Organized Against Rape Records, box 31, folder 29, SCRC, Temple University Archives.

78. United States Congress, *Federal Financial Assistance to State and Local Law Enforcement: Hearings Before the Subcommittee on Juvenile Justice of the Committee on the Judiciary, United States Senate, Ninety-Seventh Congress, Second Session, on Oversight Hearings on Proposed Legislation Providing Federal Financial Assistance to State and Local Law Enforcement Agencies, and to Review the Effects of Budgetary Reductions for Criminal Justice Assistance Programs; and on H.R. 4481 . . .* (Washington, D.C.: US Government Printing Office, 1982), 114–117.

79. "Letter from Edward G. Rendell, DA. February 24, 1984," Women Organized Against Rape Records, box 17, folder 14, SCRC, Temple University Archives.

80. Samia Cherry, interview with the author, April 3, 2019.

81. Letty Thall, interview with the author, April 10, 2019.

82. Deborah Johnson, interview with the author, April 25, 2019.

83. Lynn Moncrief to Lorraine Brantham, January 28, 1977, Women Organized Against Rape Records, box 5, folder 11, SCRC, Temple University Archives; *HOTLINE*, March 1977, Women Organized Against Rape Records, box 29, folder 4, SCRC, Temple University Archives. For more on the conflict over busing and the desegregation of Philadelphia public schools, see Matthew Countryman, *Up South*.

84. "Crisis Center Project 1975 / 1976," Women Organized Against Rape Records, box 18, folder 21, SCRC, Temple University Archives.

85. Abigail Perkiss, *Making Good Neighbors: Civil Rights, Liberalism, and Integration in Postwar Philadelphia* (Ithaca, NY: Cornell University Press, 2014), 129–130.

86. "ER Committee: WOAR Statistics on Rape 1974–1976," Women Organized Against Rape Records, box 4, folder 20, SCRC, Temple University Archives.

87. "ER Committee: WOAR Statistics on Rape 1974–1976."

88. Breines, *The Trouble Between Us*, 156–157; Valk, *Radical Sisters*, 170.

89. "Board of Directors Meeting February 21, 1978," Women Organized Against Rape Records, box 1, folder 9, SCRC, Temple University Archives.

90. "1980 Statistics," Women Organized Against Rape Records, box 2, folder 24, SCRC, Temple University Archives.

91. *HOTLINE*, October 1979, Women Organized Against Rape Records, box 29, folder 6, SCRC, Temple University Archives; Richie, *Arrested Justice*, 133; Taylor ed., *How We Get Free*, 66–67; Thuma, *All Our Trials*, 127–128; Gruber, *The Feminist War on Crime*, 87; Lindsey, *America, Goddam*, 119; Greene, *Free Joan Little*, 228.

92. Bumiller, *In an Abusive State*, 4.

93. For more on African American women serving as "bridge leaders" between the feminist movement against sexual violence and Black liberation groups, see Maria Bevacqua, "Reconsidering Violence Against Women: Coalition Politics in the Antirape Movement," in *Feminist Coalitions: Historical Perspectives on Second-Wave Feminism*, ed. Stephanie Gilmore (Urbana: University of Illinois Press, 2008), 163–177.

94. "Letter to Henrietta Tower Wurts Memorial Fund, January 5, 1977," Women Organized Against Rape Records, box 5, folder 11, SCRC, Temple University Archives; Lynn Moncrief to Rev. Frank B. Mitchell, December 22, 1976, Women Organized Against Rape Records, box 5, folder 10. SCRC, Temple University Archives; *HOTLINE*, February 1977, Women Organized Against Rape Records, box 29, folder 4, SCRC, Temple University Archives. According to Wadiyah Nelson, Black churches proved an unprofitable line for recruitment due to "an inordinate amount of resistance . . . dealing with Black-on-Black rape, because at that point it was airing [the community's] dirty laundry." Wadiyah Nelson, interview with the author, March 19, 2019.

95. Lynn Moncrief to Mattie McDaniels, December 6, 1976, Women Organized Against Rape Records, box 5, folder 10, SCRC, Temple University Archives.

96. "Brief Overview of How Community Outreach Is Implemented 10/26/76–11/14/77," Women Organized Against Rape Records, box 1, folder 5, SCRC, Temple University Archives.

97. Ruth Hall to Lynn Moncrief, August 4, 1979, Women Organized Against Rape Records, box 6, folder 7, SCRC, Temple University Archives.

98. Lynn Moncrief to Deb Friedman, August 21, 1978, Women Organized Against Rape Records, box 6, folder 7, SCRC, Temple University Archives.

99. *HOTLINE*, April 1977, Women Organized Against Rape Records, box 29, folder 4, SCRC, Temple University Archives.

100. Freedman, *Redefining Rape*, 110.

101. *HOTLINE*, April 1977, Women Organized Against Rape Records, box 29, folder 4, SCRC, Temple University Archives.

102. Thuma, *All Our Trials*, 45.

103. Bevacqua, *Rape on the Public Agenda*, 84–85; Thuma, *All Our Trials*, 2.

104. Tommi Avicoli, "Combatting Rape: Interview with Lynn Moncrief," *Drummer* [Philadelphia], March 14, 1978, 5.

105. Tommi Avicoli, "Prison Rape: Interview with Lynn Moncrief, *New Gay Life* [Philadelphia], March 2, 1978, 22.

106. Lynn Moncrief to William Fuller of Prisoners Against Rape, April 2, 1979, Women Organized Against Rape Records, box 6, folder 7, SCRC, Temple University Archives.

107. *HOTLINE*, September 1979, Women Organized Against Rape Records, box 29, folder 6, SCRC, Temple University Archives.

108. *HOTLINE*, September 1977, Women Organized Against Rape Records, box 29, folder 4, SCRC, Temple University Archives.

109. "Board of Directors Meeting, May 19, 1977," Women Organized Against Rape Records, box 1, folder 4, SCRC, Temple University Archives.

110. "GJC Crisis Center Project Quarterly Report July-September 1977," Women Organized Against Rape Records, box 18, folder 33, SCRC, Temple University Archives.

111. The term "Third World," as used by Black feminist organizations like Frances Beal's Third World Women's Alliance, refers to a sense of political affinity among non-white people of the world based on recognition of the interlocking nature of racism, sexism, and imperialism. In the case of Philadelphia WOAR's Third World Caucus (TWC), where the majority of its members and its originators were Black women, the term is used interchangeably with Black feminist. For more on the diverse uses of the term "Third World Woman" in Black political organizing in the 1970s, see Springer, *Living for the Revolution* and Farmer, *Remaking Black Power*.

112. Lee Nelson, interview with the author, April 1, 2019; Letty Thall, interview with the author, April 10, 2019; Glenavie Norton, interview with the author, April 12, 2019.

113. Wadiyah Nelson, interview with the author, May 10, 2018.

114. Joan Ashton Frye, interview with the author, May 10, 2018.

115. Samia Cherry, interview with the author, April 3, 2019.

116. Samia Cherry, interview with the author, April 3, 2019.

117. Wadiyah Nelson, interview with the author, May 10, 2018; Joan Ashton Frye, interview with the author, May 10, 2018.

118. "Third World Caucus Objectives, Adopted June 9, 1978," Women Organized Against Rape Records, box 4, folder 44, SCRC, Temple University Archives.

119. Wadiyah Nelson, interview with the author, March 19, 2018.

120. "Legal Committee, 1975–1976," Women Organized Against Rape Records, box 4, folder 26, SCRC, Temple University Archives.

121. *WOARpath*, Spring 1981, Women Organized Against Rape Records, box 29, folder 11, SCRC, Temple University Archives.

122. *HOTLINE*, April 1980, Women Organized Against Rape Records, box 29, folder 8, SCRC, Temple University Archives.

123. "Crisis Center Project 1975 / 1976," Women Organized Against Rape Records, box 18, folder 21, SCRC, Temple University Archives.

124. Wadiyah Nelson, interview with the author, March 19, 2019; "Memorandum from Lynn Moncrief to TWC, June 25, 1979," Women Organized Against Rape Records, box 4, folder 44, SCRC, Temple University Archives.

125. "Introspective Look at Our Volunteer, 1977," Women Organized Against Rape Records, box 34, folder 32, SCRC, Temple University Archives.

126. Letty Thall, interview with the author, April 10, 2019.

127. Lee Nelson, interview with the author, April 1, 2019.

128. Glenavie Norton, interview with the author, April 12, 2019.

129. *HOTLINE*, July 1977, Women Organized Against Rape Records, box 29, folder 4, SCRC, Temple University Archives. Emphasis added.

130. "Third World Caucus Objectives, Adopted June 9, 1978," Women Organized Against Rape Records, box 4, folder 44, SCRC, Temple University Archives.

131. "September 12, 1977: Third World Caucus Newsletter," Women Organized Against Rape Records, box 4, folder 44, SCRC, Temple University Archives; "Third World Caucus Newsletter January 1978," Women Organized Against Rape Records, box 4, folder 44, SCRC, Temple University Archives.

132. Berit Lakey, interview with the author, April 29, 2019.

133. *HOTLINE*, June 1979, Women Organized Against Rape Records, box 29, folder 6, SCRC, Temple University Archives.

134. *HOTLINE*, October 1979, Women Organized Against Rape Records, box 29, folder 6, SCRC, Temple University Archives.

135. "Profile of WOAR Volunteer for the Period October 1979–December 1979," box 3, folder 10, SCRC, Temple University Archives.

136. "Third World Caucus Objectives, Adopted June 9, 1978," Women Organized Against Rape Records, box 4, folder 44, SCRC, Temple University Archives.

137. "Letter to Board of Directors from Hiring Committee," Women Organized Against Rape Records, box 4, folder 44, SCRC, Temple University Archives.

138. For more on the ways in which professionalized white feminist praxis within rape crisis centers overlooked the needs of poor non-white rape victims and contributed to Black women's disempowerment within the movement, see Bevacqua, *Rape on the Public Agenda*, 83; Gottschalk, *Prison and the Gallows*, 125; Bumiller, *In an Abusive State*, 95; Richie, *Arrested Justice*, 149.

139. "Memorandum from Lynn Moncrief to Third World Caucus, June 25, 1979," Women Organized Against Rape Records, box 4, folder 44, SCRC, Temple University Archives.

140. "Administrative Team Report Fiscal Year 1980," Women Organized Against Rape Records, box 1, folder 15, SCRC, Temple University Archives.

141. *WOARpath*, January 1981, Women Organized Against Rape Records, box 29, folder 11, SCRC, Temple University Archives.

142. *WOARpath*, January 1981, Women Organized Against Rape Records, box 29, folder 11, SCRC, Temple University Archives.

143. "Volunteer Profiles (through June 1980)," Women Organized Against Rape Records, box 3, folder 11, SCRC, Temple University Archives.

144. "Training and Education Team Objectives," Women Organized Against Rape Records, box 4, folder 22, SCRC, Temple University Archives.

145. "Volunteer Training Manuals," Women Organized Against Rape Records, box 35, folder 6, SCRC, Temple University Archives.

146. "Focus: Public Education," Women Organized Against Rape Records, box 30, folder 13, SCRC, Temple University Archives.

147. *WOARpath*, January 1981, Women Organized Against Rape Records, box 29, folder 11, SCRC, Temple University Archives.

148. Sandra Long, "Rape is Color Blind," *Philadelphia Bulletin*, June 29, 1981.

149. *WOARpath*, Spring 1981, Women Organized Against Rape Records, box 29, folder 11, SCRC, Temple University Archives.

150. Richie, *Arrested Justice*, 36–37.

151. *WOARpath*, Spring 1983, Women Organized Against Rape Records, box 29, folder 17, SCRC, Temple University Archives.

152. "Letters to WOAR," Organized Against Rape Records, box 7, folder 5, SCRC, Temple University Archives.

153. Renee D. Turner, "Date Rape," *Ebony*, December 1990, 106.

154. United States Congress, *The Coming Decade: American Women and Human Resources Policies and Programs, 1979: Hearings Before the Committee on Labor and Human Resources, United States Senate, Ninety-Sixth Congress, First Session . . . January 31 and February 1, 1979* (Washington, D.C.: U.S. Government Printing Office, 1979), 823.

155. Nkenge Touré, "Special Populations Conference: Black Focus," *Feminist Alliance Against Rape Newsletter* (May / June 1977): 8.

Chapter 3

1. Nancy Gager and Cathleen Schurr, *Sexual Assault: Confronting Rape in America* (New York: Grosset & Dunlap, 1976), 203.

2. United States Congress, *The Coming Decade: American Women and Human Resources Policies and Programs, 1979: Hearings Before the Committee on Labor and Human Resources, United States Senate, Ninety-Sixth Congress, First Session . . . January 31 and February 1, 1979* (Washington, D.C.: U.S. Government Printing Office, 1979), 528.

3. "National Center for the Prevention and Control of Rape Fact Sheet, September 1977," Pauline Bart Papers, box 2, David M. Rubenstein Rare Book & Manuscript Library, Duke University.

4. Bevacqua, *Rape on the Public Agenda*, 148–149.

5. Gottschalk, *The Prison and the Gallows*, 126–127.

6. Ann Wolbert Burgess, ed., *Rape and Sexual Assault: A Research Handbook* (New York: Garland Publishing, 1985), 18–24.

7. United States Congress, *Research into Violent Behavior*, 557.

8. "Upcoming Conference," *Feminist Alliance Against Rape Newsletter* (January / February 1977): 1.

9. Nkenge Touré, "Special Populations Caucus: Black Focus," *Feminist Alliance Against Rape Newsletter* (May / June 1977): 8.

10. It is unclear how many people of color, if any, submitted applications for NCPCR funding.

11. Touré, "Special Populations Caucus: Black Focus," 9.

12. "Report from the First National Conference on Third World Women and Violence, August 1980: Overview of Third World Women and Violence," Loretta Ross Papers, SSC-MS-00504, box 5, folder 3, Smith College Special Collections.

13. See Hicks, *Talk with You Like a Woman*; Khalil Gibran Muhammad, *The Condemnation of Blackness: Race, Crime, and the Making of Modern Urban America* (Cambridge, MA: Harvard University Press, 2010); Nelson, *Body and Soul*.

14. For more on the history of white scientific professionals exploiting the bodies of Black women to build theories of sex without the perspectives of Black women themselves, see C. Riley Snorton, *Black on Both Sides: A Racial History of Trans Identity* (Minneapolis: University of Minnesota Press, 2017), 17.

15. "Mathias Bill," *Feminist Alliance Against Rape Newsletter* (winter 1974): 10.

16. Jackie MacMillan, "Update: Mathias Bill," *Feminist Alliance Against Rape Newsletter* (fall 1975): 18.

17. Bevacqua, *Rape on the Public Agenda*, 143–144.

18. Gager and Schurr, *Sexual Assault: Confronting Rape in America*, 203.

19. Gager and Schur, *Sexual Assault: Confronting Rape in America*, xiv.

20. "National Center for the Prevention and Control of Rape Fact Sheet, September 1977," Pauline Bart Papers, box 2, David M. Rubenstein Rare Book & Manuscript Library, Duke University.

21. Ronni Schier, "The War Against Rape," *For a Change Women's News*, September 19, 1977, 7.

22. "Being a Feminist Academic (1981)," Pauline Bart papers, box 23, David M. Rubenstein Rare Book & Manuscript Library, Duke University.

23. "Correspondence (feminists), 1975–1979," Papers of Susan Brownmiller, 1935–2000, MC 523, T-326, 7.10–7.12, box 7, Schlesinger Library, Radcliffe Institute, Harvard University.

24. Deb Friedman, "Where Has All the $$ Gone?," *Feminist Alliance Against Rape Newsletter* (September / October 1976): 5

25. "Biographical Information Diana E. H. Russell," Diana Russell Papers, SSC-MS-00752, box 13, Smith College Special Collections.

26. Diana E. H. Russell, "Political Actions," accessed October 7, 2019, https://www.dianarussell.com/political_actions.html.

27. Diana E. H. Russell, *The Politics of Rape: The Victim's Perspective* (New York: Stein and Day, 1974).

28. "Rape, 1979–1980," Papers of Angela Y. Davis, 1937–2017 (inclusive), 1968–2006 (bulk), MC 940, 188.6, box 188, Schlesinger Library, Radcliffe Institute, Harvard University.

29. "Letter from Diana Russell June 14, 1973," Third World Women's Alliance Records, SSC-MS-00697, box 3, folder 4, Smith College Special Collections.

30. Diana E. H. Russell, *Sexual Exploitation: Rape, Child Sexual Abuse, and Workplace Harassment* (Beverly Hills: Sage Publications, 1984), 41.

31. Russell, *Sexual Exploitation*, 33.

32. Russell, *Sexual Exploitation*, 19.

33. Jackie MacMillan, "Grants Available from NIMH," *Feminist Alliance Against Rape Newsletter* (winter 1976): 13.

34. Deb Friedman, "Where Has All the $$$ Gone?," *Feminist Alliance Against Rape Newsletter* (September / October 1976): 5.

35. MacMillan, "Grants Available from NIMH," 13.

36. "Mathias Bill," *Feminist Alliance Against Rape Newsletter* (winter 1974): 10.

37. "Upcoming Conferences," *Feminist Alliance Against Rape Newsletter* (January / February 1977): 1.

38. Deb Friedman, "NIMH Conference," *Feminist Alliance Against Rape Newsletter* (March / April 1977): 2.

39. Nkenge Touré, "Special Populations Conference: Black Focus," *Feminist Alliance Against Rape Newsletter* (May / June 1977): 8.

40. Touré, "Special Populations Conference: Black Focus," 3.

41. Touré, "Special Populations Conference: Black Focus," 3.

42. Touré, "Special Populations Conference: Black Focus," 9.

43. Touré, "Special Populations Conference: Black Focus," 8.

44. Touré, "Special Populations Conference: Black Focus," 8.

45. Touré, "Special Populations Conference: Black Focus," 8.

46. "Third World Women and Rape: Report from the First National Conference on Third World Women and Violence, August 1980," Loretta Ross Papers, SSC-MS-00504, box 5, folder 2, Smith College Special Collections.

47. Deb Friedman, "Conferences Evoke Concerns of Special Populations," *Feminist Alliance Against Rape Newsletter* (May / June 1977): 4.

48. Friedman, "Conferences Evoke Concerns of Special Populations," 4.

49. Friedman, "Conferences Evoke Concerns of Special Populations," 4.

50. Friedman, "Conferences Evoke Concerns of Special Populations," 4.

51. "Conferences Cancelled," *Feminist Alliance Against Rape Newsletter* (July / August 1977): 5.

52. United States Congress, *Research into Violent Behavior*, 404.

53. United States Congress, *Research into Violent Behavior*, 404.

54. United States Congress, *Research into Violent Behavior*, 406.

55. United States Congress, *Research into Violent Behavior*, 406.

56. United States Congress, *Research into Violent Behavior*, 406.

57. United States Congress, *Research into Violent Behavior*, 406.

58. Patricia Hill Collins, *Black Feminist Thought: Knowledge, Consciousness, and the Politics of Empowerment*, 2nd ed. (New York: Routledge, 2014), 19.

59. "San Francisco Women Against Rape & Bay Area Women Against Rape," *Plexus* (October 1974): 5.

60. Ann Bartz, "BAWAR: What to Do About Rape in the Bay Area," *Freedom News*, September 1973, 9.

61. "San Francisco Women Against Rape & Bay Area Women Against Rape," *Plexus* (October 1974): 5.

62. "News Notes: Bay Area Women Against Rape," *Feminist Alliance Against Rape Newsletter* (January / February 1977): 9.

63. Gary Rivlin, "Who Do You Trust?: Experts Say Cops Don't Rape More than Any Other Group of Citizens. They Also Don't Rape Less . . ." *Express: The Easy Bay's Free Weekly*, September 20, 1991, 22–23.

64. Thuma, *All Our Trials*, 50.

65. "Local Rapist: Stinky," *Plexus* (May 1977): 5.

66. Carolyn Craven, "A Rape Victim Strikes Back: Television Reporter Tells of Her Brutal Ordeal and Resolve to Help Capture Her Brutal Attacker," *Ebony*, September 1978, 154–160.

67. Craven, "A Rape Victim Strikes Back," 158.

68. Craven, "A Rape Victim Strikes Back," 160.

69. Springer, *Living for the Revolution*, 29.

70. Warren Hinckle, "Strange Jailing in 'Stinky' Case," *San Francsico Chronicle*, November 11, 1978; Fred Garretson, "Cops: We Had Stinky; DA: I Can't Prosecute," *Oakland Tribune*, July 14, 1979; "Stinky Case Stymied," *Plexus* (August 1979): 8.

71. Elise Cassel, "16 Months Since Last Stinky Rape Attack," *Oakland Tribune*, April 15, 1979.

72. "State of the Movement—Resources & Activists," *Plexus* (May 1979): 10–11; "Rape Group Fights for Life," *Plexus* (June 1979): 2; "BAWAR: No Replacement," *Plexus* (July 1979): 7; "BAWAR Split Goes to Suit," *Plexus* (August 1979): 1; "Hotline Needs Help," *Plexus* (October 1979): 10.

73. "Field Notes," Diana Russell Papers, SSC-MS-00752, box 6, Smith College Special Collections.

74. "Case #217–024: Zidar," Diana Russell Papers, SSC-MS-00752, box 4, Smith College Special Collections.

75. "Case #101–013: Juanida," Diana Russell Papers, SSC-MS-00752, box 1, Smith College Special Collections.

76. "Case #101–013: Juanida."

77. "Case #230–002: Ela," Diana Russell Papers, SSC-MS-00752, box 5, Smith College Special Collections.

78. "Case #320–001: Gwen," Diana Russell Papers, SSC-MS-00752, box 7, Smith College Special Collections.

79. "Case #145–013: Barbara," Diana Russell Papers, SSC-MS-00752, box 1, Smith College Special Collections.

80. "Case #421–163: Dorothy," Diana Russell Papers, SSC-MS-00752, box 10, Smith College Special Collections.

81. "Case #200–037: Margaret," Diana Russell Papers, SSC-MS-00752, box 4, Smith College Special Collections.

82. "Case # 181–019: Elmira," Diana Russell Papers, SSC-MS-00752, box 3, Smith College Special Collections.

83. "Case #235–050: Juanita," Diana Russell Papers, SSC-MS-00752, box 5, Smith College Special Collections.

84. Alternatively, their calls for stronger policing in rape-prone areas and harsher punishment of convicted rapists may have emerged from economic desperation. By mid-decade, a looming recession had spiked unemployment and municipal fiscal crises had choked the Bay Area of social services. Since policing seemed to be the only domestic service the state would consistently offer its citizens, some African American women may have seen their personal salvation from violence in a stringent crime control policy. For more on African Americans' embrace of policing in the late twentieth century, see Forman, *Locking Up Our Own*.

85. "Case #197–014: Jacquelyn," Diana Russell Papers, SSC-MS-00752, box 4, Smith College Special Collections.

86. "Case #401–008: Anonymous," Diana Russell Papers, SSC-MS-00752, box 11, Smith College Special Collections.

87. "Case #235–051: Ernestine," Diana Russell Papers, SSC-MS-00752, box 5, Smith College Special Collections.

88. "Case #246–01: Jazelle," Diana Russell Papers, SSC-MS-00752, box 6, Smith College Special Collections.

89. "Case #246–01: Jazelle."

90. "Case #420–024: Gail," Diana Russell Papers, SSC-MS-00752, box 9, Smith College Special Collections.

91. "Case #420–024: Gail."

92. "Case #307–017: Juanita," Diana Russell Papers, SSC-MS-00752, box 7, Smith College Special Collections.

93. "Case #307–017: Juanita."

94. Mary Ann Largen, "Slipping Services Through a Conservative Congress," *Feminist Alliance Against Rape Newsletter* (November / December 1978): 15.

95. United States Congress, *Research into Violent Behavior*, 427–429.

96. United States Congress, *Research into Violent Behavior*, 519–520.

97. United States Congress, *Research into Violent Behavior*, 522–523.

98. United States Congress, *Research into Violent Behavior*, 553.

99. United States Congress, *Research into Violent Behavior*, 554.

100. United States Congress, *Research into Violent Behavior*, 553.

101. United States Congress, *Research into Violent Behavior*, 553.

102. United States Congress, *Research into Violent Behavior*, 556.

103. United States Congress, *The Coming Decade*, 528.

104. United States Congress, *The Coming Decade*, 823–825.

105. Russell, *The Politics of Rape*, 14.

106. Bevacqua, *Rape on the Public Agenda*, 52.

107. Russell, *Sexual Exploitation*, 20.

108. Ronni Scheier, "The War Against Rape," *For a Change Women's News*, September 19, 1977, 7.

109. Russell, *Sexual Exploitation*, 46.

110. Russell, *Sexual Exploitation*, 83.

111. Russell, *Sexual Exploitation*, 84.

112. Russell, *Sexual Exploitation*, 99: 20 percent of the all the non-white women raped by non-white men reported, compared to 14 percent of white women raped by non-white men, 7 percent of non-white women raped by non-white men, and 5 percent of white women raped by white men.

113. Russell, *Sexual Exploitation*, 99. Compared to Jewish women (9 percent), Asian women (8 percent), non-Jewish white women (7 percent), or Native American women (0 percent).

114. Russell, *Sexual Exploitation*, 92.

115. Russell, *Sexual Exploitation*, 93.

116. Russell, *Sexual Exploitation*, 98.

117. Russell, *Sexual Exploitation*, 99.

118. Russell, *Sexual Exploitation*, 143.

119. Russell, *Sexual Exploitation*, 143.

120. Russell, *Sexual Exploitation*, 289.

121. Burgess, ed., *Rape and Sexual Assault*, 21.

122. United States Congress, *Victims of Rape: Hearing Before the Select Committee on Children, Youth, and Families, House of Representatives, One Hundred First Congress, Second Session, Hearing Held in Washington, DC, June 28, 1990* (Washington, D.C.: U.S. Government Printing Office, 1990), 209.

123. Gail E. Wyatt, "The Sexual Abuse of Afro-American and White-American Women in Childhood," *Child Abuse and Neglect* 9, no. 4 (1985): 507–519; Gail E. Wyatt, "The Relationship Between Child Sexual Abuse and Adolescent Sexual Functioning in Afro-American and White American Women," *Annals of the New York Academy of Science* 528 (1988): 111–122; Gail E. Wyatt, "Reexamining Factors Predicting Afro-American and White American Women's Age at First Coitus," *Archive of Sex Behavior* 18, no. 4 (1989): 271–298; Gail E. Wyatt and M. Newcomb, "Internal and External Mediators of Women's Sexual Abuse in Childhood," *Journal of Consulting and Clinical Psychology* 58, no. 6 (1990): 758–767; Gail E. Wyatt, D. Guthrie, and C. M. Notgrass, "Differential Effects of Women's Child Sexual Abuse and Subsequent Sexual Victimization,"

Journal of Consulting and Clinical Psychology 60, no. 2 (1992): 167–173; Gail E. Wyatt and M. Riederle, "Sexual Harassment and Prior Sexual Trauma Among African American and White American Women," *Violence and Victims* 9, no. 3 (1994): 233–247.

124. United States Congress, *Victims of Rape*, 29.

125. United States Congress, *Victims of Rape*, 29.

126. United States Congress, *Victims of Rape*, 29.

127. United States Congress, *Victims of Rape*, 30–31.

128. United States Congress, *Victims of Rape*, 27–28.

129. United States Congress, *Victims of Rape*, 94–95.

Chapter 4

1. Nkenge Touré, interview by Loretta Ross, transcript of video recording, December 5, 2004, Voices of Feminism Oral History Project, Sophia Smith Collection, Smith College, 35.

2. Nkenge Touré, interview with the author, October 16, 2018.

3. Nkenge Touré, interview with the author, October 16, 2018.

4. "Report from the First National Conference on Third World Women and Violence (1981)," Loretta Ross Papers, SSC-MS-00504, box 5, folder 3, Smith College Special Collections.

5. Chris Myers Asch and George Derek Musgrove, *Chocolate City: A History of Race and Democracy in the Nation's Capital* (Chapel Hill: University of North Carolina Press, 2017), 394–395.

6. Nkenge Touré, interview by Loretta Ross, 42.

7. Nkenge Touré, interview by Loretta Ross, 99.

8. Lynn Sacco, "Sanitized for Your Protection: Medical Discourse and the Denial of Incest in the United States, 1890–1940," *Journal of Women's History* 14, no. 3 (2002): 80–104; Nancy Whittier, *The Politics of Child Sexual Abuse: Emotion, Social Movements, and the State* (Oxford: Oxford University Press, 2011), 119; Freedman, *Redefining Rape*, 130, 160.

9. Robin D. Stone, *No Secrets, No Lies: How Black Families Can Heal from Sexual Abuse* (New York: Broadway Books, 2004), 29.

10. Loretta Ross, interview by Joyce Follet, transcript of video recording, November 3, 2004, Voices of Feminism Oral History Project, Sophia Smith Collection, Smith College, 46–48.

11. Whittier, *The Politics of Child Sexual Abuse*, 61.

12. Florence Rush, "The Sexual Abuse of Children," in *Rape: The First Sourcebook for Women*, ed. Noreen Connell and Cassandra Wilson (New York: Plume Books, 1976), 66.

13. Gager and Schurr, *Sexual Assault*, 46.

14. Philip Jenkins, *Moral Panic: Changing Concepts of the Child Molester in Modern America* (New Haven, CT: Yale University Press, 1998), 118; Meiners, *For the Children?*, 167–169; Renfro, *Stranger Danger*, 33.

15. Greene, *Free Joan Little*, 225–226.

16. Shaw, *What a Woman Ought to Be and Do*, 210–219; Crystal Sanders, *A Chance for Change: Head Start & Mississippi's Black Freedom Struggle* (Chapel Hill: University of North Carolina Press, 2016), 57.

17. Linda Gordon, *Heroes of Their Own Lives: The Politics and History of Family Violence: Boston, 1880–1960* (New York: Viking Press, 1988); Jenkins, *Moral Panic*; Stephen Robertson, *Crimes Against Children: Sexual Violence and Legal Culture in New York City, 1880–1960* (Chapel Hill: University of North Carolina Press, 2005); Freedman, *Redefining Rape*, 148–149.

18. Jenkins, *Moral Panic*, 94.

19. Whittier, *The Politics of Child Sexual Abuse*, 23.

20. Rush, "The Sexual Abuse of Children," 66.

21. Gager and Schurr, *Sexual Assault*, 46.

22. Whittier, *The Politics of Child Sexual Abuse*, 32–34. Not to be confused with the Community Action Programs (CAPs) of the "war on poverty."

23. "Daddy Said Not to Tell: Dynamics of Child Sexual Assault," *Aegis* (September / October 1978): 45.

24. "Daddy Said Not to Tell," 46.

25. Sacco, "Sanitized for Your Protection."

26. Burgess, ed., *Rape and Sexual Assault*, 20.

27. Judith Lewis Herman, *Father-Daughter Incest* (Cambridge, MA: Harvard University Press, 1981), 206–207.

28. Herman, *Father-Daughter Incest*, 67.

29. At the same time, Herman insisted that "many of the first, most daring, and most honest contributions to the public discussion of incest were made by Black women, and much of our work has been inspired by theirs." In the footnotes, Herman cited Maya Angelou's *I Know Why the Caged Bird Sings* (1969) and Toni Morrison's *The Bluest Eye* (1970) as examples.

30. Gail Elizabeth Wyatt, "The Sexual Abuse of Afro-American and White-American Women in Girlhood," *Child Abuse & Neglect* 9 (1985): 513–518.

31. Richie, *Arrested Justice*, 90–92.; Gruber, *Feminist War on Crime*, 52–58.

32. Melba Wilson, *Crossing the Boundary: Black Women Survive Incest* (Seattle: Seal Press, 1994), 8.

33. Kimberle Crenshaw, "Mapping the Margins: Intersectionality, Identity Politics, and Violence Against Women of Color," *Stanford Law Review* 43, no. 6 (1991): 1259.

34. "Daddy Said Not to Tell, Part II," *Aegis* (November / December 1978): 7.

35. "Daddy Said Not to Tell, Part II," 8.

36. "Daddy Said Not to Tell, Part II," 9.

37. As scholar Linda Gordon notes, the hesitance of child protection agencies to call upon heavy-handed state intervention in sexually abusive households stemmed from disbelief of girls who accused their male relatives of sexual abuse. A related reluctance to deprive the family of a male breadwinner also prevented child savers from calling for the incarceration of abusive fathers. Gordon, *Heroes of Their Own Lives*, 220–224.

38. "Daddy Said Not to Tell, Part II," 8.

39. Dorothy Roberts, *Shattered Bonds: The Color of Child Welfare* (New York: Basic Books, 2001), 16–17; Meiners, *For the Children?*, 40, 64.

40. Stone, *No Secrets, No Lies*, 16.

41. Hicks, *Talk with You Like a Woman*, 42–43; Muhammad, *The Condemnation of Blackness*, 103.

42. "The Negro Family: The Case for National Action," Office of Planning and Research, United States Department of Labor, March 1965, www.dol.gov/asp/programs/history/webid-meynihan.htm.

43. Stone, *No Secrets, No Lies*, 179.

44. Stone, *No Secrets, No Lies*, 182.

45. Stone, *No Secrets, No Lies*, 182.

46. Stone, *No Secrets, No Lies*, 181–184.

47. Stone, *No Secrets, No Lies*, 184.

48. Stone, *No Secrets, No Lies*, 194.

49. Stone, *No Secrets, No Lies*, 204–206.

50. Marilyn Marshall, "How to Protect Your Children from People They Trust," *Ebony*, November 1986, 52.

51. Tashmica Torok, "Casting Aspersions," in *Love WITH Accountability: Digging up the Roots of Child Sexual Abuse*, ed. Aishah Shahidah Simmons (Chico: AK Press, 2019), 274.

52. Whittier, *The Politics of Child Sexual Abuse*, 84–85.

53. Whittier, *The Politics of Child Sexual Abuse*, 90, 94.

54. Whittier, *The Politics of Child Sexual Abuse*, 87.

55. Whittier, *The Politics of Child Sexual Abuse*, 76–77.

56. Jenkins, *Moral Panic*, 127.

57. Douglas J. Besharov, "Overreach of the Guardian State," *Wall Street Journal*, April 2, 1983.

58. Roberts, *Shattered Bonds*, 16; Meiners, *For the Children?*, 64.

59. Renfro, *Stranger Danger*, 5–6.

60. Scholar Philip Jenkins has argued that media attention to child sexual abuse in the late 1970s and early 1980s fit Stuart Hall's classic definition of a moral panic, in which "the official reaction . . . is out of all proportion to the actual threat offered . . . 'experts' perceive the threat in all but identical terms, and appear to talk 'with one voice' of rates . . . and the media representations stress 'sudden and dramatic' increases . . . and 'novelty' above and beyond that which a sober, realistic appraisal could sustain." See Jenkins, *Moral Panic*, 6.

61. Nancy Whittier contends that the race-neutral feminist analysis of child sexual abuse ignited a seemingly race-neutral moral panic in which "the African American press . . . was virtually indistinguishable from white women's magazines." Upon closer inspection, the coverage in the Black press evoked subtle differences owing to the Black community's complex historical relationship with incest. See Whittier, *Politics of Child Sexual Abuse*, 119.

62. Gruber, *The Feminist War on Crime*, 109.

63. Renfro, *Stranger Danger*, 57.

64. Russell Watson, "A Hidden Epidemic: Sexual Abuse of Children is Much More Common than Most Americans Suspect," *Newsweek*, May 14, 1984, 30–36.

65. Walter Leavy, "How to Protect Your Child from Molesters," *Ebony*, May 1981, 117–122.

66. The feminist race-neutral analysis of child sexual abuse, in conjunction with the inroads made by Black anti-rape organizers in the 1970s, may have emboldened the Black press to participate in the discourse. They necessarily approached the issue with the entirety of its cultural and historical context in tow. Black news outlets may have covered child rape and molestation as a self-conscious rebuttal to the stereotypical dyad of abusive, unloving Black fathers and negligent, careless Black mothers. By engaging Black parents in the project of protecting Black children from molestation and abuse, these publications asserted that Black parents would go to the same lengths as their white counterparts to ensure their safety.

67. Renfro, *Stranger Danger*, 87.

68. Jenkins, *Moral Panic*, 132–133.

69. Jane Roberts Chapman and Barbara Smith, "Response of Social Service and Criminal Justice Agencies to Child Sexual Abuse Complaints," in *Response: To the Victimization of Women and Children* 10, no. 3 (1987), Pauline Bart Papers, box 82, David M. Rubenstein Rare Book & Manuscript Library, Duke University.

70. Chapman and Smith, "Response of Social Service and Criminal Justice Agencies."

71. Chapman and Smith, "Response of Social Service and Criminal Justice Agencies."

72. Chapman and Smith, "Response of Social Service and Criminal Justice Agencies."

73. National Legal Resource Center for Child Advocacy and Protection, American Bar Association, Young Lawyers Division, "Child Sexual Abuse: Legal Issues and Approaches," September 1980, Center for Women Policy Studies subject files on domestic violence, 1975–1985, MC 1095, 1.6, box 1, Schlesinger Library, Radcliffe Institute, Harvard University.

74. "Incest-Punish the Mother?," *Aegis* 37 (1983): 48–49.

75. "Incest-Punish the Mother?," 48–49.

76. "Alarming Number of Victims of Childhood Sex Abuse," *Washington Post*, March 30, 1983, D.C.6.

77. Michel Marriott, "Child Sexual Abuse: Hidden Crimes Come Out of the Closet," *Washington Post*, June 8, 1984, A1.

78. Marriott, "Child Sexual Abuse," A16.

79. Roberts, *Shattered Bonds*, 59.

80. Renfro, *Stranger Danger*, 9.

81. Valk, *Radical Sisters*, 163.

82. Valk, *Radical Sisters*, 170.

83. Valk, *Radical Sisters*, 170.

84. "Rape crisis centers (Elizabethann O'Sullivan), 1972–1977, 1997," Papers of Susan Brownmiller, 1935–2000, MC 523, T-326, 22.10, box 22, Schlesinger Library, Radcliffe Institute, Harvard University.

85. Nkenge Touré, interview by Loretta Ross, 40–41.

86. Nkenge Touré, interview by Loretta Ross, 40–41.

87. Nkenge Touré, interview by Loretta Ross, 40–41.

88. Nkenge Touré, interview by Loretta Ross, 35–36.

89. Loretta Ross, interview by Joyce Follet, 33–34.

90. Whittier, *The Politics of Child Sexual Abuse*, 177.

91. Loretta Ross, interview by Joyce Follet, 48.

92. Nkenge Touré, interview by Loretta Ross, 13.

93. Nkenge Touré, interview by Loretta Ross, 12.

94. Nkenge Touré, interview by Loretta Ross, 13.

95. Nkenge Touré, interview by Loretta Ross, 17.

96. Nkenge Touré, interview by Loretta Ross, 38.

97. "Interview: Black Women and Rape," *Feminist Alliance Against Rape Newsletter* (November / December 1976): 10.

98. "Interview: Black Women and Rape," 12.

99. "Interview: Black Women and Rape," 14.

100. Athelia Knight, "Activists Seek Probe in Ward Murder," *Washington Post*, November 8, 1980, C1.

101. "In Memorium: Yulanda Ward, 22 Years Old," *Aegis* 31 (winter / spring 1981): 80–81.

102. Thuma, *All Our Trials*, 151–154.

103. "Judgment on Justice," *Feminist Alliance Against Rape Newsletter* (September / October 1977): 5.

104. Valk, *Radical Sisters*, 163.

105. "Orientation Packet 1975," Deb Friedman Collection of Feminist Anti-violence Records, SSC-MS-00795, box 1, folder 2, Smith College Special Collections.

106. "Take Back the Night March Statement of Purpose 1981," Deb Friedman Collection of Feminist Anti-violence Records, SSC-MS-00795, box 1, folder 1, Smith College Special Collections.

107. "Take Back the Night March Statement of Purpose 1981."

108. Nancy McDonald, "DC Center Faces Funding Cut," *Feminist Alliance Against Rape Newsletter* (November / December 1976): 21.

109. Thuma, *All Our Trials*, 139.

110. Nkenge Touré, interview with the author, October 16, 2018.

111. Natalia Mehlman Petrzela, *Classroom Wars: Language, Sex, and the Making of Modern Political Culture* (New York: Oxford University Press, 2015), 186.

112. McDonald, "DC Center Faces Funding Cut," 21.

113. Loretta Ross, interview by Joyce Follet, 120.

114. Whittier, *The Politics of Child Sexual Abuse*, 82.

115. Martha Langelan, "Don't Cut Funds for Rape Prevention," *Washington Post*, June 28, 1981, D6.

116. Loretta Ross, interview by Joyce Follet, 120.

117. Carlos Sanchez, "D.C. Rape Crisis Center Was Among First in U.S.," *Washington Post*, September 23, 1989, B5.

118. Asch and Musgrove, *Chocolate City*, 377.

119. Asch and Musgrove, *Chocolate City*, 380.

120. Asch and Musgrove, *Chocolate City*, 394–395.

121. Nkenge Touré, interview with the author, October 16, 2018.

122. William E. Smart, "A Child Should Be a Zebra in a Collection of Zebras," *Washington Post*, November 13, 1983, B5.

123. Nkenge Touré, interview with the author, October 16, 2018.

124. Nkenge Touré, interview with the author, October 16, 2018.

125. "Staying Safe," *Aegis* 39 (1985): 37.

126. Nkenge Touré, "Special Populations Caucus: Black Focus," *Feminist Alliance Against Rape Newsletter* (May / June 1977): 8.

127. Roberts, *Shattered Bonds*, 236–237, 273–274.

128. "Violence Against Black Women: Breaking the Silence," Nkenge Touré Papers, SSC-MS-00563, box 8, folder 1, Smith College Special Collections.

129. "Staying Safe, 1984," Nkenge Touré Papers, SSC-MS-00563, box 4, folder 16, Smith College Special Collections.

130. "Child Sex Abuse Curriculum (1984)," Nkenge Touré Papers, SSC-MS-00563, box 4, folder 17, Smith College Special Collections.

131. Ferentz Lafargue, "On Moving Forward," in *Love WITH Accountability: Digging Up the Roots of Child Sexual Abuse*, ed. Aishah Shahidah Simmons (Chico: AK Press, 2019), 51.

132. Sandy Rovner, "When Saying No Is Not Enough," *Washington Post*, May 4, 1984, B5.

133. Loretta Ross, interview by Joyce Follet, 120.

134. Nkenge Touré, interview with the author, October 16, 2018.

135. Loretta Ross, interview with the author, September 27, 2018.

136. "Child Sex Abuse Curriculum (1984)," Nkenge Touré Papers, SSC-MS-00563, box 4, folder 17, Smith College Special Collections.

137. "Staying Safe, 1984," Nkenge Touré Papers, SSC-MS-00563, box 4, folder 16, Smith College Special Collections.

138. "Staying Safe, 1984."

139. "Child Sex Abuse Curriculum (1984)," Nkenge Touré Papers, SSC-MS-00563, box 4, folder 17, Smith College Special Collections.

140. "Child Sex Abuse Curriculum (1984)."

141. "Staying Safe, 1984."

142. "Child Sex Abuse Curriculum (1984)."

143. "Staying Safe, 1984."

144. "Staying Safe, 1984."

145. Meiners, *For the Children?*, 186–187; Renfro, *Stranger Danger*, 143.

146. Donna Murch, *Living for the City: Migration, Education, and the Rise of the Black Panther Party in Oakland, California* (Chapel Hill: University of North Carolina Press, 2010), 127; Farmer, *Remaking Black Power*, 162.

147. Emily Thuma, "Lessons in Self-Defense: Gender Violence, Racial Criminalization, and Anticarceral Feminism," *Women's Studies Quarterly* 43, nos. 3 & 4 (fall / winter 2015): 52–71.

148. Meiners, *For the Children?*, 9–10.

149. Lynn Roberts, "Becoming Each Other's Harvest," in *Love WITH Accountability: Digging Up the Roots of Child Sexual Abuse*, ed. Aishah Shahidah Simmons (Chico: AK Press, 2019), 86.

150. "Staying Safe, 1984."

151. Murch, *Living for the City*, 178.

152. Nkenge Touré, interview by Loretta Ross, 53.

153. Nkenge Touré, interview by Loretta Ross, 52.

Chapter 5

1. Phyllis Pennese, interview with the author, April 22, 2019. Historian Dawn Flood notes that despite their best efforts to transform rape into "a potential arena for interracial and cross class feminist cooperation . . . many white women had difficulty understanding how the legacy of racial discrimination affected biased prosecutions of sexual violence and could not comprehend why Black feminists were sometimes reluctant to join the imagined bonds of universal sisterhood." See Flood, *Rape in Chicago*, 155.

2. Edith Herman, "A 'Forgotten' Story of Pain in the Inner City," *Chicago Tribune*, July 15, 1979, M3.

3. Herman, "A 'Forgotten' Story of Pain in the Inner City."

4. Ronald Tate, "Rape: Usually an Unreported Crime," *Chicago Defender*, August 13, 1980, 3.

5. Ronald Tate, "Trauma Bypasses Economic Barriers," *Chicago Defender*, August 14, 1980, 3.

6. Tate, "Trauma Bypasses Economic Barriers."

7. Historian Anne Gray Fischer has argued that police escalated the criminalization of sex workers in American cities like Boston and Atlanta during the 1970s and 1980s as a manifestation of "broken windows" policing, which aggressively surveilled and pursued harmless infractions as a means preventing more destructive forms of crime and restoring falling property values. In both cities, Black sex workers bore the brunt of this heavy-handed criminalization. Fischer, *The Streets Belong to Us*, 139.

8. Alan P. Henry, "Policemen Hit on Black Rape Cases," *Chicago Sun-Times*, August 19, 1982, 28.

9. Mary Scott Boria to Saundra Bishop, April 10, 1985, HERS (Health Evaluation & Referral Service) Records, box 2, folder 17, Special Collections and University Archives, University of Illinois at Chicago.

10. Mary Scott Boria, interview with the author, June 13, 2018.

11. Sylvia Rush, interview with the author, January 23, 2019.

12. Phyllis Pennese, interview with the author, April 22, 2019.

13. Beryl Fitzpatrick, interview with the author, February 1, 2019.

14. Boria to Bishop, April 10, 1985.

15. Taylor, "Rape Crisis Centers Reduced."

16. United States Congress, *Victims of Crime: Hearings Before the Subcommittee on Criminal Justice of the Committee on the Judiciary, House of Representatives, One Hundredth Congress, First Session, on H.R. 2786, H.R. 3352, and H.R. 3678 . . . September 30, October 6, and December 11, 1987* (Washington, D.C.: U.S. Government Printing Office, 1987), 197.

17. Gruber, *The Feminist War on Crime*, 100. The victims' rights movement charged that the American criminal justice system was unduly preoccupied with protecting the rights of defendants at the expense of crime victims, who were routinely disregarded and mistreated by law enforcement officials. See Gottschalk, *The Prison and the Gallows*, 79; Kohler-Hausmann, *Getting Tough*, 255; Jill Lepore, "The Rise of the Victims' Rights Movement," New Yorker, May 21, 2018, https://www.newyorker.com/magazine/2018/05/21/the-rise-of-the-victims-rights-movement.

18. Bevacqua, *Rape on the Public Agenda*, 168.

19. United States Congress, *Legislation to Help Crime Victims*, 4.

20. Scholars have extensively documented President Reagan's heavily racialized campaigns to demonize welfare recipients and the devastating effects of welfare state retrenchment on Black Americans. See Annelise Orleck, *Storming Caesars Palace: How Black Mothers Fought Their Own War on Poverty* (Boston: Beacon Press, 2005); Michelle Alexander, *The New Jim Crow* (New York: The New Press, 2012); Marisa Chappell, *The War on Welfare: Family, Poverty, and Politics in Modern America* (Philadelphia: University of Pennsylvania Press, 2012); Tamar W. Carroll, *Mobilizing New York: AIDS, Antipoverty, and Feminist Activism* (Chapel Hill: University of North Carolina Press, 2015).

21. Lois Haight Herrington, et al., *President's Task Force on Victims of Crime: Final Report* (Washington, D.C.: U.S. Government Printing Office, 1982), ii.

22. Herrington, et al., *President's Task Force on Victims of Crime*, 5–6.

23. United States Congress, *Victims of Crime*, 149–151.

24. "Department of Justice Factsheet for VOCA," Women Organized Against Rape Records, box 20, folder 10, Special Collections Research Center, Temple University Archives.

25. United States Congress, *Victims of Crime*, 1.

26. United States Congress, *Victims of Rape*, 56.

27. "VOCA 1986–1987," Women Organized Against Rape Records, box 20, folder 10, SCRC, Temple University Archives.

28. United States Congress, *Victims of Rape*, 19.

29. United States Congress, *Victims of Crime*, 18.

30. Flood, *Rape in Chicago*, 1.

31. Jacquet, *The Injustices of Rape*, 21–23.

32. Jacquet, *The Injustices of Rape*, 104.

33. Bevacqua, *Rape on the Public Agenda*, 100.

34. "Women's Anti-Rape Group: Brief History; Minutes, October 9, 1971–February 22, 1973," Records of New York Women Against Rape, 1971–1984 (inclusive), 1971–1975 (bulk), MC 353, 1, box 1, Schlesinger Library, Radcliffe Institute, Harvard University.

35. United States Congress, *Victims of Rape*, 57.

36. "June 20, 1986: Letter from PA Commission on Crime and Delinquency to Judy Turetsky (WOAR President) Awarding VOCA Funds to 86-VF-05–2523," Women Organized Against Rape Records, box 20, folder 10, SCRC, Temple University Archives; "June 7, 1988: Letter from PA Commission on Crime and Delinquency Awarding WOAR VOCA Funds for 88-VF-05–2985 (new number) for $56,970," Women Organized Against Rape Records, box 20, folder 14, SCRC, Temple University Archives.

37. "Direct Service Staff Meeting Minutes Nov 28, 1988," Women Organized Against Rape Records, box 12, folder 19, SCRC, Temple University Archives.

38. "Direct Service Staff Meeting Minutes Nov 28, 1988."

39. "Victims of Crime Act Performance Report April 1, 1987–September 30, 1987," Women Organized Against Rape Records, box 20, folder 14, SCRC, Temple University Archives.

40. "ICASA Coalition Commentary, 1987–1988," Pauline Bart Papers, box 70, David M. Rubenstein Rare Book & Manuscript Library, Duke University.

41. Gottschalk, *The Prison and the Gallows*, 79–86; Kohler-Hausmann, *Getting Tough*, 6.

42. Marissa Chappell, *The War on Welfare: Family, Poverty, and Politics in Modern America* (Philadelphia: University of Pennsylvania Press, 2010), 21.

43. Chappell, *The War on Welfare*, 202.

44. Gottschalk, *The Prison and the Gallows*, 127.

45. "Application Procedures," National Association of Crime Victim Compensation Boards, accessed December 27, 2019, http://www.nacvcb.org/index.asp?sid=5. For more on the arduous process of applying for victim's compensation, see Susan J. Brison, *Aftermath: Violence and the Remaking of a Self* (Princeton, NJ: Princeton University Press, 2002), 81–91.

46. Dána-Ain Davis, *Battered Black Women and Welfare Reform: Between a Rock and a Hard Place* (Albany: State University of New York Press, 2006), 41–42. Black feminist scholar Beth Richie explains that Black women living in poverty are rarely accorded the status of deserving victims. More often, they are "blamed, stigmatized, or, worse, criminalized because of their abuse." According to Richie, state entities refuse to see poor Black women as a victimizable population because "prevailing social ideology about family, motherhood, sex, and race make it easy to attribute responsibility to [poor Black women] for their predicament." See Richie, *Arrested Justice*, 24, 122.

47. "The Exchange: A Forum on Domestic Violence," National Woman Abuse Prevention Center, Washington, D.C., vol. 3, no. 2 (spring / summer 1989), Women's newsletter and periodical collection, 1923–2011 (inclusive), 1970–1995 (bulk), Pr-4, carton 4, Schlesinger Library, Radcliffe Institute, Harvard University.

48. "Crime Victim Compensation: An Overview," National Association of Crime Victim Compensation Boards, accessed December 27, 2019, http://www.nacvcb.org/index.asp?sid=5.

49. "Victim Compensation," *Feminist Alliance Against Rape Newsletter* (May / June 1977): 7.

50. Fischer, *The Streets Belong to Us*, 149, 158–159.

51. Kali Gross, "African American Women, Mass Incarceration, and the Politics of Protection," *Journal of American History* 102, no. 1 (June 2015): 25.

52. Lisa Newmark, Judy Bonderman, Barbara Smith, and Blaine Liner, *National Evaluation of State Victims of Crime Act Assistance and Compensation Programs* (Washington, D.C.: Urban Institute, 2003), 101.

53. *National Evaluation of State Victims of Crime Act Assistance and Compensation Programs*, 98; Catherine J. Whitaker, *Black Victims* (Washington, D.C.: U.S. Department of Justice, Bureau of Justice Statistics, 1990), 2.

54. *National Evaluation of State Victims of Crime Act Assistance and Compensation Programs*, 99.

55. Gruber, *The Feminist War on Crime*, 108.

56. Gruber, *The Feminist War on Crime*, 96.

57. Bevacqua, *Rape on the Public Agenda*, 86.

58. United States Congress, *Mental Health Systems Act Hearings Before the Subcommittee on Health and the Environment of the Committee on Interstate and Foreign Commerce, House of Representatives, Ninety-Sixth Congress, First Session, on H.R. 4156 . . . and H.R. 3986 . . . June 14, 25, and 26, 1979* (Washington, D.C.: U.S. Government Printing Office, 1979), 394.

59. Bevacqua, *Rape on the Public Agenda*, 153.

60. United States Congress, *Legislation to Help Crime Victims*, 195.

61. United States Congress, *Victims of Crime*, 185.

62. United States Congress, *Victims of Crime*, 187–188.

63. *Victim-Witness Support Center News*, vol 1, no. 3, The Victim-Witness Support Center, Washington, D.C., (June 1981), Women's newsletter and periodical collection, 1923–2011 (inclusive), 1970–1995 (bulk), Pr-4, carton 4, Schlesinger Library, Radcliffe Institute, Harvard University.

64. Gruber, *The Feminist War on Crime*, 102.

65. "First Conference: NCASA," *Aegis* (September / October 1979): 44.

66. "NCASA Resolutions 1979–1988," Pauline Bart Papers, box 16, David M. Rubenstein Rare Book & Manuscript Library, Duke University.

67. "NCASA Resolutions 1979–1988."

68. "WOARpath May 1989," Women Organized Against Rape Records, box 30, folder 7, SCRC, Temple University Archives.

69. "WOARpath May 1989."

70. Gail Sullivan, "Funny Things Happen on Our Way to Revolution," *Aegis* (spring 1982): 14.

71. Phyllis Pennese, interview with the author, April 22, 2019. Ironically, Pennese at times felt more at ease in the predominantly white lesbian coalition than within the Women of Color Caucus, where she regularly encountered the homophobia of her Black female colleagues.

72. Mary Scott Boria, interview with the author, June 13, 2018.

73. Richie, *Arrested Justice*, 150.

74. Though these organizations were almost exclusively white-operated, Black women's groups such as the League of Black Women and the National Alliance of Black Feminists incorporated rape prevention and counseling into their agendas and collaborated with their white counterparts. See Flood, *Rape in Chicago*, 141–142.

75. Hanke Gratteau, "Few Places to Go for Aid After Rape," *Chicago Defender*, July 28, 1982, 4.

76. United States Congress, *Victims of Crime*, 43.

77. Robert McClory, "Up Against Sex Crime," *Chicago Reader*, July 17, 1981, 8–23.

78. Tim Franklin, "City, State Among Worst in Helping Rape Victims," *Chicago Tribune*, August 19, 1982, A11.

79. Tony Fortenberry, "Rape: Chicago's Black Disgrace," *Chicago Defender*, April 11, 1981, 2.

80. "CSASN Mission Statement," HERS Records, box 2, folder 16, Special Collections and University Archives, University of Illinois at Chicago. Though CSASN's leadership was solidly African American and the majority of the community workers they trained were based in Black

neighborhoods, CSASN also targeted Latina women, particularly in the Pilsen neighborhood. Soyla Villicana of Mujeres Unidas Para Acion was an early member of CSASN.

81. "Proposal for CSASN," HERS Records, box 1, folder 7, Special Collections and University Archives, University of Illinois at Chicago.

82. "Statement to the Community Development Block Grant Coordinating Committee, April 14, 1984," HERS Records, box 1, folder 7, Special Collections and University Archives, University of Illinois at Chicago.

83. "Letter August 16, 1984," HERS Records, box 2, folder 16, Special Collections and University Archives, University of Illinois at Chicago; Sylvia Rush, interview with the author, January 23, 2019.

84. Mary Scott Boria, interview with the author, June 13, 2018; Saundra Bishop, interview with the author, July 3, 2018. For more on Harold Washington's mayoralty, including his interracial coalition building and attempts to break Chicago's notorious Democratic political machine, see Gordon K. Mantler, *The Multiracial Promise: Harold Washington's Chicago and the Democratic Struggle in Reagan's America* (Chapel Hill: University of North Carolina Press, 2023).

85. Mary Scott Boria, interview with the author, June 13, 2018; the Chicago Panthers did little to encourage Boria to develop critical perspectives on Black women and rape. Historian Dawn Flood affirms that in Chicago, "Black nationalist men asserted that charges of intraracial rape amounted to a betrayal of the race, even though many Black Chicago women viewed silence about sexual violence at the hands of Black men as a betrayal of Black sisterhood." See Flood, *Rape in Chicago*, 141.

86. Mary Scott Boria, interview with the author, June 13, 2018.

87. Mary Scott Boria, interview with the author, June 13, 2018.

88. Beryl Fitzpatrick, interview with the author, February 1, 2019; NABF held its first meeting as an unofficial chapter of the National Black Feminist Organization on June 19, 1974, at the Loop YWCA, the epicenter of Chicago anti-rape activity during the 1970s. See Springer, *Living for the Revolution*, 53.

89. Beryl Fitzpatrick, interview with the author, February 1, 2019.

90. Phyllis Pennese, interview with the author, April 22, 2019.

91. Mary Scott Boria, interview with the author, June 13, 2018.

92. For more on the culture of dissemblance, see Darlene Clark Hines's classic article "Rape and the Inner Lives of Black Women in the Middle West."

93. Mary Scott Boria, interview with the author, June 13, 2018.

94. Saundra Bishop, interview with the author, July 3, 2018; Mary Scott Boria, interview with the author, June 13, 2018.

95. Phyllis Pennese, interview with the author, April 22, 2019.

96. Scholar A. Finn Enke has demonstrated how the geography of midwestern cities like Chicago, conditioned by generations of racial segregation, isolated Black women from feminist institutions that emerged during the 1960s and 1970s. This contributed to the perception of women's liberation as an exclusively white and middle-class phenomenon. A. Finn Enke, *Finding the Movement: Sexuality, Contested Space, and Feminist Activism* (Durham, NC: Duke University Press, 2007), 85–86.

97. Phyllis Pennese, interview with the author, April 22, 2019.

98. "CSASN Steering Committee Meeting Minutes April 29, 1985," HERS Records, box 3, folder 28, Special Collections and University Archives, University of Illinois at Chicago.

99. Sylvia Rush, interview with the author, January 23, 2019.

100. "Third World Women and Violence by Loretta J. Ross, August 1980," Loretta Ross Papers, SSC-MS-00504, box 5, folder 2, Smith College Special Collections.

101. Sylvia Rush, interview with the author, January 23, 2019.

102. Beryl Fitzpatrick, interview with the author, February 1, 2019.

103. Beryl Fitzpatrick, interview with the author, February 1, 2019.

104. Beryl Fitzpatrick, interview with the author, February 1, 2019.

105. "CSASN Application for DHS Funding Under the Auspices of YWCA Chicago," HERS Records, box 2, folder 16, Special Collections and University Archives, University of Illinois at Chicago.

106. "Chicago Sexual Assault Service Network 1985–1986," HERS Records, box 2, folder 17, Special Collections and University Archives, University of Illinois at Chicago.

107. "CSASN Training Subcommittee Meeting 8/13/1984," HERS Records, box 2, folder 16, Special Collections and University Archives, University of Illinois at Chicago.

108. Mary Scott Boria to Saundra Bishop, April 10, 1985, HERS Records, box 2, folder 17, Special Collections and University Archives, University of Illinois at Chicago.

109. "Edgewater Uptown Community Mental Health Center (1984)," HERS Records, box 2, folder 16, Special Collections and University Archives, University of Illinois at Chicago.

110. "Edgewater Uptown Community Mental Health Center (1984)."

111. "Status Report February 21, 1985," HERS Records, box 2, folder 17, Special Collections and University Archives, University of Illinois at Chicago.

112. Linnet Myers, "Daley to Laud 25 for Help to Women," *Chicago Tribune*, October 5, 1987, B7.

113. Some scholars regard the turn toward service provision in the 1980s as a misstep that hastened the anti-rape movement's deradicalization. Nancy Matthews claims that during the 1980s "women with social welfare backgrounds," many of them African Americans, joined the anti-rape movement in substantial numbers. Consequently, "the work became more imbued with a social welfare orientation" at the expense of the radical feminist critique of patriarchal violence that galvanized the movement in the first place. Kristen Bumiller agrees that that service-centered programs operated by social welfare professionals "narrowly focused on individualistic forms of problem solving" and as a result were "not rooted in a collective understanding of this violence or a sense of interconnectedness of women's problems as expressed by early grassroots organizers." Their scholarship bookends the "narrative of the anti-rape movement's decline," in which an apolitical social service model supplanted and neutralized radical feminism. See Matthews, *Confronting Rape*, 155; and Bumiller, *In an Abusive State*, xiv, 12.

114. Gail Sullivan, "Funny Things Happen on Our Way to Revolution," *Aegis* 34 (1982): 19–20.

115. Carrie Baker and Maria Bevacqua question the equation of social service provision with deradicalization, reminding scholars that "the provision of such services was vital to the victims and survivors who needed them most." See Carrie N. Baker and Maria Bevacqua, "Challenging the Narrative of the Anti-Rape Movement's Decline," *Violence Against Women* 24, no. 3 (2018): 357.

116. Mary Scott Boria, interview with the author, June 13, 2018.

117. Sylvia Rush, interview with the author, January 23, 2019.

118. See Nancy Naples, *Grassroots Warriors: Activist Mothering, Community Work, and the War on Poverty* (New York: Routledge, 1998); Orleck, *Storming Caesar's Palace*; Nelson, *Body and Soul.*

119. In many respects, CSASN's community-based counseling on the South and West Sides of Chicago resembled the People's Free Medical Clinics embraced by the Black Panther Party during the 1970s. As scholar Alondra Nelson has shown, free health clinics were not evidence of the "deradicalization" of the Panthers as their agenda migrated from armed self-defense to community survival programming. They were alternative institutions built in response to the inadequacies of the for-profit healthcare system that attacked systemic racism by promoting "self-health" and community control of medical care. They often appropriated government funds to achieve this. See Nelson, *Body and Soul*, 105.

120. Writer Alice Walker first coined the term "womanist" in 1979. Often used interchangeably with "Black feminist," "womanist" refers specifically to a subset of Black feminist theory that centers the everyday experiential knowledge of Black women. It distinguishes itself from more organizational forms of Black feminism and mainstream white feminism by entrusting Black women with the survival of the Black community as a whole, rather than focusing solely on eliminating gender oppression. It is often affiliated with Black lesbianism, spirituality, and Black nationalist discourses. See Alice Walker, *In Search of Our Mothers' Gardens: Womanist Prose* (San Diego: Harcourt, Brace, Jovanovich, 1983); Katie G. Cannon, *Black Womanist Ethics* (Atlanta: Scholar's Press, An American Academy of Religion Book, 1988); Collins, *Black Feminist Thought*, 42.

121. Phyllis Pennese, interview with the author, April 22, 2019.

122. Beryl Fitzpatrick, interview with the author, February 1, 2019.

123. Mary Scott Boria, interview with the author, June 13, 2018.

124. Mary Scott Boria, interview with the author, June 13, 2018.

125. Sylvia Rush, interview with the author, January 23, 2019.

126. Renee D. Turner, "Rape: The Myths and Realities," *Ebony*, October 1988, 112.

127. Turner, "Rape: The Myths and Realities," 112.

128. Renee D. Turner, "Date Rape," *Ebony*, December 1990, 104.

129. Turner, "Date Rape," 104.

130. Turner, "Date Rape," 106.

131. "Letters to the Editor," *Ebony*, December 1988, 18.

132. "Letters to the Editor," *Ebony*, February 1991, 186.

133. Cheryl W. Thompson, "Donors Skirt Issue When It Comes to Funding Women's Aid Agencies," *Chicago Tribune*, November 18, 1992, A6.

Chapter 6

1. Deborah S. Pinkey, "Power to Her People," *American Medical News*, December 15, 1989, 36; Byllye Avery, interview by Loretta Ross, transcript of video recording, July 21, 2005, Voices of Feminism Oral History Project, Sophia Smith Collection, Smith College, 24–25.

2. Byllye Avery, "Breathing Life into Ourselves: The Evolution of the National Black Women's Health Project," in *The Black Women's Health Book: Speaking for Ourselves*, ed. Evelyn C. White (Seattle: Seal Press, 1994), 7–8; "Vulnerability to premature death" refers to geographer Ruth Wilson Gilmore's influential definition of racism. Ruth Wilson Gilmore, *Golden Gulag: Prisons, Surplus, Crisis, and Opposition in Globalizing California* (Berkeley: University of California Press, 2007), 28.

3. "Program: First National Conference on Black Women's Health Issues, June 24–26, 1983," Black Women's Health Imperative Records, SSC-MS-00487, box 2, folder 28, Smith College Special Collections.

4. Byllye Avery, "Black Women's Health: A Conspiracy of Silence," *Sojourner*, January 1989, 15–16; Martha Scherzer, "Byllye Avery and the National Black Women's Health Project," *The Network News / National Women's Health Network* (May / June 1995): 4.

5. For more on the connection between physical and mental health in survivors of abuse, see Bessel A. Van der Kolk, *The Body Keeps the Score: Brain, Mind, and Body in the Healing of Trauma* (New York: Penguin Books, 2015).

6. Avery, "Black Women's Health," 16.

7. Scherzer, "Byllye Avery and the National Black Women's Health Project," 4; Jael Miriam Silliman, Marlene Gerber Fried, Loretta Ross, and Elena R. Gutiérrez, *Undivided Rights: Women of Color Organize for Reproductive Justice* (Boston: South End Press, 2004), 72.

8. Susan L. Smith, *Sick and Tired of Being Sick and Tired: Black Women's Health Activism in America, 1890–1950* (Philadelphia: University of Pennsylvania Press, 1995), 18; Nelson, *Body and Soul*, 88–80.

9. Jennifer Nelson, *More than Medicine: A History of the Feminist Women's Health Movement* (New York: New York University Press, 2015), 128.

10. "NBWHP 7th Annual Conference, July 16–18, (1993) Detroit, Michigan," Loretta Ross Papers, SSC-MS-00504, box 18, folder 7, Smith College Special Collections; "10th Anniversary Homecoming Celebration, June 30–July 3, 1994," Black Women's Health Imperative Records, SSC-MS-00487, box 4, folder 9, Smith College Special Collections; "Annual Meeting, June 22–25, 1995, Baltimore, Maryland," Black Women's Health Imperative Records, SSC-MS-00487, box 4, folder 20, Smith College Special Collections.

11. "Letter from Pam Freeman," Loretta Ross Papers, SSC.MS.00504, box 18, folder 15, Smith College Special Collections; "Agenda for NBWHP Community Meeting, December 6, 1995," Black Women's Health Imperative Records, SSC-MS-00487, box 1, folder 2, Smith College Special Collections; "California Black Women's Health Project Info 1998," Black Women's Health Imperative Records, SSC-MS-00487, box 1, folder 24, Smith College Special Collections.

12. Alondra Nelson identifies a "long medical civil rights movement" that stretches from nineteenth century public health practitioners to the Black Panther clinics of the 1970s. Black healthcare activists collectively maintained that the mainstream professionalized medical establishment was profoundly racist in its treatment of Black people, alternately ignoring their health issues and subjecting them to unethical experimentation. Black healthcare activists challenged medical discrimination through parallel institution-building, pushing for integration, and practicing a "politics of knowledge." See Nelson, *Body and Soul*, 24; Scherzer, "Byllye Avery and the National Black Women's Health Project," 6.

13. Bevacqua, *Rape on the Public Agenda*, 169–172.

14. Gottschalk, *The Prison and the Gallows*, 151–152.

15. United States Congress, *Violence Against Women: Victims of the System: Hearing Before the Committee on the Judiciary, United States Senate, One Hundred Second Congress, First Session, on S. 15, a Bill to Combat Violence and Crimes Against Women on the Streets and in Homes, April 9, 1991* (Washington, D.C.: U.S. Government Printing Office, 1991), 201.

16. Thuma, *All Our Trials*, 7.

17. Victoria Law, "Against Carceral Feminism," *Jacobin*, accessed September 27, 2019, https://web.archive.org/web/20200109164449/https://jacobinmag.com/2014/10/against-carceral-feminism/.

18. Loretta Ross, interview by Joyce Follet, 151–152.

19. "Building a Movement Against Racism (1983)," Loretta Ross Papers, SSC-MS-00504, box 4, folder 4, Smith College Special Collections.

20. "Breaking the Conspiracy of Silence: Preaching the Gospel of Sisterhood," Loretta Ross Papers, SSC-MS- 00504, box 4, folder 1, Smith College Special Collections.

21. Greene, *Free Joan Little*, 187.

22. Loretta Ross, interview by Joyce Follet, 203.

23. Pinkey, "Power to Her People," 35.

24. Loretta Ross, interview by Joyce Follet, 206.

25. Byllye Avery, interview by Loretta Ross, 83.

26. Byllye Avery, interview by Loretta Ross, 29.

27. Jacquet, *Injustices of Rape*, 76, 81, 94.

28. Byllye Avery, interview by Loretta Ross, 29.

29. Deborah R. Grayson, "'Necessity Was the Midwife of Our Politics': Black Women's Health Activism in the 'Post'–Civil Rights Era (1980–1996)," in *Still Lifting, Still Climbing: African American Women's Contemporary Activism*, ed. Kimberly Springer (New York: New York University Press, 1999), 144.

30. Loretta Ross, interview by Joyce Follet, 204.

31. Loretta Ross, interview by Joyce Follet, 206.

32. Loretta Ross, interview by Joyce Follet, 206.

33. White, *Too Heavy a Load*, 27.

34. Greene, *Free Joan Little*, 197–198.

35. Byllye Avery, interview by Loretta Ross, 55.

36. "Equal But Still Not on the Same Level," Black Women's Health Imperative Records, SSC-MS-00487, box 1, folder 19, Smith College Special Collections.

37. "Resource Roundup: Health Factsheet on Black Women," Loretta Ross Papers, SSC-MS-00504, box 17, folder 10, Smith College Special Collections.

38. For more on how the Reagan Administration accelerated the devaluation of Black life, see Orleck, *Storming Caesars Palace*; Chappell, *The War on Welfare*; Murakawa, *The First Civil Right*; Tamar W. Carroll, *Mobilizing New York: AIDS, Antipoverty, and Feminist Activism* (Chapel Hill: University of North Carolina Press, 2015); Hinton, *From the War on Poverty to the War on Crime*.

39. "Equal But Still Not on the Same Level."

40. Avery, "Black Women's Health," 15–16.

41. Avery, "Black Women's Health," 15–16.

42. As quoted in Greene, *Free Joan Little*, 199.

43. For more on the history of organizing among Black women public housing tenants, including around sexual violence, see Rhonda Y. Williams, *The Politics of Public Housing: Black Women's Struggles Against Urban Inequality* (New York: Oxford University Press, 2004); and Levenstein, *A Movement Without Marches*.

44. Marie Rasheed, "The Self Help-Process Works, If You Let It," *Vital Signs* (February 1989): 14.

45. Cheryl Boykins, "Developing Self Help Groups in Public Housing," *Vital Signs* (February 1989): 14.

46. Diana L. More and Hanifa Shoatz-Bey, "From the Community: Center for Black Women's Wellness," *Vital Signs* (February 1989): 11.

47. Lisa Levenstein, *They Didn't See Us Coming: The Hidden History of Feminism in the Nineties* (New York: Basic Books, 2020), 91–92.

48. INCITE!, *The Revolution Will Not Be Funded*, xiii.

49. Robert L. Allen, "From Black Awakening in Capitalist America," in *The Revolution Will Not Be Funded: Beyond the Non-Profit Industrial Complex*, ed. INCITE! Women of Color Against Violence, 2nd ed. (Durham, NC: Duke University Press, 2017), 52–56.

50. Nichell J. Taylor, "Crime Seminar Asks: If We Don't Take Charge, Who Will?," *In Town Extra* (Atlanta, GA), January 11, 1991.

51. Taylor, "Crime Seminar Asks: If We Don't Take Charge, Who Will?"

52. Taylor, "Crime Seminar Asks: If We Don't Take Charge, Who Will?"

53. For more on the distinctions between fast and slow violence, see Rob Nixon, *Slow Violence and the Environmentalism of the Poor* (Cambridge, MA: Harvard University Press, 2011), 2–3.

54. Krista, "The Whitewashing of the Grady Rape Crisis Center," *The Great Speckled Bird* (Atlanta, GA), July 1, 1974, 14.

55. Krista, "The Whitewashing of the Grady Rape Crisis Center."

56. Willoughby Mariano, "Grady Releasing 1,000 Rape Kits Withheld from Law Enforcement," *Atlanta Journal-Constitution*, September 23, 2016, https://www.ajc.com/news/state—regional-govt—politics/grady-releasing-000-rape-kits-withheld-from-law-enforcement/lmNadPDErZa3CNBQmiEE0H/.

57. Newbille departed the project in 1995 and was replaced by Scott, who shuttered the project's Atlanta headquarters to take up permanent residence in the Washington, D.C. office. Silliman et al., *Undivided Rights*, 77; Evan Hart, "Building a More Inclusive Women's Health Movement: Byllye Avery and the Development of the National Black Women's Health Project, 1981–1990" (PhD diss., University of Cincinnati, 2012).

58. Cynthia Newbille-Marsh, "Women Against Violence" *Vital Signs* (October 1991): 3.

59. "Black Women's Health Imperative," Black Women's Health Imperative, accessed November 25, 2019, https://web.archive.org/web/20200109165520/http://www.Blackwomenshealth.org/about-us/our-story/_print_y.html.

60. Loretta Ross, interview by Joyce Follet, 217–220; Byllye Avery, interview by Loretta Ross, 41–43.

61. Grayson, "Necessity Was the Midwife of Our Politics," 134–135.

62. Cynthia Newbille, "Women Against Violence," *Vital Signs* (October 1991): 3.

63. Newbille, "Women Against Violence."

64. Newbille, "Women Against Violence."

65. Byllye Avery to Anita Hill, November 7, 1991, Black Women's Health Imperative Records, SSC-MS-00487, box 4, folder 4, Smith College Special Collections.

66. "National Black Women's Health Project Sixth Annual Meeting Notes," Black Women's Health Imperative Records, SSC-MS-00487, box 1, folder 4, Smith College Special Collections.

67. "Issue Panel: Black Women's Health; The Impact of Violence, the Challenges of Hearing," June 26, 1992, Los Angeles, CA, MP3, 151:50, Black Women's Health Imperative Records, SSC-MS-00487, box 1, folder 38, Smith College Special Collections.

68. "Issue Panel: Black Women's Health; The Impact of Violence, the Challenges of Hearing."

69. Ritchie, *Invisible No More*, 118–120.

70. "Issue Panel: Black Women's Health; The Impact of Violence, the Challenges of Hearing."

71. Bevacqua, *Rape on the Public Agenda*, 169–172.

72. Gruber, *The Feminist War on Crime*, 146–148.

73. Loic Wacquant, *Punishing the Poor: The Neoliberal Government of Social Insecurity* (Durham, NC: Duke University Press, 2009), 64.

74. Gruber, *The Feminist War on Crime*, 149.

75. Greene, *Free Joan Little*, 232.

76. Levenstein, *They Didn't See Us Coming*, 8.

77. United States Congress, *Crimes of Violence Motivated by Gender: Hearing Before the Subcommittee on Civil and Constitutional Rights of the Committee on the Judiciary, House of Representatives, One Hundred Third Congress, First Session, November 16, 1993* (Washington D.C.: U.S. Government Printing Office, 1994), 2–3.

78. "Action Packet: Violence Against Women Act, 1999," Records of Legal Momentum, 1978–2011, MC 727: Vt-240: DVD-73, 106.10, box 106, Schlesinger Library, Radcliffe Institute, Harvard University.

79. Bevacqua, *Rape on the Public Agenda*, 170.

80. INCITE!, *The Revolution Will Not Be Funded*, 119.

81. INCITE!, *The Revolution Will Not Be Funded*, 11.

82. Bumiller, *In an Abusive State*, 164–165.

83. United States Congress, *Crimes of Violence Motivated by Gender*, 19; United States Congress, *Violence Against Women*, 321.

84. Gottschalk, *The Prison and the Gallows*, 152; INCITE!, *The Revolution Will Not Be Funded*, 119; Thuma, *All Our Trials*, 8; Gruber, *The Feminist War on Crime*, 148; Levenstein, *They Didn't See Us Coming*, 8; Greene, *Free Joan Little*, 235–236.

85. Gruber, *The Feminist War on Crime*, 148.

86. INCITE!, *The Revolution Will Not Be Funded*, 119.

87. Nancy Whittier, "Carceral and Intersectional Feminism in Congress: The Violence Against Women Act, Discourse, and Policy," *Gender & Society* 30, no. 5 (2016): 792, 809.

88. "Letter to Byllye Avery from Women's International League for Peace and Freedom, 1991," Black Women's Health Imperative Records, SSC-MS-00487, box 1, folder 34, Smith College Special Collections.

89. "Letter to Byllye Avery from Women's International League for Peace and Freedom, 1991."

90. "103rd Congress House Vote Description," Black Women's Health Imperative Records, SSC-MS-00487, box 2, folder 16, Smith College Special Collections.

91. Opposition to the death penalty has been one of the few points of political collaboration between the feminist movement against sexual violence and the Black freedom struggle. Jacquet, *Injustices of Rape*, 179–181.

92. *Hill Briefs*, vol. 1, no. 6 (June 1995), Black Women's Health Imperative Records, SSC-MS-00487, box 2, folder 37, Smith College Special Collections.

93. *Hill Briefs*, vol. 1, no. (June 6, 1995).

94. Chappell, *The War on Welfare*, 1.

95. Chappell, *The War on Welfare*, 8–10.

96. *Hill Briefs*, vol. 1, no. (June 6, 1995).

97. *Hill Briefs*, vol. 1, no. (June 6, 1995).

98. *Hill Briefs*, vol. 1, no. (June 6, 1995).

99. *Hill Briefs*, vol. 1, no. (June 6, 1995).

100. "Annual Meeting, June 22–25, 1995, Baltimore, Maryland," Black Women's Health Imperative Records, SSC-MS-00487, box 4, folder 20, Smith College Special Collections.

101. "California Black Women's Health Project Info 1998," Black Women's Health Imperative Records, SSC-MS-00487, box 1, folder 24, Smith College Special Collections.

102. “California Black Women’s Health Project Info 1998.”

103. INCITE!, *The Revolution Will Not Be Funded*, 119.

104. Levenstein, *They Didn’t See Us Coming*, 94.

Epilogue

1. Levenstein, *They Didn’t See Us Coming*, 93–94.

2. Whittier, “Carceral and Intersectional Feminism in Congress,” 798–799.

3. Levenstein, *They Didn’t See Us Coming*, 167.

4. Lacey M. Sloan, “Two Movements, Two Paths, One Goal,” *Revolution: A Semi-annual Journal for Those Working to Stop Sexual and Domestic Violence* 1, no. 1 (winter 2006): 4.

5. Loretta Ross, interview with the author, September 27, 2018.

6. Richie, *Arrested Justice*, 155.

7. Thuma, *All Our Trials*, 159.

8. INCITE!, *The Revolution Will Not Be Funded*, 119.

9. Richie, *Arrested Justice*, 93–94.

10. Gruber, *The Feminist War on Crime*, 193–194.

11. Levenstein, *They Didn’t See Us Coming*, 182.

12. INCITE! Women of Color Against Violence and Critical Resistance, “INCITE!-Critical Resistance Statement | INCITE!,” accessed September 8, 2023, https://incite-national.org/incite-critical-resistance-statement/.

13. Ibid.

14. Richie, *Arrested Justice*, 155.

15. INCITE! Women of Color Against Violence, *Color of Violence: The Incite! Anthology* (Boston: South End Press, 2006); INCITE!, *The Revolution Will Not Be Funded*.

16. Levenstein, *They Didn’t See Us Coming*, 94.

17. Levenstein, *They Didn’t See Us Coming*, 95.

18. Zahara Hill, “A Black Woman Created the ‘Me Too’ Campaign Against Sexual Assault 10 Years Ago,” *Ebony*, October 18, 2017, https://www.ebony.com/news/black-woman-me-too-movement-tarana-burke-alyssa-milano/#axzz53KgRevKC. For a complete recounting of Tarana Burke’s activist trajectory, see Tarana Burke, *Unbound: My Story of Liberation and the Birth of the #MeToo Movement* (New York: Flatiron Books, 2021).

19. “Get To Know Us | History & Inception,” Me Too Movement, accessed January 26, 2021, https://metoomvmt.org/get-to-know-us/history-inception/.

20. Levenstein, *They Didn’t See Us Coming*, 192.

21. Tarana Burke, “Purpose,” Just Be Inc., accessed February 10, 2021, https://justbeinc.wixsite.com/justbeinc/home.

22. Hill, “A Black Woman Created the “Me Too” Campaign Against Sexual Assault 10 Years Ago.”

23. Larry Neumeister, Jennifer Peltz, Michael R. Sisak, “Jury Finds Trump Liable for Sexual Abuse, Awards Accuser $5M,” *Associated Press*, May 9, 2023, https://apnews.com/article/trump-rape-carroll-trial-fe68259a4b98bb3947d42af9ec83d7db.

24. Gruber, *The Feminist War on Crime*, 12–14.

25. Sandra E. Garcia, “The Woman Who Created #MeToo Long Before Hashtags,” *New York Times*, October 20, 2017, https://www.nytimes.com/2017/10/20/us/me-too-movement-tarana-burke.html.

26. Gruber, *The Feminist War on Crime*, 8–9.

27. Elizabeth Adetiba, "Tarana Burke Says #MeToo Should Center Marginalized Communities," *The Nation*, November 17, 2017, https://www.thenation.com/article/archive/tarana-burke-says-metoo-isnt-just-for-white-people/.

28. Liz Rowley, "The Architect of #MeToo Says the Movement Has Lost Its Way," *The Cut*, October 23, 2018, https://www.thecut.com/2018/10/tarana-burke-me-too-founder-movement-has-lost-its-way.html.

29. Adetiba, "Tarana Burke Says #MeToo Should Center Marginalized Communities."

30. Adetiba, "Tarana Burke Says #MeToo Should Center Marginalized Communities."

31. Tarana Burke, "Media Kit," Me Too Movement, accessed February 10, 2021, https://metoomvmt.org/stay-informed/media-kit/.

32. Tarana Burke, "Statistics," Me Too Movement, accessed February 10, 2021, https://metoomvmt.org/learn-more/statistics/.

33. Tarana Burke, "Glossary," Me Too Movement, accessed February 10, 2021, https://metoomvmt.org/learn-more/glossary/.

34. Beryl Fitzpatrick, interview with the author, February 1, 2019.

35. Loretta Ross, interview with the author, September 27, 2018.

36. Samia Cherry, interview with the author, April 3, 2019.

37. Sylvia Rush, interview with the author, January 23, 2019. R. Kelly was indicted on ten counts of aggravated criminal sexual abuse weeks after her interview. In 2022, he was convicted on multiple charges involving child sexual abuse. As of 2024, he is serving a thirty-one-year combined sentence.

38. Phyllis Pennese, interview with the author, April 22, 2019.

39. Loretta Ross, interview with the author, September 27, 2018.

40. Mary Scott Boria, interview with the author, June 13, 2018.

41. Mary Scott Boria, interview with the author, June 13, 2018.

42. "About RAINN," Rape, Abuse, & Incest National Network (RAINN), accessed February 10, 2021, https://www.rainn.org/about-rainn.

INDEX

ACKNOWLEDGMENTS

Writing a dissertation can be a lonely and formidable endeavor under the best of circumstances. The COVID-19 pandemic struck exactly one year prior to my defense, which made completing the dissertation exponentially more difficult. Thankfully, I had an unshakable support system in place both within and beyond Rutgers to anchor my mind and buoy my spirits that year. Amid the devastation and uncertainty, I was inordinately fortunate to secure an assistant professorship at Mercy University in Dobbs Ferry, New York. There, I took my first tentative steps to transforming a scrappy but promising dissertation into a publishable book manuscript. Once again, the support of colleagues, friends, and families made the transformation possible. Here, I would like to thank those who comprised my support system in all its phases.

First and foremost, my thanks go to my dissertation advisor, Johanna Schoen. From my first graduate colloquium to the final round of chapter revisions, she has been infinitely generous, patient, and supportive. She is a model for the qualities that make the best academics: unflinching honesty, engaged scholarship, and human kindness. Her faith in my project has been unwavering. I also thank my dissertation committee. The graduate colloquiums offered by Rachel Devlin and Donna Murch laid the intellectual bedrock for this project. From drafts to defense, they asked the exact right question at the precise time to push my analysis to the next level. Lisa Levenstein was enthused by this project from our first conversation at the Berkshire Conference of Women Historians in 2017 and consistently offered sage advice thereafter. Though not an "official" member of my dissertation committee, Jennifer Mittelstadt has always made herself available to me. Her intellectual and professional guidance have been invaluable.

The seed of this book was planted at The College of New Jersey, my first intellectual home. The stellar faculty in the History and Women's & Gender Studies Departments recognized my raw potential and encouraged me to pursue my PhD. Annie Nicolosi, Cynthia Paces, Robert McGreevey, Jon

Landreau, and Marla Jaksch treated me like a scholar long before I would dare describe myself as one. My heartfelt thanks go out to them for mentoring me long after their professional duties to me ended.

From Rutgers University to Mercy University and beyond, I have been blessed with colleagues who have nurtured this project at every stage of its development. Those who participated in the Women's and Gender History Seminar from fall 2016 through spring 2017 and the U.S. and African American History Seminar of spring 2017 made Rutgers History Department the best place I can imagine for "doing" gender history. The students and faculty participants of the Rutgers Center for Historical Analysis' Black Bodies Seminar 2017–2018 also open-handedly shared their insights with me and significantly strengthened Chapter 2. The Black Atlantic Dissertation Writing Group offered accountability and camaraderie at crucial stages of the writing process for Chapter 6. Special thanks go out to Julia Bowes, Cameron Bunker, Kaisha Esty, Marlene Gaynair, Tracey Johnson, Carie Rael, Anna Richey, Bren Sutter, Dara Walker, Pamela Walker, Meagan Wierda, Brenna Yellin, and Amy Zanoni. Thank you for your generosity and friendship. I hope I helped you half as much as you helped me. The faculty of the School of Liberal Arts have made Mercy University a comfortable academic home. Ben Abelson, Elise Arnold-Levene, K. Patrick Fazioli, Dana Horton, Soonyi Lee, Maureen MacLeod, Andrés Matias-Ortiz, Robert Murray, Virginia Coleman Prisco, Laura Proszak, and Peter West have provided cogent feedback and warm words of encouragement. I have also benefitted from an incredible network of scholars outside of my home institutions. Desiree Abu-Odeh, M. Aziz, Molly Brookfield, Joshua Crutchfield, Anastasia Curwood, Cheryl Dong, Anne Gray Fischer, Dawn Rae Flood, Gillian Frank, Estelle Freedman, Cheryl Hicks, Clay Howard, Cat Jacquet, Caitlyn Jones, Melanie Newport, Paul Renfro, Gillet Rosenblith, Emily Thuma, Kidada Williams, Tiana Wilson, and Cookie Woolner have advanced this project in ways great and small. Any impact this book might make is indebted to their bottomless intellectual generosity; their top-rate scholarship on race, sexuality, and violence in the modern United States; and their human kindness.

The creation of this book, from research to revision to production, was facilitated by several professionals and organizations who deserve the highest praise. I am grateful to the Graduate School of New Brunswick, the Rutgers Center for Historical Analysis, the Rutgers Oral History Archives, Smith College Libraries, the P.E.O. International, the New-York Historical Society, the Andrew W. Mellon Foundation, the Warren and Beatrice Susman

Endowment, the Schlesinger Library on the History of Women in America, and the William F. Olson Chair in Civic and Cultural Studies for providing financial and scholarly support for this project. Thanks also goes to the helpful and knowledgeable archivists at Smith College Special Collections, the Special Collections Research Center at Temple University, the Sallie Bingham Center at Duke University, the Special Collections and University Archives at the University of Illinois Chicago, the Schlesinger Library on the History of Women in America, and the National Museum of African American History and Culture. At the University of Pennsylvania Press, Bob Lockhart and Margot Canaday instantly grasped this book's key interventions and never wavered in their enthusiasm for it. They expertly steered the book through proposals, peer review, multiple rounds of revision, and production, as did the indispensable Penn Press workers. I am deeply grateful to them and the anonymous reviewers whose incisive commentary shaped this book manuscript.

I cannot thank enough the women who took time out of busy days and hard-earned retirements to answer a cold call from a Rutgers graduate student and discuss their activist pasts with me over the phone, via Zoom, in their living rooms, and at coffee shops: Saundra Bishop, Mary Scott Boria, Samia Cherry, Beryl Fitzpatrick, Joan Ashton Frye, Deborah Johnson, Berit Lakey, Lee Nelson, Wadiyah Nelson, Glenavie Norton, Phyllis Pennese, Loretta Ross, Sylvia Rush, Letty Thall, and Nkenge Touré. I am honored to preserve the memory of your lifelong struggles for justice.

My friends and family ensured that my sanity remained intact despite the slings and arrows of life in academia. They were always on-hand to dry my tears, ease my nerves, and share my laughter, even from the other side of the planet. Thank you to Alison and Kevin Wiesner for teaching me the value of persistence and reminding me to make time to celebrate your victories. My greatest debt of all is to my husband, Steven Thompson. He has lived with this project for as long as I have, and without complaint. As a librarian by training, he has materially contributed to this book by tracking down sources, proofreading drafts, formatting chapters, and indexing the final production. I cannot begin to enumerate all he has given me as a partner. Thank you for all the evenings and weekends sacrificed, all the delicious meals prepared while I hunched over my desk, all the cat pictures sent to me while I traveled, and all the pep talks when I felt like quitting. None of this would have been possible without you.